FOREVER YOUNG

After nearly thirty years as BBC Radio 2's top presenter and with over five million listeners, Jimmy Young said his last 'bye for now' at the end of 2002, the end of a legendary programme.

Traditionally a very private man, he now reveals the truth behind his controversial departure from the BBC, and also the story of his life. He tells of a difficult childhood, often plagued by illness and dogged by his parents' unhappy marriage. He reveals that behind his success lie two stormy marriages and several affairs. His initial breakthrough as a singer came quickly but disappeared almost as fast. In 1960 he began to turn his luck around as a radio broadcaster. With the *JY Programme*, Jimmy Young broke the mould with his mix of music, recipes, chat and current affairs.

Told in his unmistakable warm and intelligent voice, this is a fascinating and candid account of a lifetime in showbusiness and the private man behind one of Britain's best-loved public figures.

FOREVER YOUNG

SIR JIMMY YOUNG

WINDSOR

First published 2003
by
Hodder and Stoughton
This Large Print edition published 2004
by
BBC Audiobooks Ltd
by arrangement with
Hodder and Stoughton Ltd

ISBN 0 7540 9553 3

British Library Cataloguing in Publication Data available

Printed and bound in Great Britain by
Antony Rowe Ltd., Chippenham, Wiltshire

ACKNOWLEDGEMENTS

Nick Lom. A fine lawyer and a great friend who has battled tenaciously and successfully on my behalf for many years. Shimon Cohen. A wise adviser, a wonderful friend, and a gritty fighter. When the going gets tough Shimon gets going. John Gurnett. I'm truly blessed with good friends. John produced the *JY Prog* for many years and was a tower of strength on our broadcasting trips around the world. The *Prog* has ended but our friendship flourishes. Lesley, Ann and John, and Brenda and Ralph who have always been there for us and who gave such great support to Alicia during my long illness in 2002.

For Alicia, for everything

CONTENTS

INTRODUCTION

Did I jump or was I pushed? That was the question posed by many of my listeners when the press broke the news that I was 'standing down' from my five-days-a-week Radio 2 *JY Prog*. The answer—guessed correctly by almost everybody—was that I was pushed. You don't voluntarily leave a programme whose listening audience you have increased from 2.5 million to 5.75 million and which is still going up. And you certainly don't leave 5.75 million listeners who are asking you not to go.

It was around 1998 that the first leaks about my enforced departure from Radio 2 began to appear. Actually it's very surprising that they hadn't appeared earlier, because the moves to replace me seem to have started several years before that. I am by nature a trusting soul—far too trusting, my friends tell me—so of course I was the last to know about the manoeuvring the BBC was allegedly carrying out behind my back.

When Jim Moir arrived as Controller of Radio 2 in November 1995 he told me that he would like me to take more time away from the microphone. It fell short of saying, 'You're fired', but it conveyed a very strong message. In other words, forget the fact that the *JY Prog* is an enormous success; forget the fact that all the leading politicians and captains of industry fight to get on it and that it has broadcast to the acclaim of its peers from all around the world; forget the fact that it attracts so much of the press coverage desired by Radio 2.

1

The underlying message seemed to be yes, the *JY Prog* is still excellent, the listening figures are excellent and you are an excellent broadcaster—but we would like to replace you. I agreed that I would take a further two weeks a year away from the microphone.

Time passed and I was invited to lunch. However, the message had changed. Pleasantries were exchanged and then, quite out of the blue, Jim admitted he had made a mistake by asking me to take more time away from the microphone. I interpreted that to mean that he hadn't yet found somebody to replace me but, while he continued his efforts to get rid of me, he would rather like me to forego my two weeks' extra holiday. I declined.

In the old days, the choosing of my holiday replacements had been a much more friendly affair. Replacements were chosen for their high-profile name value to Radio 2. Names like Neil Kinnock, Ken Livingstone, David Frost and Charles Kennedy, whose presence might attract listeners while I was away but who obviously had no interest in taking over the programme because they had other fish to fry elsewhere. However, that policy was being changed. Now people who were hired as replacements were largely figures who would give their eye-teeth to take over my programme, and most of them didn't bother to hide the fact. Jim was enjoying enormous success in changing other programmes, but he didn't quite manage that in the twelve-to-two slot.

In fact the *JY Prog* format was deceptively simple. All I did was chat, interview, play records and then pick up, read on sight and broadcast telephoned-in reaction and comment. Oh and, by the way, you needed a sense of humour and warmth.

I also self-operated. In other words I operated the machinery as well. Self-operating demands a certain amount of skill and dexterity and, even at the advanced age of eighty-one, I've been described by various excellent studio managers as 'shit-hot on the buttons'. Most of my stand-ins didn't even attempt it. One broadcaster who did try to emulate me by self-operating unfortunately had the habit of forgetting to close the microphone after he'd finished speaking. He was saved from broadcasting oblivion by the quick thinking and action of his studio manager.

As I say, the programme format was simple. Putting all its ingredients together and making them work successfully was another matter altogether. When it became obvious that Radio 2's intention was to replace me, the reaction was immediate. Outraged listeners contacted every senior BBC administrator they could think of, from the Chairman down to the Radio 2 Controller, demanding a change of policy, and the popular papers took up the cry, 'Save our Jim'. Particularly embarrassing for the BBC were the protests from younger listeners, whom the Beeb claimed I was failing to attract to my programme—protests on the Radio 2 website, of all places—that they should 'Save our Jim'. I was even telephoned at home one morning in 1998 and asked to participate in the *Big Breakfast* television programme on Channel 4, where a furious sixteen-year-old was demanding— on behalf of herself and her teenage friends—that the BBC get its hands off Jimmy Young. Over dinner one evening a very high-up BBC executive told me that at the height of the furore senior politicians were hammering on his door to deliver a message that couldn't have been clearer: 'What the f—— do you think you're doing? Have you gone f——ing mad or something?'

The BBC, considerably shaken, pompously replied, 'There is a world of difference between sacking someone and not renewing their contract.' It appeared to me, and to my listeners, that the end result was exactly the same. Such was the strength of the protests against my programme being axed that the BBC had to resort to deceit to justify it. Listeners who were furious at my enforced departure sent letters of protest to the Corporation. One wrote to tell me that the Powers That Be at the BBC were implying to listeners that after twenty-eight years of doing the *JY Prog* I had decided to retire. That statement was, quite simply, a falsehood. I cannot tell you how sad it makes me that the BBC should tarnish its reputation for honesty and fairness by feeling it must lie about something as unimportant as dropping one of its contract artists.

I often reflect that, whatever the future may hold, life has certainly provided me with a weird and wonderful journey so far. I'll return to that story later, but let's leave it for a while and go back to when it all began.

CHAPTER ONE

THE BAKER'S BOY

I was born on 21 September 1921 in Woodside Street, Cinderford, in the Forest of Dean in Gloucestershire. My parents were Frederick George Young and Gertrude Jane Young (*née* Woolford). I weighed only four pounds and was not expected to live. My mother and father decided to name me Leslie Ronald. Well, no harm in that— they are perfectly respectable names. However, I never was, and still am not, called Leslie by my family. I was always known to my father and mother, my grandparents, and all the aunts and uncles in my grandparents' extended family as Jim. It was always 'Our Jim' did this or 'Our Jim' did that. Never Leslie, always Jim. Don't ask me why they didn't christen me Jim in the first place. I haven't the faintest idea.

The county of Gloucestershire, and perhaps the Forest of Dean in particular, is beautiful, and there are many pretty towns in the Forest. However I cannot honestly say that my birthplace was, or even now is, one of them. Cinderford was at that time very dependent on the coal mining industry. It always struck me, and still does, as being a town that has had to survive the hard way.

I too had to learn to survive, for I was always a frail child and had more than my fair share of childhood illnesses. When I was just five, and on holiday with my parents at Weston-super-Mare, I suddenly suffered agonising pain. I collapsed and

5

my father had to carry me indoors. It was rheumatic fever. Into hospital I went, where the doctors decided that tonsils were causing the problem. They removed them and, I'm happy to say, removed the problem with them. However, my medical problems were far from over.

Aged seven, I managed to suffer from bronchitis, pleurisy and double pneumonia at the same time. I was confined to bed and by my side was placed the fashionable 'cure' of the time for pneumonia, a kettle that belched out steam hour after hour. This was supposed to do fantastic things for your lungs. I suspect it just did for your lungs. With one foot in the grave it was singularly unfortunate that my bedroom overlooked a graveyard. So from time to time I was able to hear the sad tolling of the church bell and watch mourners, clothed in black, slowly following the coffins of their loved ones. I was wondering, of course, even at that tender age, how long it would be before my own family was following me.

Legend has it that, given up for dead by our doctor, I was saved by doses of a herbal cure. This involved crushing a plant called house leek which grew up walls and then feeding me the juice. 'Give him that night and morning and his temperature will go down,' said the locals to my parents. They did. It did. And a miracle was declared, although the lifelong legacy has been a weak chest.

I was too young, and too ill, for some of the traumas of the 1920s to impinge on me. For instance I was just five at the time of the ill-fated General Strike, and only eight in 1929 which saw the start of the Great Depression. My companions in primary school seemed to be as reasonably well

6

shod and clothed as I was, and I never saw any evidence to support claims of the 'We couldn't afford shoes in which to go to school' variety, although for some families that may have been true. Perhaps I was fortunate in my choice of parents. My father and his brother Gilbert owned Young Bros, Bakers and Confectioners, a business which continued successfully through the 1920s and most of the 1930s, so I was sheltered from the financial hardship which many faced during those years. In fact my father was doing so well that we were able to move from Woodside Street to a semi-detached house at 95 Church Road. It had four small rooms and a tiny basement kitchen with whitewashed walls and a copper in it. The copper was an important feature of houses in those early days, and in our family it served a dual purpose. The family wash was done in it on a weekly basis, but it had an annual use as well. Every year into it went the Christmas puddings for boiling, and they were the tastiest I've ever had. For me, Christmas was the best time of the year. Hordes of children from my mother's side of the family filled the house, and we would all play Blow Football on the kitchen table. For an only child it was wonderful to have such company.

Usually I had to make my own entertainment— and remember, this was before the days of television and my own family didn't even possess what was then called a wireless set. Sometimes I would hide myself away in my grandfather's greenhouse at the bottom of the garden. Like many small boys I was fascinated by railway engines and used to pretend I was a train driver by stoking up the greenhouse boiler until it belched out black smoke. It didn't do the plants a lot of good, of course—nor my popularity with my grandfather. In the evenings, after going to bed I often used to lie there in the dark and watch the lights of the buses going up and down the distant hills. It was entertainment of a sort, but it was also very lonely.

Although Cinderford was daily becoming more depressed my father's business continued to prosper and we were able to move from 95 Church Road to the house next door, No. 97, which had an extra room. Good news indeed in what were, generally, bad times. Perhaps one of the reasons my father was doing well was because he used me instead of employing extra staff. Other kids came out of school and went home. I didn't. Dad used to meet me in the bread van at the school gates and I had to help with delivering the bread before we went home. Then, for me, it was supper followed by homework. 'Little man, you've had a busy day' was a popular song at the time and I felt it could have been written for me. It got worse. 'After school' became 'before school' as well. And sometimes I even found myself delivering bread during the school lunch break. This was the first real cloud on my childhood horizon.

Meanwhile all of us in primary school were faced with the scholarship exam, the eleven-plus of those days. This was the exam which, fairly or unfairly, was seen as dividing the sheep from the goats. If you passed you went to the prestigious East Dean Grammar School. If you failed you didn't. Given my prolonged absence from school due to illness, plus my extra duties delivering bread, could I catch up sufficiently to pass? I worked very hard but still wasn't sure whether I could do it.

The exam results were sent directly to your parents, and on the day they were announced I went home from St White's Primary School feeling extremely apprehensive. However, the tea table was a very cheerful sight. I saw delicious-looking strawberries and cream, a rare treat in those days— but were my exam results good enough for me to be included in the feast, I wondered.

My father wasn't the most demonstrative of men and, as we pulled out the chairs to sit down for tea, my fears were not eased when he said, 'You made a right mess of that exam, didn't you?'

My heart sank. So the worst had happened. I had failed. I had worked as hard as I possibly could, and it had all been for nothing. 'Oh, are the results in?' I asked weakly, expecting and fearing that I was about to hear bad news.

'They certainly are,' said my father. 'Come in here.'

He led me into the kitchen. Standing there was the shiny-bright, gleaming, brand-new bicycle I had been promised if I passed. Dad said we couldn't afford a top-of-the-range Raleigh bike so mine was a Hercules, which cost one pound less than a Raleigh. I didn't care. It was mine, and I was the happiest kid in the neighbourhood as I zoomed around on it. And as I zoomed I reflected that, despite all the illness and absence from school, I'd managed to make it after all. I was actually on my way to the grammar school. To the school blazer and cap with the letters E.D.G.S. proudly inscribed on them and the school motto '*Sicut Arbor Lucem Petimus*'—'Like a tree we seek the light.' Some of you reading this will already be screaming, 'Elitist!' Fortunately that was not the reaction of most people in 1932. Most people then were willing to give a pat on the back for hard work done and examinations passed.

Life wasn't all studying, of course. I enjoyed my tennis as well—and so, indeed, did Dad. He played at the posh club. All white flannels and cut-glass accents. The scruffy-looking public court was a couple of hundred yards away and that's where we juniors played, also looking scruffy. Dad was in the middle of an upmarket mixed doubles one evening when a voice with a Forest of Dean burr drifted across. 'Thou dost always say as we be a-cheating,' it said, prompting one of the ladies in Dad's game to cry out, 'Good Lord, just listen to that simply dreadful accent.'

Dad didn't comment. Well, he couldn't really. He knew who it was. I arrived home and walked straight into a walloping great clout around the ear.

'What was that for? What's wrong?' I yelped.

'I'll tell you what's wrong,' said Dad. 'We've got to do something about your speech.'

Actually he didn't do anything about my speech. My education in the University of Life and my travels around the world did what was necessary. But I've never really lost that Gloucestershire accent. Nor do I wish to. It's a nice soft burr that sounds warm and friendly. It's easy on the ear, and I have no doubt it's been an enormous asset for me in my broadcasting career.

While education was a necessity, my passion was for music. I was born into, and surrounded by, music. Although I was an only child my grandfather on my mother's side married twice and, including adoptions, had sixteen children. In due course they also had children, and most of them could sing or

10

play an instrument, or both. And almost all of us were taught to read music—something which was to prove a great asset for me later on. This brought about the family belief that, if necessary, we could probably perform the *Messiah* in the Baptist chapel without needing to call on outside help. My father sang in choirs, and had done so at the prestigious Three Choirs Festivals, held in rotation at Gloucester, Worcester and Hereford Cathedrals. My mother not only sang, but also played and taught both the organ and piano. She began playing the organ in church at the age of seven and continued to do so up to the age of eighty. And she still took piano pupils at home until three days before her death in June 1972 at the age of eighty-two.

At sixteen I dreamed of making music my career, although I never really believed it would happen. I certainly never thought that I would end up being, for a short while, a pop idol making hit records. Nor that a dramatic change of direction would mean that, as one career ended, another, as a current affairs and political interviewer, would begin.

Meanwhile, at school, there were some compensations for me as I began to get involved in various activities. I worked out in the gym and was pretty good at it. Some friends and I, about a dozen of us, formed our own little boxing club. We didn't have a proper ring but we did have a shed, and in it we tried to knock spots off each other. I also joined the school amateur dramatics group and, in one presentation, played the hero, complete with tights and whitewashed wooden sword. Perhaps best of all, when I was about thirteen I discovered girls.

She was an East Dean Grammar School girl who wore the regulation gymslip and black stockings. (I can hear my male readers' heavy breathing already.) She had knock knees and her toes turned in, a combination which for some strange reason I found most attractive and very sexy. However, I had received a very strict upbringing at home and I'm afraid our relationship never really progressed beyond holding hands and going for long walks. None the less, our mini-romance convinced me that I really should acquire some social graces. Like being able to dance, for instance.

One of our bread delivery men was a tall, slim, suave Cinderford man-about-town and I set about conning him into teaching me. After a great deal of effort and persuasion on my part, he agreed to help me. The trouble was that he insisted on taking the man's part. This meant that I was always going backwards. So, although the lessons gave me the basic idea of what was required, I had to remember to reverse the instructions when dancing with a real girl. We used actually to hold the people we were dancing with in those days, and it was a huge pleasure to hold a beautiful, soft, cuddly young woman after enduring my bony, and very uncuddly, tutor.

Because of all the time I was spending helping in my father's business, my school work had been suffering. Some of my teachers thought my poor progress was due to lack of effort and application on my part, but that was simply not true. I was doing so much work for my father that I had little time left to study. The easiest, although not the wisest, course seemed to be to leave school and join my father's business full-time. And so at the age of fifteen, and against the strong advice of my teachers, that is what, with my father's agreement, I did.

It was about a year later when my father and I had our little brush with the law. I had been driving Dad's bread van in little country lanes and quiet back streets since I was twelve. It had started off as a sort of game. Dad would say, 'Move it up a bit, Jim', and I'd drive the van a few yards to our next port of call. I took to driving easily and was very good at it. In those days there was no driving test—you simply applied for a licence. The starting age was seventeen and my father applied for a licence for me—adding two years on to my age. I got my licence, and thus from the age of fifteen I was driving quite openly around the Forest helping Dad deliver the bread. I was still only sixteen when, driving-wise, my life came to a grinding halt. We had been shopped.

I was driving through the centre of Cinderford when, although there was nothing wrong with my driving, a policeman stopped me and I knew the game was up. My father and I appeared in court. His licence was suspended. I was banned from having a licence until I was seventeen. Dad was very cross because he was forced to hire someone else to drive him. But then, he was at least partly responsible for getting us in that position in the first place, so he couldn't really complain too much.

Working in the bakery involved me making up the dough in the evening in a huge mixer. It then stood through the night in the bread troughs to ferment, and in the morning we took it out and got on with making it into loaves. Since making the dough involved humping around very heavy sacks of flour it's a wonder that, at my tender age, I didn't do myself a mischief. And, having done that, going to bed and getting up at four in the morning to start work again wasn't too much fun either. However, even as I delivered the bread or worked in the bakehouse I knew that the bakery business was not for me. It may have been my father's intention, and desire, that I should follow him into the family business, but my mind was firmly set on a very different course.

Music was my ambition and I was determined that, if possible, it should be my life. The first positive step towards achieving my ambition was to join the church choir. In fact not merely to join it but to make sure I got to sing the solos as often as possible. I used to practise singing them in the empty chapel with Mum playing the organ, which gave me a head start over my rivals when it came to auditioning for the real thing.

My father was a member of a local amateur dramatic society and I managed to persuade him that it would be a good idea if I joined as well. Once in, I beavered away to such good effect that, when the society put on Gilbert and Sullivan's *The Gondoliers*, I landed the second tenor part while Dad, quite rightly, had the tenor lead. At the tender age of seventeen this was the first time I had played love scenes on the stage—or anywhere else, come to that—and I found it a most enjoyable experience. Among other things, it involved clasping to my teenage chest a very pretty leading lady, aged about thirty, with auburn hair and a stunning figure. I had always longed to be in showbiz and, if you'll pardon the pun, that clinched it!

Back in the 1930s much of this do-it-yourself entertainment was a necessity where we lived, because there wasn't very much fun to be had in Cinderford without it. This was especially true of our family. My mother's side was very religious— some might say obsessively religious. For instance, my grandfather wouldn't allow shoes to be polished on Sundays, so they had to be polished on Saturday in preparation for church on Sunday. Sewing was also banned. Grandad never explained why the Good Lord should want to forbid us to clean or sew on Sundays, and none of us had the courage to ask. He also believed that cinemas were evil places where the devil lurked in the darkness, and my grandfather's beliefs were imposed with an iron will on the whole of the family. So, since Cinderford had only one cinema, and I had been indoctrinated into believing that the devil was living in it, I was almost thirteen before I plucked up enough courage to sneak in to see a film.

A tiny, deeply religious woman, my mother seemed frail but had a great inner strength, probably provided by her total and absolute faith. She had a great sense of humour and fun and she laughed a lot. And she had many, many friends who adored her. Apart from her love for me, her life centred on her religion and her music. Both of them were there for her in Cinderford and I knew she was unlikely to move away from the area. Several times, in later years, I suggested that she should join me in London, but her roots and her friends were in the Forest of Dean and that is where she stayed for the rest of her life. I often feel that she died with one wish unfulfilled—the wish to see me as I am now, happily and permanently linked to a woman who is in every sense committed to me, and to whom I too am totally committed.

*   *   *

Unfortunately, by the late 1930s relationships of this kind had ceased to be part of the Young household. For much of the time now I was living in a cold, silent atmosphere with parents who, unless they were rowing, did not talk to each other except through me. I had a father who was seldom at home because he was with another woman, and a mother who was sitting at home alone either doing the business books or sewing or knitting and often crying. My home life, such as it was, was falling apart. In 1939 my parents told me they had decided to get divorced.

The stark reality facing me was that my father had left home to live with his mistress and I couldn't see myself realising my ambitions if I stayed behind in Cinderford. Thoroughly confused and needing to think through my future, I left home and sought temporary accommodation with friends of my mother's not far away in Newport. But clearly I couldn't impose on them for long. I had no academic qualifications. In fact I had no training for anything other than working in a bakehouse or delivering bread, jobs which I had never enjoyed and to which I certainly didn't want to return.

So what was I to do?

CHAPTER TWO

RITES OF PASSAGE

Aged eighteen days short of eighteen years, I felt boxed into a corner when suddenly, aurally and visually, I sensed that there might be an escape route. It was supplied aurally by Mr Neville Chamberlain on Sunday, 3 September 1939 when I heard him declare on the wireless that we were at war with Germany. Visually it came simply by looking out of my window. Immediately opposite, and looking very inviting just at that moment, was an Army barracks.

At a stroke, or more accurately at a glance, my problem was solved. Since I would be called up eventually, why not solve all my problems right now? The Army could supply me with a job, clothing, food and accommodation, so why didn't I simply walk across the road and join up? I packed my few belongings into my pathetic little suitcase, burned my bridges by telling my Newport friends that I was off to join the Army, and walked across to the barracks.

The soldier at the entrance introduced me to a friendly-looking sergeant who asked whether I had had breakfast.

'No, sir,' I replied.

He escorted me to a huge dining hall packed with soldiers who were all tucking in with great gusto. The noise level was high. The atmosphere was warm. I began to feel that perhaps this might be a home for me after all. And that was before we

17

even got to the food. When we did it turned out to be double eggs and bacon, sausages, beans and toast. And seconds if you could manage it. I had seldom eaten as well as this, even at home, and I decided there and then that, if this was the way the Army lived, it would do me very nicely thank you very much.

Breakfast over, my friendly sergeant and I got down to the serious business of joining up. It didn't take very long.

'How old are you? he asked.

'Seventeen, sir,' I replied.

'I'm afraid you're too young,' he said. 'Come back when you're eighteen.'

Easier said than done. In fact, now I had a big problem. I had already informed my friends of my intention to join the Army and I'd taken my few worldly possessions with me. I didn't want to slink back with my tail between my legs. As I walked out of the Army barracks my stomach was comfortably full but it wouldn't stay that way for long. I had very little money and nowhere to sleep that night. I had to find a home, but if the Army wouldn't have me who would?

I pondered the question as I walked along clutching my little stiffened cardboard suitcase. I didn't fancy the Navy. All that pitching and tossing and Hello Sailors. That only left the Air Force—and, blow me down, what should I see before me but an RAF recruiting office. I went in and announced that I would like to join the Royal Air Force.

'How old are you?' asked the friendly RAF recruiting sergeant.

'Eighteen, sir,' I replied. (I'm a quick learner.)

18

'Right,' he said. 'Just give me all your details and then go home and we'll send for you in due course.'

'I'm afraid I can't do that, sir,' I replied. I explained that my home life had fallen apart, which was true, and then I stretched the truth a little by saying that I literally had nowhere to sleep that night. With all my worldly goods in my battered little suitcase I obviously looked the part, and by the end of the afternoon I was on a train heading for the huge RAF depot at Padgate, just outside Warrington in Lancashire.

Since most of the airmen at Padgate were volunteer reservists who were considerably older than me, my transition from boyhood to manhood was very swift. Until that time I had rarely drunk alcohol. Within a week they'd fixed all that and I was carousing around Warrington with the rest of them.

I had been at Padgate for about three weeks when I was summoned to the guardroom. The message was that my father was there to see me. Apparently my mother's friends in Newport had told her I'd joined up. She'd contacted my father and he, probably appalled by the swift and dramatic consequences of the marital break-up, had traced me through the Air Force. When I met him at the guardroom he promptly burst into tears. But it was too late for tears. I was in for the duration of the war, however long that might be. My father and I went out for dinner in Warrington that evening, but it was an uncomfortable time we spent together. I was no longer a boy. In a very short time I had grown up. I was a young man and our lives were now set on very different courses. His life was with his new wife and family. I was on

19

my way to God knows where with the RAF.

And so I settled down to service life, drilling and marching with a pack on my back. In some strange way I enjoyed it, though sometimes after a strenuous route march I was too exhausted to do anything other than collapse in full kit and boots on to my bed and sleep the sleep of the dead. Around midnight, some of my boisterous and more energetic fellow squaddies would return to camp, full of booze and bonhomie, and shake me back into life. Then I'd strip down to my underclothes, climb between the blankets and sleep on like a baby until reveille. In later life one of my big problems has been insomnia. A few tough route marches around London with a full pack should cure that nicely. But then again, perhaps not.

So what was the RAF planning to do with this young chap from Cinderford? Back in Newport when I signed on I had volunteered for air crew, hoping to become a pilot. If I was going to fly in something I wanted to drive it myself—I have never been a good passenger. So it was off down south to Bexhill by the sea in Sussex where there was an air crew training centre. Most of the hotels had been taken over by the RAF and I was billeted in one of them. We did our press-ups and physical jerks in the swish and streamlined De La Warr Pavilion, but the first objective was to master Morse code. However by this time it was the middle of winter, bitterly cold, with huge waves breaking over the sea front and lashing us with freezing spray. It did its damage. It wasn't long before I was laid low with the thing that has laid me low all through my life—that chest.

It soon became obvious to my masters in the

RAF that I was never going to make a pilot as long as I breathed—or ceased to breathe, as seemed likely at one stage. And so, as a 'sporty type', I was posted to Uxbridge in Middlesex where, weak chest or no weak chest, I trained as a physical training instructor. Taking the course at the same time were an assortment of British sporting names from all fields, including flyweight title challenger Peter Kane. This underlined for me the wisdom of the service maxim, 'Never volunteer for anything', especially if it involves getting into a boxing ring. You never know whom you might meet. I enjoyed boxing, although not with Peter Kane, but my main interest was rugby and I was about to get the chance to pursue that much further.

On completion of the course I was posted to Compton Bassett in Wiltshire—sounds delightful, doesn't it? In fact it was a group of wooden huts in the middle of a bleak and wintry Salisbury Plain. A colleague there was Les Howe, who had played soccer for Tottenham Hotspur. There was also Jack Hesketh, who was to become a firm friend— but our immediate area of mutual interest was rugby. Jack was a member of a very famous rugby league family. His father, Tom, was a director of Wigan Rugby League Club and, formerly, a player of great distinction himself. Jack and I played rugby together at Compton Bassett and, when I spent weekend leaves at his home in Wigan, we did our training at Wigan's famous Central Park. Jack was kind enough to say he thought I had great potential, but training at Central Park was the nearest I got to actually wearing Wigan's cherry and white. However, some years later I received notification that I had been elected an honorary

21

life member of the Wigan Rugby Social and Working Men's Club at Central Park. An honour which is my sole entry in *Who's Who* under 'Clubs'. I should also record that an English rugby union captain said kind words about my rugby-playing abilities, but more of that later.

Compton Bassett also saw a brief reunion with my father. By a strange coincidence he had moved with his mistress, now his wife, to nearby Bradford on Avon, where he had taken over a newsagent's and tobacconist's shop, and we met from time to time. However, it was also while I was at Compton Bassett that his wife presented him with twins. A new wife and a new family, then. It was clear that I had made the right decision to try to create a new life for myself on my own.

There was always great rivalry between the services, particularly between the Army and the RAF. So when, as sometimes happened, we entertained Army visitors in the corporals' mess, it was no vicarage tea party. I'm a fairly small fellow and I was certainly the smallest of our bunch at Compton Bassett. So if any Army guest felt like getting a bit stroppy, little Corporal Young was usually the first victim. But one such trouble-maker lived to regret it. In the mess there was a stove, and when you stoke up a service stove you work at it until the top is glowing red and almost transparent with white-hot heat. So, perhaps with fond memories of warming up the plants in my grandfather's greenhouse, one evening, having stood just about as much as a human being can endure, I uplifted this particular visitor and planted him on the stove. He had to be taken to hospital, but a good time was had by all, as they say in the local papers, and I became a legend at Compton Bassett overnight.

It was in February 1941 that I received notification that I had been posted abroad where, as a single man, I would serve for four years. It's difficult to describe the shock to my system. Not very long ago I had been a baker's boy in Cinderford for whom the fourteen-mile journey to Gloucester was an adventure. Now I was to travel four thousand miles to India and stay there for several years. I would go out aged nineteen and return aged twenty-three. I would have lived for all that time in a different environment, in a different lifestyle, in a vastly different culture. No doubt I would learn things from the experience, but I doubted that it was the ideal way to complete the transition from boyhood to manhood. How wrong I was.

We sailed out from Greenock in a blacked-out convoy escorted by warships and, as we sat lazily around on deck, the journey almost assumed the air of a pleasure cruise. That is if you could forget the obvious dangers from the German submarines that were sinking so much Allied shipping.

Durban, at the southern tip of South Africa, was a beautiful sight as we steamed towards it in the darkness. Our ship was still blacked out and we had sailed from a Britain that showed no lights once evening came. People stumbled about with torches in their hands. Cars had tiny slits of light where there used to be headlamps. Once indoors, you couldn't switch on a light until the blackout curtains had been drawn. The slightest chink of light would bring an angry air-raid warden hammering on your door. No street lamps, no cheerful advertising signs. Now here was Durban, a twinkling, blazing mass of light, a welcome oasis of brightness on a long, dark voyage. The contrast was almost unbelievable. Then it was on through the Indian Ocean, rather safer than the Atlantic, until we arrived at Bombay, the Gateway to India.

The impact on a country boy from the Forest of Dean was simply enormous. For a start there was the smell. Not that it was unpleasant, but it was certainly very different from home. And yet, of course, this now *was* home. And it was going to be home for the next four years.

I still didn't know where I was going to end up and I, along with many hundreds more, spent several weeks in a transit camp just outside Bombay while the authorities decided what to do with us. I was still the Virgin Airman—a situation that some of my colleagues were keen to bring to an end. In my ignorance, or innocence, I had no idea where six of them were taking me one steamy evening near the Bombay waterfront. They led the way along a narrow side street, then through a door into a long, dark hall that eventually gave way to a wide, winding staircase. I was last in the line when we reached the top, and suddenly I got the feeling that this was an unsavoury kind of place and I didn't like the atmosphere one little bit. There was only one thing to do. Scarper. This was obviously one of those places they had warned us about. There was nothing prudish about it. If the Military Police caught me I was for the chop.

I hurried back down the staircase and into the pitch darkness of the hall. There a hand suddenly reached out and grabbed me. I could just make out the faint outline of a peaked cap—a military policeman. 'I want you!' he growled. 'You're in the Air Force, aren't you?' My months of physical training instruction were about to come into their own. The MP had my left arm in his right hand. I whipped my other arm smartly round, broke his grip on me, punched him in the face and ran, hurtling out through the door and into the street.

If the Compton Bassett rugby team could have seen me they would have been proud. Whistles blew, and soon there were four MPs trying to catch up with me. Believe me, they stood no chance. The fear of a military prison forced me on. In the darkness I outpaced them and escaped arrest.

Later, search parties went round the camp, as the MPs tried to identify this young upstart who had messed up the sour looks of one of their upstanding lads. No one recognised me. The darkness had saved me and I felt not a little pleased with myself. Doubly so, in fact. Out of my six colleagues who stayed on and sampled the fun and games, four subsequently had to enlist the help of the Medical Officer. Retribution for trying to lead a pure young airman astray, I reckoned.

It was eventually decided that, along with several others, I should begin my posting in India at the RAF station at Drigh Road, Karachi. We were to get there by train.

The train journey from Bombay to Karachi involves crossing the Sind desert. And should you be reading this as you are doing exactly that, travelling in your twenty-first-century super-duper air-conditioned luxury carriage, I can hear you saying, 'So—what's the problem?' You should try doing it in a wooden carriage with wooden benches instead of seats and no glass in the windows. The

25

carefully tended parts of Bombay are green. The Sind desert is not, and the sand swirled in through the spaces where the windows should have been. It also swirled up your nose and down your throat. It found, and filled, every orifice. We passed small towns where every house had a metal wind funnel sticking out of the roof in a desperate attempt to catch any little passing breeze that might help to cool the place. The only bit of good news was that you could buy a bathful of ice and put it in your train compartment. The theory was that it would cool the air. We paid for a bathful and put our feet in it. Heaven. But such was the heat that in fifteen minutes it had melted. Not much of a bargain, really.

Eventually we arrived in Karachi. It was not green and cared for in the way that Bombay had been, but it was on the coast and there was a nice sea breeze blowing. Maybe it wasn't going to be too bad after all. What I didn't know was that Drigh Road was a very long thoroughfare leading straight back into the Sind desert. However, as long as you kept your eyes peeled for the bugs, scorpions and snakes the camp itself was quite comfortable.

There were a couple of good things about Karachi. One was that we managed to establish a thriving concert party and dance band, so I was able to keep my hand in at the showbusiness that I hoped to join after the war. The other was that we had an excellent rugby team. Our captain was Bob Stirling, a forward of such outstanding talent that he captained England. Bob led from the front, and we did our best to live up to the excellent example he set. Many years later, when asked to comment on my singing, Bob said that he didn't know too much about music but he really remembered me best as a gutsy, courageous and nippy wing three-quarter. I'm only too happy to accept that assessment from an England captain.

We took on other Air Force units and the Army. The officers and gentlemen of the Dragoon Guards were around those parts at that time and rather fancied themselves at rugby. It was, therefore, an immense delight always to beat them. One officer and gentleman, however, did get his own back. Somewhat frustrated because I had scored a few tries, he came in with a short arm tackle that severely damaged my nose. I have had two operations on it and still can't breathe properly!

What with the concert party and rugby activities, my two years at Karachi passed quickly. I was then posted to a hill station called Chakrata. Hill stations were where troops would come for rest and recuperation leave, and I was sent to help set up entertainment for them. There was no rugby at Chakrata. The camp was perched on a small plateau eight thousand feet up a mountain, and kicking for touch would have cost a fortune in lost balls. However, there were other skills to learn—and I set about learning them with considerable enthusiasm.

Just one mile from Chakrata was Kailana, which differed from Chakrata in one crucial respect. It was full of women. They were servicemen's wives, considered too delicate to be with their husbands in the stifling heat of the plains, and therefore waiting in the cool beauty of the hills for their husbands to visit them. And not all were cool. Some were distinctly warm and cuddly and missing the joys of married life. They were also willing to share some of those joys, on a temporary basis, with us lonely airmen. Aged twenty-two, I was selected for further education by a charming lady some fifteen years older. I was a Virgin Airman and she saw it as her duty to teach me the things a young man should know about the art of pleasing a woman. I like to think that she was a successful teacher.

CHAPTER THREE

LEARNING THE HARD WAY

In 1945, with my four not entirely wasted years served, I was posted back home. My ambition to become a professional singer was still as strong as ever and on my return to England I pursued it. To the detriment of my personal life, I'm afraid.

My first stop on my return was at a hospital near Sleaford in Lincolnshire where I was admitted with a minor ailment. An operation was performed on a delicate part of my anatomy—without an anaesthetic—which was both painful and unsuccessful. When they thought I was all right to face the world again I went on sick leave to my father's home at Bradford on Avon. This marked another important moment in my life. The time I spent with my father and his new family convinced me that, even if he had wanted me to, becoming a part of his personal and business life again was just not possible. Too much water had passed under the bridge. He had built a new life for himself and, quite simply, it would be both unfair and unwise for me to try to insert myself into it.

No, the hard reality of life was that I would come out of the RAF to nothing. My mother was still in Cinderford, but there was no future for me there. I was on my own. I had to stand on my own two feet and make a new life for myself. So far, then, I had faced facts and made a rational decision. However, I was still a confused young man and, probably influenced by my happy liaison in India, I was about to make an irrational one.

Horizontal patients often develop a crush on vertical nurses. When I was in hospital I had been looked after by Wendy, a very attractive young woman with a great sense of humour. I was a vigorous young man who had learned to enjoy female company and the comforts of home during my two years at Chakrata. Add to that the fact that I now had no home to go to, and the outcome was almost entirely predictable. Wendy and I dated, and in 1945 we got married.

I still didn't have a job, but Wendy's brother Marcel, a hairdresser, came to our rescue. He was kindness itself and gave me a job managing one of his London businesses. You might think that with all this I would be satisfied. But no—my obsession with making music my career would destroy our marriage.

I managed Marcel's shop, but my heart wasn't in it. I spent all my lunch hours in the Denmark Street area around Charing Cross Road, the heart of London's Tin Pan Alley. In those days music publishers dominated the scene, feeding songs to artists, record companies and the airwaves (whereas today many top singers publish their own songs and issue their own records). So I used to

29

lurk around their offices, trying to get someone interested enough to push me in the right direction. It was a heartbreak way to spend a lunch break. Sometimes I might get a few words with a publisher. Sometimes I went back to the shop without even having been able to set foot in an office.

Wendy and I had originally set up home in one room in Barrow Road, Streatham, but then moved to another a little better in Eastcote, which was where we were living when our daughter, Lesley Ann, was born in 1947. Clearly one room was now hardly ideal, so brother-in-law Marcel stepped in to help us again and said that we could have the flat above another of his hairdressing establishments, Margaret's, in Warren Drive, Tolworth, in Surrey.

With hindsight I think I would have been a prime specimen for a psychiatrist at this stage. One part of me was going through the motions of trying to appear normal and settle down in a mundane nine-to-five job. The other, much larger, part had no intention of doing anything of the kind. It was totally set on getting me into showbusiness and, come hell or high water, no matter the damage inflicted on me or anybody else, it was going to get me there.

Thus normal, dull Leslie Ronald Young applied to the Ministry of Education for a one-year teacher training course and was accepted. What was more, while I was waiting for the course to start I was offered, and accepted, a job as a temporary civil servant at the Ministry of Education's offices in Lennox Gardens, off Sloane Street. But showbiz-obsessed Jimmy Young (as 'Our Jim' from Cinderford had now become in that area of his life) was never cut out to be a civil servant. So, even while working for the Min. of Ed., I continued to haunt music publishers' offices and to audition for anybody who was willing to listen to me.

I auditioned twice for top theatrical agent Lillian Aza. She was wonderfully kind and helpful and arranged for me to audition for the BBC. Initially I failed, and Lillian received a letter informing her that the BBC considered that Mr Young had no future in broadcasting. However, I managed to secure another audition and this time I passed. But that was when I discovered the BBC's quaint system. What I had passed was just an audition. I was now required to take a 'seeded' audition. It seemed to me a bit like the Grand National. Having successfully survived Becher's Brook you then discovered that you had to jump the Chair.

Anyway, I successfully cleared both hurdles and in due course I received a letter, dated 16 June 1948, from the BBC's Joy Russell-Smith. It read, 'Following your audition on the 11th June, I am pleased to be able to tell you that you have gained the requisite number of marks and have, therefore, passed successfully. It now remains to be seen whether you can be used in broadcasts. Directly I have further news I will, of course, let you know.' I cannot now remember whether the then naïve me actually cheered, believing that in a matter of a few weeks I should be on the wireless. But if I did I shouldn't have. The key sentence in the letter was, of course, 'It now remains to be seen whether you can be used in broadcasts.' It seems they decided that I couldn't and they didn't. Meanwhile I plugged on at the Min. of Ed. while still driving music publishers and agents mad.

Then came the magic day when one agent actually said yes. He operated from very seedy offices in Soho. Let's put it this way. If your daughter was a dancer looking for work you wouldn't be too happy if she was looking to find it in this office. The offer was for me to appear for a week on a variety bill at Deal in Kent, and my salary was to be £15. I worked out that by getting off early from work and getting the first train back I could just about do Deal without losing my job, so I accepted.

Audiences at Deal were practically non-existent, and in the communal dressing room the human half of a dog act complained that we weren't going to get paid. A tired old music hall singer observed, 'I don't know what *you're* moaning about. You can always eat the act. But what about us?' It was my first encounter with the ability of pros to laugh in the face of adversity. It was a quality I admired. And I was going to need it myself many times in the future. I never got paid for the week at Deal, of course, but that did nothing to dim my determination. So I continued to slog on at the Min. of Ed. and haunt music publishers whenever I could.

The year 1949 was to prove an eventful one for me. In fact it was a year which changed my life both professionally and domestically. I received a phone call one day from a pianist named Bill Williams. Bill was not a star name but was much respected in the music business. He played at a club in South Molton Street in London's West End, and was looking for someone to stand in for him for one night while he earned better money at a gig elsewhere. I was nervous about saying yes, but my enthusiasm was such that I would have said yes to conducting the London Philharmonic.

The date was a festive occasion. The object of the exercise for the patrons was to get sloshed and fall about the floor, which suited me. I bashed away to try to be heard above the din. I sang and there was applause, and the evening was quite a party. It must have been a success, because Bill called me again on the phone within a few weeks with another offer—to play and sing every evening at the Nordic Club by the Thames at Hampton Court. He had been offered the job but couldn't accept, so he recommended me.

Soon the strain of the life I was now leading was really beginning to tell on Wendy and me. Rushing home when the day's work was through. Then rushing off to Hampton Court to play piano until whatever hour of the night was necessary. Then home to bed at Tolworth . . . and up again and into the same routine, day after day. Something had to give—and it did. As a recipe for financial advancement, working all day and half the night may be good thinking. As a recipe for marital happiness it's just the opposite.

But by now I thought I could see my musical career opening up, and my obsession with that took over completely. As ever, I was determined to succeed—whatever the damage to myself and others. As the unhappiness I was causing in our marriage grew I abandoned home, wife and baby daughter and went to live a pretty unhappy domestic life in a bedsit with a gas ring in Surbiton. I think I probably viewed my lonely existence there as a punishment for the way I was treating Wendy and Lesley.

Fortunately, after we were divorced Wendy remarried, and I was delighted. Perhaps in her new marriage she would find the happiness that I had not given her in ours. Wendy also suggested that it would be better for Lesley if she was legally adopted by her new stepfather, and I agreed.

It was to be many years before I saw Lesley again. She grew up without my knowing her. In fact, it was as a young woman that she rang me one day from London's Heathrow airport where she was seeing friends off to America. I was fearful that, when we met, her feelings towards me would be bitter because of the way I had abandoned her as a baby. Fortunately she is such a warm, loving person that those fears never materialised.

In fact, although I didn't know it at the time, Lesley too had suffered a considerable shock. She grew up thinking that her stepfather was her real father. Because of my high media profile, I was referred to as 'he' or 'him'. As in, 'Did you hear what *he* said this morning?' Fairly naturally— Lesley being an extremely bright lady who has attained both BA and MA status—she started to wonder who this mysterious 'he' was. She asked around and found out, and in due course found me.

I'm a very lucky man. In spite of the bumpy ride over the early years there is no trauma or bitterness. Just a very loving, warm closeness between Lesley, my wife Alicia and myself.

*   *   *

Meanwhile, back in 1949, into my life that June came a quiet, unassuming man named George

34

Inns. George had started in radio as a call boy with the BBC and was now a senior and highly respected producer. He strolled into the Nordic Club and, after listening to me play and sing for a while, asked if I would like to join him for a drink. He asked me if I had ever broadcast. I recalled my BBC auditions and the great silence that followed them and George, having made some sympathetic noises, promised to see if there was anything he could do about it. I went back to the piano, George eventually went home, and I wondered whether I should ever see or even hear from him again.

Within a few weeks he was back again, this time with John Hooper, another BBC producer. I discovered later that George had been raving about this fantastic young fellow named Jimmy Young working at the Nordic Club. 'He should be broadcasting,' said George, and he had talked John into coming along to listen.

Not only that but, knowing I had no money, George paid for me to make a demonstration record to play to someone higher up the scale at the BBC. A few days later George was back at the club again, saying that he thought I could do better. So we made another record. This time he was happier with the result and said he would contact me when he had any news.

The news came in June. Mr Inns had made an appointment for me to see a man called Jim Davidson. Mr Davidson was a very important person indeed. He was the Assistant Head of the BBC's Variety Department. He could launch, or not launch, careers. He was also a blunt, brusque, rough Australian and he frightened the life out of me.

Mr Inns went with me into Mr Davidson's office. I received a grunted greeting. Side one of my record was listened to in silence. In fact, Mr Davidson was busy with his managerial correspondence and I wondered if he was even listening. Side two went on. Again silence. Until it finished when Mr Davidson said, 'Put the first side on again.'

I had not been invited to have a seat, so I stood there in silence while my future was being decided. Midway through the replay of side one I saw Mr Davidson press a buzzer. 'That's it,' I thought. 'I'm about to be thrown out.' A secretary appeared and Mr Davidson said, 'Fetch the book.'

I hadn't the faintest idea what was going on, and Mr Inns leaned against the office wall looking as though he was wishing he'd never started all this in the first place. The book was placed on Mr Davidson's desk and he opened it. He flicked through a few pages and then suddenly said to me, 'What are you doing on 9 August?'

'Nothing, sir,' I replied.

'Right,' said the great man. 'Thank you, George.' We were dismissed.

Outside the office we paused in the corridor. Mr Inns said, 'I've never seen anything like that in all my years with the BBC.'

I still had no idea how the meeting had gone, so I said, 'What happened, then, Mr Inns?'

He replied, 'You've got a broadcast on 9 August.'

I was to share a programme with the Ronnie Pleydell Orchestra. I would be singing and playing four songs and so, for help with my very first broadcast, I turned to the music publishers whom I

36

had been driving mad for so long. And to one publisher who had been particularly helpful. He was Cliff Adams, who would later mastermind the long-running and very successful *Sing Something Simple* programme but who then worked at the famous publishers Campbell Connelly.

These were the infamous days of what was called 'plug money'. Some music publishers would pay popular broadcasters back-handers—cash to feature their songs on air. In other words, to 'plug' them. A scandal blew up when certain greedy bandleaders with a thirty-minute broadcast decided to play one chorus per song seque—in other words, without a break in between. You can get an awful lot of songs into thirty minutes like that. And at, say, £20 plug money per song it was a lucrative business. A number of BBC producers decided that, since they were the ones handing out the broadcast dates in the first place, they'd like a slice of the back-hander action as well. At least one got fired as a result.

But at this time I wasn't even in 'the business' as a full-time pro, so I knew nothing of all that. Suffice to say that if you had to sing four songs on a broadcast it was a good idea to ensure that they came from four different publishers. It's true that all four could pay plug money, but somehow it didn't seem as obvious as if all your songs came from the same publisher.

Cliff Adams, an extremely good piano player himself, coached me. And although I didn't realise it, also plugged me at the same time. Thus it was that when my great day, 9 August 1949, arrived, I sat at the piano with four Campbell Connelly songs to sing. Accusations of plug money could have killed my career before it even got started. However, I was naïve and innocent and that may have been what saved me.

Singing with the Ronnie Pleydell Orchestra that day was a young lady named Sally Douglas. Realising how nervous I was, she very kindly stood by the piano and turned my music for me while I played and sang. Sally was very soon to play a much bigger part in my life. More of that later.

Meanwhile the broadcast was a great success, and job offers flooded in. It was decision time. Either I clung on to my day job and played at showbusiness as a part-time amateur, or I took a deep breath and plunged in at the deep end. It was no contest from the start. I said goodbye to the Min. of Ed. and my prospects of becoming a teacher with no regrets. For better or worse, it was now showbusiness success or bust.

One of the most famous bandleaders at that time was Ray Martin, who later had a huge international hit record with 'Blue Tango'. Ray wanted a female and a male singer for his weekly BBC broadcasts with the Northern Variety Orchestra from Manchester. He already had the female, and asked if I would be interested in becoming his male vocalist. You bet I would. What I didn't know until I got to Manchester was that his female vocalist was Sally Douglas. It already seemed as though fate was at work.

Sally was tall, Junoesque and rather affected in manner. She wore ornate spectacles with upswept sides and smoked cigarettes through a long holder. In fact, with hindsight it is difficult to imagine anyone less suited to me. However, she was an experienced vocalist who had sung with many top-line bands and I must confess I found her absolutely fascinating to talk to. Our friendship developed into an affair but Sally always made it clear to me that, just because we were sleeping together, she didn't expect me to marry her. It was almost as though she was warning me off. If I'd had the sense I was born with I would have listened.

It would be wrong to describe ours as a 'love' affair. It was more a 'business' affair, but it led Sally and me to Marylebone Registry Office just the same. I can't remember much about the marriage ceremony, except that it was all over very quickly. Then Sally had to dash off to Manchester for a broadcast. We spent our wedding night two hundred miles apart. Not a very promising start to our marriage, and it was to get worse.

My new friend from my first broadcast, Ronnie Pleydell, had landed, subject to audition, the resident bandleader job at the very fashionable Trocadero in Shaftesbury Avenue. However, the management refused to pay for a singer unless he or she could play an instrument as well, so Ronnie asked if I would like to join him as his second pianist and singer. When I pointed out that his band's library didn't contain any arrangements for two pianos, Ronnie quite reasonably replied that, while he and I knew that, the Trocadero management didn't.

And so we auditioned. The band was on the stage. Management was sitting out front. The band went first. Then I sang.

'Very good,' said management. 'Could we now hear something with Mr Young playing piano?'

Fortunately the pianos were arranged so that the sharp ends pointed towards the dance floor where management was sitting. I say 'fortunately' because that meant they couldn't see the keyboards.

'One, two, one, two, three, four,' called Ronnie. Away went the band. Mr Young waved his hands over the keyboard and we got the job.

We were comfortably installed at the Trocadero when Ronnie had to fly to America urgently on a business trip. He asked me to stand in as bandleader while he was away. By this time I had figured out that you didn't need to be an ace musician to be a bandleader. As cynical musicians often observed, 'Most punters—and some bandleaders—can't tell a crotchet from a hatchet.' Management of a dining-and-dancing restaurant hate to think they are paying a band that nobody wants to dance to. What was needed was the ability to judge what tempo of music would attract diners on to the dance floor and, once you'd got them there, the ability to chat them up. So, having decided what we were going to play, I would get the band started, then turn my back and let them get on with it. Meanwhile I attended to the social side with the customers.

I took to this role like a duck to water, and very soon came an offer to step up the ladder. I was invited to form a trio to play in a new club called the Carousel, which was about to open in the basement of the very fashionable dining-and-dancing restaurant 96 Piccadilly.

Most musicians receiving such an offer would have been over the moon. I had only been in the entertainment business for less than a year and it frightened the life out of me. Because of my temporary promotion to bandleader at the Trocadero my wage there had gone up from £12 to

£15 per week. In addition, I was earning about £15 per week from broadcasts. An impressive total of £30 a week. Would I be better off staying where I was on my 'guaranteed' £30 a week, rather than taking a gamble on a new club which might not succeed? But colleagues who had been in the music world far longer than me pointed out that nothing is guaranteed in our business. It's extremely high-risk. You can be flavour of the month today, and out on your ear with nothing tomorrow. The advice I got was that, if a step up the ladder was offered, I should accept the risk and grab it with both hands.

I jumped in at the deep end and accepted. However, even though it meant I would keep less money for myself, I had the good business sense to hire a bass player and a guitarist who I hoped would make up for my shortcomings as a pianist. Bass player Arthur Watts and guitarist Roy Plummer were acknowledged in the music business as being at the very top of the profession. Both were very much in demand for recording sessions, and I was relieved and flattered when they agreed to join me.

Jack and Daphne Barker, just about the biggest cabaret act in London's West End at the time, provided the floor show and the Carousel quickly became the 'in' place to be. It was packed every night. At two o'clock one morning Roy Plummer leaned over the piano to me and uttered the immortal words, 'You've obviously got something because this place is always full, but I don't know what it is. You certainly can't play the bloody piano.'

Well, in my own defence I suppose I should say

that I also sang, and it was in the Carousel that I got my first break in a national newspaper. I had noticed that a short, round, bespectacled gentleman had become a regular at the club, and one night he came over to the piano. He invited me, at our next break, to join him at his table for a drink. I went over and he introduced himself as Arthur Christiansen, editor of the *Daily Express*. Chris, as I later came to know him, said he was very impressed with my playing and singing and said he was personally going to write an article about me for the *Express*. I was perhaps too naïve at the time fully to appreciate what an honour it was to have the editor—and a legendary editor at that—write it himself. I was proud in later years to be able to count myself among his many friends.

Clearly I was quickly making a name for myself, and Jack and Daphne Barker asked me to join them, with my band, in a new club they were to open in Swallow Street, near Piccadilly Circus. It was another challenge that I accepted, and it went well. So well that, early in 1951, my old bosses at 96 Piccadilly invited me to return to lead a larger band in their main dining-and-dancing restaurant.

Into the club one evening came a stocky young gentleman named Alan Freeman. Not Alan 'Fluff' Freeman, the DJ and performer, but a behind-the-scenes Alan Freeman, a clever and ambitious entrepreneur. In an era when huge companies like Decca and EMI dominated the recording scene Alan had taken the gamble of starting up a small recording company which he called Polygon. He had signed only two artists. One was bandleader Ray Martin. The other was a young lady called Petula Clark. Alan asked if I would like to join him.

Neither of the two giants seemed to be interested in me and so, fairly quickly, I said that I would. We released two records that were greeted with little enthusiasm, but Alan seemed prepared to persevere with me. Anxious not to release three flops in a row I hung back, hoping for some kind of a miracle. I again took to haunting the offices of music publishers, looking for potential hit material, and one day the miracle arrived.

I was sitting in the office of a music publisher named Allan Holmes when he burst through the door laughing and waving a sheet of music in the air. 'I've got it, Jim,' he said. 'I've got just the right song for you. It's a hit. It can't miss. It's even got your name in the title.' He waved the music in front of me. The title was, 'Too Young'.

I sat down at the piano in Allan's office and played and sang it. I was convinced. His publishing instincts were right. I was sure it was the song I had been waiting for, and the sooner I recorded it the better. Fortunately Alan Freeman agreed. After all, he had to pay for the recording session.

But first we needed someone very special to arrange and orchestrate the music, and to conduct the orchestra at the recording session. On several broadcasts I had worked with a young, brilliant, although unknown staff arranger for a music publisher, and I was sure he was the man for the job. He had never conducted an orchestra before and, as he told me some years later, was so terrified that, prior to the big day, he spent a lot of time in front of a mirror at home practising. His name was Ron Goodwin. And although he may have been terrified in 1951 he went on to become world-famous for his superb film scores including

43

Those Magnificent Men in Their Flying Machines.

For reasons best known to himself, but probably budget, Alan Freeman had chosen the Conway Hall in Red Lion Square, Holborn as the venue for the recording. The Conway Hall is well known as a venue for radicals to make fiery speeches. It is not well known as a recording studio suitably equipped for making hit records. However, that's where we were and we just had to make the best of it.

The recording equipment was frighteningly primitive. Even in 1951 it would have been laughed at by one of the major recording companies. Alan, Ron and I heaved and sweated a portable bag of tricks into a tiny room off the side of the stage. The means of communication between the suits in the control room and me on the stage was an ex-Army surplus field telephone.

The orchestra was assembled on the floor of the hall and the stage curtain was closed so that not too much of the orchestra sound was picked up on my microphone. This meant, of course, that I could no longer see Ron. He and his orchestra were on one side of the curtain and I was on the other. The whole set-up struck me as being straight out of a Heath Robinson cartoon. No way were we going to be able to produce a hit record in these conditions.

How wrong can you be?

At the time that I recorded 'Too Young' Jack Jackson was Britain's top disc jockey, and millions listened every Saturday to his late night radio show. So influential was Jack's show that it was said that if he played your record once and it was commercial you had a hit on your hands. If he played it twice you would reach number one.

Jack would play your record only if he liked it. If

44

he didn't like it, no amount of persuasion or pressure would make him change his mind. He was offered three versions of 'Too Young'. One was by Nat King Cole, one by Steve Conway, and the third was mine. He chose mine, and he played it not once, or even twice, but on three successive Saturdays. Orders flooded in and they swamped Alan Freeman's tiny Polygon label. In those days the giant recording companies controlled the pressing and distribution of records, and they certainly weren't going to press mine if they could help it. However, although Alan may have lacked clout he didn't lack guts. He kept on trying and eventually found a place out in Amersham, in Buckinghamshire, that would press our version.

But Alan found it impossible to keep up with the demand from record dealers and, lacking distribution facilities, I was never going to outsell Nat King Cole. However, I didn't suffer too much, if at all. Record charts had yet to be invented. The popularity guide then was a sheet music best-selling list. 'Too Young' went to number one. I was getting the vast majority of the airplays, so I got a lot of the kudos and press coverage that went with the hit.

I was now one of the hottest recording prospects around, in competition with the really big recording names of the day—Frankie Laine, Slim Whitman, David Whitfield, Doris Day and Perry Como. Unfortunately, I was too new in the business and too naïve to realise it. There was I, still playing and singing away for the same money in Jack and Daphne Barker's club, which was packed with people who'd come to hear me sing 'Too Young'. I didn't have an agent or adviser, so nobody had told me that I could be earning at least ten times more singing the same songs in theatres.

Every night at the club tables were booked by executives from the major record companies. HMV, Philips, Columbia and Decca were all eager to woo me away from Alan Freeman's tiny Polygon. Alan, naturally and rightly, pleaded with me to stay and I, letting my heart rule my head, made a decision which was almost fatal for my career. I turned down all the recording giants who, with their muscle, know-how, greater access to potential hit songs and, most important of all, their distribution, could do so much more for me. Alan had discovered me and given me my first break, and I decided I owed it to him to stay.

Loyalty is a highly commendable trait, but ours can be a cold, unforgiving business. You don't get bonuses for loyalty. It's a high-risk job with no built-in pension plan. Mistakes tend to get savagely punished, and I had just made a major mistake. It was to take four years and a change of record label before I would have another major hit record. Four long, hard, depressing years during which my spirits and my confidence sank so low that I almost disappeared from the business altogether.

By 1953 it was clear that I was struggling with Polygon, and Alan Freeman and I amicably agreed that I should try my luck elsewhere. I signed for the giant Decca label, and the instant result underlined what a huge mistake I had made by turning them down in 1951. In 1953 Frank Chacksfield recorded on Decca, and got to number two in the hit parade with an instrumental written by Charlie Chaplin and called 'Limelight'. Words were added, and it became 'Eternally'. It wasn't exactly the hit song we were looking for but it would do to be getting on

46

with, and so I recorded it. It got to number eight in the Top Twenty, and at least put a temporary halt to my downward slide towards recording oblivion.

Meanwhile I had to earn a living, and that meant touring theatres. Singers like Dickie Valentine and Ronnie Hilton were doing big business. The difference was that they were consistently producing hit records, which I wasn't. It wasn't that I always did bad business, it was just that I didn't always do good business. And playing to a theatre that's only half full in some dreary town doesn't stimulate the adrenaline too much. This was particularly the case when your fortunes were so low that the only way you could get work was by 'putting in your own bill'.

It worked like this. Managers who were no longer willing to pay me a salary would let me take a percentage, usually 55 per cent, of the box office take, out of which I had to pay the cast and sometimes the costs of printing and posters as well. Since managements would insist on a strong supporting cast you simply had to hope that there would be enough left over at the end of the week to make it worthwhile working. I can assure you from bitter experience that on many occasions there wasn't.

I thought it highly ironic that, when I had to put in the bill for a week at the Dudley Hippodrome, I had, as my fourth top of the bill, the man who had helped to make my 'Too Young' a hit—Jack Jackson. I paid Jack £175 for the week. Then there were the second and third top to pay, plus the rest of the cast. On Saturday evening I walked on to the stage knowing that, even if I filled the house for both Saturday performances—which I didn't—I would still lose £300 on the week.

You still have to go on, sing your heart out and look as though you're enjoying every minute of it, even though you feel as though you've just been kicked in the guts—or worse—by a horse. 'Put it down to experience' was the advice from the old pros whose wages I was paying. Well, they say you can't buy experience but you can certainly pay for it. As I was finding out the hard way.

Of course, life was not all doom and gloom. It never is where pros are involved, as was emphasised when I came to play a week at the Hackney Empire. Moss Empire Theatres, who owned it, had just announced that they were going to close theatres during the summer because business slumped so badly when customers went away on holiday. As I walked off stage after closing the first house the stagehands were sitting around having their evening tea-and-sandwich break. However, their usual cheery smiles and banter were missing. In fact they looked decidedly depressed. When I asked why they were looking so miserable I received a reply which was a classic example of showbiz black humour.

'It's this new Moss Empire policy, Jim,' said one of them. 'They're going to close their theatres for eight weeks in the summer. Then, if that's a success, they're going to close them altogether.'

CHAPTER FOUR

NUMBER ONE AT LAST

Since my career was so stalled in the UK I wondered if I could learn something by finding out how things were done in the USA. In the early fifties it was rare to find a British record in the US best-seller lists. America was where most of the hit records were coming from. Those were the days of Johnnie Ray, Frankie Laine, Guy Mitchell and Al Martino. There was no way that I was going to crack America all on my own, but that I went at all gives some idea of how desperate we were.

Decca Records were marketed in America by London Records, who said they would shepherd me around New York and show me the ropes. Funds were so low at the time that I couldn't afford to take Sally with me. She stayed at home close to the phone in case some monumental stroke of good fortune should suddenly turn up. And so I set out on my lonely voyage of discovery.

London Records were as helpful as they could be in the circumstances. They did all the things that record companies are supposed to do for visitors. They took me to do guest appearances on disc jockey shows in New York, Boston and Philadelphia, but you do those for no money and nobody offered me gainful employment. One highlight, although still a non-productive one, was that they had arranged for me to meet Perry Como. At the time Como was not only one of America's most successful recording artists but also a huge star on television.

I sat in the control box with his team as he recorded his television show, clutching my recording of 'Too Young' which I had brought along in the hope that he would hear it and be impressed enough to give me a spot on his show. When I met him after he'd finished recording he was charm itself. You couldn't wish to meet a nicer guy. He took my record away to play in his dressing room. An assistant brought it back later along with complimentary remarks about it. But I never did make it on to the Perry Como television show.

I got my revenge later. In 1956 Como released a song called 'More'. I recorded it too. Perry's version, on HMV, got to number ten and stayed in the charts for eleven weeks. My version, on Decca, got to number four and stayed in the charts for seventeen weeks. I was really chuffed about that, and it seemed to have stung Perry. Shortly afterwards Frank Lee, who was my recording manager at Decca at the time, happened to be shown around a studio in America in which Como was recording. Perry was in mid-song but broke off to say, 'You won't find any material for Jim in here, Frank.' When Frank relayed the story to me I was amazed to think that a giant like Como would even acknowledge a bite in his ankle from a minnow like me. None the less, it was nice to know that I *had* bitten him.

All that my US trip had actually produced were three lousy, lonely weeks. However, as I prepared to head for home I got a phone call from London. It was from the PR man I had hired to try to put the best possible gloss on my visit. Communications between American and British showbusiness weren't as instant then as they are now, and in those days it was possible to plant a story without it being checked on too closely. Accordingly, he had dreamed up a scenario that I had been a big hit on some important shows. Also that I had earned substantial sums of dollars which, knowing that I would be in demand there, I had left in the United States for use on future visits.

So following my 'successful' American trip Sally and I sat in our draughty flat in London's Maida Vale, hoping the phone would ring with offers. It didn't, but one morning the doorbell did. I opened the door, and standing there was a man who didn't look in the least like Lew or Leslie Grade, super-agents. He wore a black jacket and pinstriped trousers. He also wore a bowler hat. He had a briefcase under his arm. He said, 'May I speak to Mr Jimmy Young, please?'

Nursing the hope that he might be an agent in disguise, I said, 'I am he.'

'Oh, good,' he said. 'I am from the Commissioners of Inland Revenue. Now about your American trip and all this money you earned and which you have left there . . .'

It took a long time to convince him that there wasn't any money and it was all a bit of a desperate showbusiness hype to revive a flagging career. By the time I'd finished I think he was actually rather sorry for me. But then, come to think of it, so was I. I simply had to do something about my lack of hit records. It was now 1955 and, apart from my number eight with 'Eternally' in 1953, I had been without a major hit for four years. I was convinced it was nothing to do with my singing. This was a business problem that I had to solve. And I had to

51

be pretty damned quick about it.

The man getting all the hits on Decca in the early 1950s was David Whitfield. He had seven records in the Top Ten, including two number ones in 1953 and 1954. He even smashed his way into the American Top Ten as well. Now it's true that David had a magnificent voice. However, I couldn't help wondering about a few other important factors, too. Who at Decca Records was steering the hit material David's way? Who was masterminding his recording sessions? And who was then promoting his record so successfully?

The answer was a man who was a genius at all those things. His name was Bunny Lewis. I had known Bunny for many years, and although I had never actually worked with him, I was convinced that he was the man to sort out my problems. We met and came to an arrangement whereby he would supervise the whole process of my record-making from start to finish. This meant from the submission and selection of potential recording material right through to the exploitation of the finished record.

That I had made the correct business decision became clear almost immediately. Bunny called me one morning and asked me to go along to his office to talk about a song. As I walked in he handed me some sheet music. I sat down at the piano and played and sang it. Afterwards I said, 'I think that is going to be the most enormous hit, and the sooner we record it the better.' Bunny agreed. It was the title song from an undistinguished B-movie about the trials and tribulations of life in prison, and it was called 'Unchained Melody'.

Bunny very quickly arranged a recording session

at Decca's studios in Hampstead, and I could hardly wait for the day to arrive because I was convinced that this was the song that could put me back in the Top Ten again. And with a bit of luck perhaps even the number one spot. Most singers seemed to prefer recording in the afternoon. I always preferred recording in the morning, and the session was booked from 10am to 1pm.

On the morning in question I woke up with a bellyache. I thought it was a bit of a nuisance but no more than that. I took the usual antacid remedies and expected it to go away. It didn't. In fact it got worse and, by the time I arrived at the studio, I even began to wonder whether it might be something rather worse than a mere stomach ache. But pros learn to live with pain, and so at 10am the recording session began. However, as it progressed so did the pain. Doubled over, I began to resemble a human hairpin. I have always been fairly good at diagnosing my ailments, so the moment arrived when I said, 'I've got appendicitis.'

Of course everybody roared with laughter. By everybody I mean the engineers, the musicians, musical director Bob Sharples and Decca's Dick Rowe who was in charge of the session. Dick's comment was, 'Silly old sod!' Dick was to achieve worldwide fame in later years as the man who turned down the Beatles. He was wrong about me as well.

The session finished at 1pm and I was back home by 1.30. Four hours later I was in London's University College Hospital having an emergency operation for appendicitis. It required twenty-four stitches and left a scar that is of interest to doctors even to this day. Fortunately I don't very often suffer illnesses which require an abdominal examination, but when I do they almost always say, 'That's a very interesting wound—how did you get it?' However, as I lay in hospital nursing my interesting wound at least I could reflect on a job well done. We had made an excellent record of 'Unchained Melody'. It was a winner, and Bunny Lewis would do a magnificent job of promoting it. All was well with the world.

Oh no it wasn't. Unknown to me, Machiavellian forces were at work. In America a singer named Al Hibbler and a bandleader named Les Baxter were both in the charts with 'Unchained Melody', and their versions had already been released over here. But I had Bunny Lewis in my camp now. He would be promoting my record, so surely all would be well? Not necessarily. Things in the record business are not as simple as that. The first visible evidence of things going wrong came when Al Hibbler went into the record charts at number fifteen. Les Baxter quickly followed him. I was nowhere to be seen. So I faced the ludicrous position whereby, thanks to Bunny Lewis, I was getting most of the airplays but the other two were selling the records.

I sat at home wondering what had gone wrong and what I could do about it. Then one morning I received a telephone call from a man in Glasgow. I had never met him, and I still haven't met him, but without his telephone call I wouldn't be writing this book. He was the director of Scotland's biggest record wholesalers and his message was blunt: 'What the bloody hell is going on with this record of yours?' I asked him to explain.

He said, 'I can't get your record and all my retailers are moaning at me. All we can get are

Al Hibbler and Les Baxter. But people don't want Hibbler or Baxter—they want you. They're crying out for your record. If we could get your record you'd be number one up here tomorrow. What the hell is going on at Decca?'

I didn't know the answer so I passed the problem on to my agent who said he would speak to his friend Edward Lewis, later Sir Edward, the top man at Decca. The answer we received was that all the presses allocated to my record had suffered mechanical failure. Put simply, they had all broken down. However, Mr Lewis assured us that the problem would now be speedily rectified.

Anecdotes within the record business suggested that the situation had little to do with the mechanical failure of my presses and much more to do with contractual differences between Decca and Brunswick, for whom Hibbler recorded. Decca pressed and marketed Brunswick in Britain, so in effect Hibbler, although in competition with me, was under the same flag as me. The stories reaching my ears were that Brunswick were unhappy with the way Decca were promoting their artists. Hibbler was number one in America and Decca had better make him a success in Britain or else. Thus a little mechanical trouble with my presses, while no doubt unintentional, would not be unwelcome.

The anecdotes may have been completely wrong, and I shall probably never know for sure what was actually going on behind the scenes, but the call to Mr Lewis produced dynamic results. Within three weeks I was number one. Al Hibbler had to be content with number two.

Getting a number one hit record, especially for

an artist who's not had a real hit for four years, is wonderful. However, it brings problems. How do you follow a number one hit? Simple, really. Make another number one hit. I had been lucky with one title song from a film—might I be lucky with another one?

Unchained had been a B-movie. *The Man from Laramie* was certainly not B-status, because it starred James Stewart. But it too had a title song with which I thought we might be able to do something. Far be it from me to criticise song writers or film producers, but I thought the way they had treated the song in the film was totally wrong. Not to put too fine a point on it, I thought it had great potential but they had thrown it away. They had recorded it as a very slow ballad with orchestra and choir, causing the *Daily Mirror* critic to comment, 'It might just as well be The Man From The Coal Board for all the fire some get into it.'

I don't know whether I could claim to have put some fire into it, but we certainly brightened it up a bit. We put a nice, bright, catchy rhythm behind it and 'The Man from Laramie' shot me up to the top of the charts again. And thus I became the first British recording artist to hit the number one spot twice in a row.

CHAPTER FIVE

FATE TAKES A HAND

The *New Musical Express* confirmed my rehabilitation. In its Top-selling Artists in Britain list for 1955 Ruby Murray was number one and Jimmy Young was number two. Trailing behind were some distinguished names. Frankie Laine was number three, David Whitfield number nine, Tony Bennett number thirteen, Dean Martin number sixteen and, would you believe, trailing in at number seventeen Frank Sinatra. I was to enjoy further recording success later in 1955 with 'Someone on Your Mind' at number thirteen, and I did even better in 1956 when 'Chain Gang' got to number nine and 'More' reached number four.

I was always painstaking in making my records. Sometimes a session would go easily—in the case of 'Too Young' we got the master on the first take. Other times I would have to work hard at it.

In those days there were basically two ways of making a record, but you had to choose which road you were going down before the recording session started. And once you had declared your intention you couldn't change. One way was that you didn't sing on the session—you just recorded the orchestra. In other words you laid down what was called a backing track. The orchestra then went home and you put your vocal on the track.

With this method, the advantage for the orchestra was obvious. They got to go home early. The advantage for the vocalist was that you could

57

sing along to the backing track as many times as you liked until you got it right. The other method, which I preferred, was simply to sing with the orchestra until you got it right. If the session went smoothly and easily, that was fine. If the session proved difficult, it could lead to frayed nerves.

We were certainly having a difficult time following the second method one very hot day at the Decca studios in Hampstead. There was a large orchestra in the studio. The rhythm section was right next to the stairs leading up from the studio floor to the control box. Take followed take and, after each one, on the talk-back the metallic voice of Frank Lee, my recording manager, would say, 'Come up to the box and hear that one, please.' The orchestra leader and I would then trudge wearily up the stairs, past the rhythm section. The orchestra would talk among themselves, desperately hoping that this really would prove to be the master so they could all go home.

Meanwhile, up in the box we would listen, discuss, and then decide that it wasn't really as good as we would like. The next thing the weary orchestra would hear was Frank Lee's voice saying, 'Just one more, please.' This seemed to go on for ever, and eventually it proved just too much for our bass player.

Jack Collier wasn't just any old bass player—he was widely regarded as one of the very best in the business. He also had a biting sense of humour. Jack was right next to the stairs leading up to the control box. As I passed behind him yet again he remarked casually to the orchestra, but in a voice you could have heard all over Hampstead, 'You know, they don't press this Jimmy Young's records.

He makes them all individually.' Predictably, of course, the orchestra roared with laughter and I thought to myself, 'Thank God for the pros' sense of humour.' It can so often defuse tense situations.

*   *   *

My return, twice, to the top of the record charts in 1955 had led to a complete change in my fortunes. Suddenly I was flavour of the year. Top theatres were clamouring for my services. In Derby fans threw red roses on to the stage and police had to be called out to control the crowds. At the Winter Gardens in Bournemouth fans again covered the stage with red roses. Yes, I know that in later years Tom Jones got knickers, but I didn't know that at the time.

The euphoria also led to me landing the starring role in my first pantomime. I was to star with Hylda Baker in *Robinson Crusoe* at the Grand Theatre, Wolverhampton. Miss Baker had been a top-of-the-bill star around the music halls for a long time. I was simply a new boy from the recording world. Yet, although I hadn't asked for it, I was booked as the top of the bill. Quite naturally Miss Baker was not best pleased, and she made her displeasure clear to the management. They solved the problem by printing two posters. In one I was top of the bill. In the other set Miss Baker was top. They made sure it was a copy of the latter set that went up on Miss Baker's dressing room wall.

Unfortunately the problem was not so easily solved in the theatre. Miss Baker had insisted that she should have the star spot in the running order. In other words, that her act should follow mine.

She hadn't reckoned with all the little 'Men from Laramie' who would be in the audience. Posses of little boys in cowboy hats and suits and carrying cap pistols were in regular attendance. Hylda's act was full of adult humour and therefore pretty boring for little boys. And bored little boys with cap pistols tend to shoot them. I didn't mind them shooting the Man from Laramie—that was par for the course. But after I'd left the stage they punctured Hylda's act with gunfire as well.

I got the impression that she didn't enjoy it. However, the pantomime was an immense success and set up a new box office record for the theatre, so everybody was pleased.

*　　　*　　　*

While 'Chain Gang' and 'More' did well in the charts in 1956, some very different sounds were going on in the background. The writing was on the wall for many ballad singers like me. Back in 1954, for instance, Bill Haley and his Comets had got to number four with 'Shake Rattle and Roll', and he had reached number one in October 1955 with 'Rock Around the Clock'. An even bigger threat was to arrive in May 1956. Here was a rocker who could sing ballads as well. His name was Elvis Presley and he not only rocketed his way to number two in May 1956 with 'Heartbreak Hotel' but went on to become one of the most successful recording artists of all time.

However, in 1956 my career was still continuing successfully and I was booked to top the bill in a summer season at the Coventry Theatre. It was a summer season that was to change my life.

By this time my second marriage, based as it was more on business than on love, had completely fallen apart. Sally and I had even come to an agreement that when I returned from touring I wouldn't go back to our flat. Fate now seemed to take a hand in bringing things to a head.

I was getting bouts of pneumonia with worrying frequency, and was nearly dying on an annual basis. Towards the end of one tour I was again terribly ill, but because I'd agreed not to go back to the flat I had booked into a hotel in London's Victoria. The doctor who was looking after me thought there was every indication that, this time, I really would die. Neither he nor the hotel management thought that dying there was a good idea, so he went personally to see Sally and asked if I might return home. She agreed, although she moved out after I began to improve. That really was the end of the line for Sally and me. We were divorced, and she went off to America where she married an English science professor who was teaching there.

I mentioned earlier that this year's summer season changed my life. That was because of Jane. One of the dancers in the show, she was tall, blonde and very beautiful. She had wonderful poise and presence and a voice to match the rest of her qualities. In short, she was a stunner—a head-turner wherever she went.

Strangely, almost perversely, although we were attracted to each other it was Jane's flatmate Carol with whom I had an affair in 1956 when Sally and I were moving towards a divorce. I've often wondered whether it was because I still had some faint hope of saving my marriage that I didn't plunge into an affair with Jane. Almost as though I knew that, with Jane, it wouldn't be a brief affair. It would be for real—and I wasn't ready for that. But fate had other ideas.

While I was ill in the hotel in Victoria I was looked after by Pip Norman, who was a mate of mine from my years in India in the RAF and was now managing a business for me. One day I opened my eyes and thought I was hallucinating. There was someone else standing in the hotel room with Pip. She was wearing an attractive blue and white striped raincoat and she looked absolutely beautiful. It was Jane. I had no idea how she had discovered where I was, but I was delighted that she had found me. It was as though we were destined to be together, and subsequently we lived happily together in London for almost two years.

There were those who said that Jane was in love with me because I was a big name and top of the bill. Well, it's true that when we first met I was top of the bill at an important theatre, but I was now losing my big-name status. I was still topping bills, but at some pretty crummy venues. In spite of which Jane not only stuck by me, she wanted to marry me. But as a two-time loser in marriage I was in no mood to risk a third time and, ironically, by the time I had come round to thinking that perhaps marriage to Jane might actually be a good idea she was no longer in love with me. One day Jane departed. She didn't leave a note. There was no fond farewell. She just wasn't there any more, and I was on my own again.

I took it very badly. I began to drink far too much, and by the beginning of 1960 I was back at rock bottom. No hit records, nor any prospect of one. My finances were low and my spirits desperately so. One of my friends, concerned about me, suggested I should consult an astrologer named Katina Theodossiou. I felt it was grasping at straws, but at that stage I was willing to try anything.

I wrote to her under my little-known legal name of Leslie Ronald Young, giving all the required information such as my date and time of birth and my mother's date and time of birth. Katina had never met me and obviously had no idea that Leslie Ronald Young was Jimmy Young. Back came a reading that contained details such as: 'You have lost a parent, either by death or divorce. You do an artistic job. If you are married it is quite possible that you will be divorced this year. If you are single there is somebody you will want to marry this year, but you won't. In fact your affair will break up.' Her reading was so accurate that I decided I must meet her.

By coincidence Katina lived exactly opposite me in Weymouth Street. I made an appointment, walked across the road and rang her doorbell. When Katina opened the door she said, 'Oh! You're Jimmy Young—so everything in my reading falls into place more than ever.'

We sat down to go through her predictions more thoroughly. She said, 'You are going to be bigger than ever in the future, but your career is not going to be dependent on your singing or your music. You are going to be introducing things and people. You are going to be interviewing people, and you are going to be a tremendous success.'

When she paused I said, 'Well, you're certainly right about the breaking up of my love affair. But as for your predictions about work, I must tell you

63

that this is only February and I've no work in the book at all for this year apart from two weeks of introducing *Housewives' Choice*, a record request programme for the BBC, in June. In fact I've been wondering whether to leave showbusiness and use the small amount of capital I have left to do something else—but don't ask me what.' I added that I was so depressed that I had been collecting sleeping pills, although I doubted that I would have the courage or the inclination to swallow them.

Katina's reaction was to burst into laughter. She said, 'For you to even contemplate suicide is absolutely ridiculous! It would be impossible for you to do it. It's just not in your make-up at all.' She added, 'One thing is certain. You will always be associated with showbusiness in some shape or form for the rest of your life. And I repeat that you are going to be a bigger success than you have ever been before, but in a different way.' She finished by saying, 'Incidentally, when I say the rest of your life I mean that you are going to live to be so old that they will have to take you out into a field and shoot you.'

But despite these optimistic predictions for my future, the present was as bad as ever. Everything that could go wrong was going wrong. Not only had I lost my lover, but I was about to lose my agent as well. He was an absolutely charming and very successful man named Ian Bevan, and very shortly after my meeting with Katina he rang and asked if I would pop in to see him.

Of course I would. I hadn't expected Katina's forecast of an upturn in my fortunes to happen quite so quickly. In fact it turned out to be a very different sort of interview. In the nicest, most gracious way he could manage Ian was throwing me out. He said, 'Look, Jim, I've booked you the two weeks of *Housewives' Choice* but I just can't book you anywhere else. Nobody's interested. I really do think it would be better if you tried to get yourself another agent. If you can't get placed elsewhere my door is always open, but perhaps a change of agent would bring you a change of luck.'

As it happened, I was just about to have a stroke of good luck—albeit in my personal life rather than my business life. Knowing that I was at an all-time low, some friends of mine asked me out. Gerry and Iris Bourne were associated with the annual ice pantomimes at the Wembley Pool, and they invited me to the arena one evening when excerpts from the pantomime were to be screened on television. In charge of the make-up was Eve. She was tall, slim and blonde and we were attracted to each other. We dated and I discovered that she was a really genuine and absolutely super person. We never actually lived together but we became very close, and remained so for many years. Eventually we parted, but I'm happy to say that she has found happiness with someone else and we are still in touch as friends.

On the business front, I had listened to what Katina had to say during our meeting, and had come to a decision. She had been so accurate on other details in my life about which she couldn't possibly have known that I decided I would stick it out till June, introduce my two weeks of *Housewives' Choice* and see what happened.

CHAPTER SIX

THROWING THE SCRIPT AWAY

I often wonder if there can possibly be any other business that is as uncertain as the one in which I've managed to survive for so long. Is there any other profession where you continually balance on the tightrope of uncertainty, often measuring job security in a matter of months, or even weeks? One thing is certain. You have to do the very best you can in the work you've got and hope it will lead on to other things. That was the mood, but much more of hope than of expectation, in which I approached *Housewives' Choice*. I went to the studio for day one with mixed feelings. Joy that at last I was working again. Fear that these ten programmes would be the last broadcasting I would ever do. I certainly never dreamed that those two weeks would give my almost dead career the kiss of life.

Before I'd even finished the first week my phone began to ring with offers of work. That had not happened for a very long time. The first call came from Arthur Muxlow at EMI, whose slogan boasted that they were the biggest recording organisation in the world. EMI took broadcasting time to advertise and promote their records on Radio Luxembourg, and Arthur was in charge of that area of their business. He asked if I would like to present two of those programmes every week, an offer that I very quickly accepted.

Perhaps at this juncture I should explain the importance of Radio Luxembourg to the record business. At that time the BBC had a virtual monopoly on broadcasting in the UK. By virtue of its charter obligation to inform, educate and entertain it had to cover a very wide range of broadcasting, of which disc jockey programmes were only a small part. It had also entered into agreements with record companies over what was called 'needle time' that restricted the number of records it could play.

Radio Luxembourg, which broadcast on 208 metres from the Duchy of Luxembourg between Belgium and Germany, had no such restrictions, and disc jockey programmes formed the core of its output that was aimed towards the UK. It's true that reception was far from perfect—it came and went, and sometimes disappeared altogether—but in some ways the almost clandestine nature of listening to it added to its popularity. It was just what the doctor ordered for record companies and record fans.

My second week of presenting *Housewives' Choice* awakened interest within two departments of the BBC itself. I received a call from the Gramophone Department offering me a weekly disc jockey programme, and another from the Popular Music Department (I couldn't help wondering whether there was an Unpopular Music Department) inviting me to do a weekly morning singing show. It looked as though, thanks to just two weeks of *Housewives' Choice*, an entirely new career was opening up for me.

By the end of 1960 the music trade papers were saying such things as 'Jimmy Young is beaming with justifiable delight over his recent emergence as an extremely successful and much sought after disc jockey.' The *New Musical Express* nominated me 'The surprise choice as this year's most enjoyable disc jockey'. As the old saying goes, nothing succeeds like success, and in 1961 I seemed to be popping up everywhere.

I appeared to have developed a knack of discovering and promoting new talent. On a radio show called *Younger than Springtime* I introduced the Springfields, who subsequently had two Top Ten hits. Then in 1963 Dusty Springfield went solo and enjoyed a string of big international hits between then and 1970. My life got ever busier, and in 1963 I was doing five disc jockey shows a week for Radio Luxembourg plus one for the BBC. I was also presenting a television programme devoted to discovering new talent. We introduced to television future hit record-makers like the Bachelors, Clodagh Rodgers and the Swinging Blue Jeans.

Everything was happening for me as a presenter. Then, out of the blue, I received a call from Columbia Records, to whom I was still under contract. They wanted me back in the studio to make a new record. I wasn't too happy about the idea, because I had moved away from the recording scene and into a different world where I was very happy. However, under my contract Columbia could insist on me making one more record for them, so I had no option but to agree.

Norman Newell, my recording manager at Columbia, had been a friend of mine for many years and was also a man of considerable song-writing talent. He had written, or helped to write, a string of hits over the years. Norman had great confidence in a new song he had written with the intention of it being the A-side of my new record. Frankly, after playing and singing it I was not impressed. However, I agreed to do it—provided that I could put a song of my own choice on the B-side. For years I had fancied an old number called 'Miss You', written by what I thought sounded like a firm of solicitors: Tobias, Tobias, Tobias. This seemed like my chance to record it.

As usual we had booked a three-hour recording session and, since Norman was in charge, he made sure we tackled his song first. It was one of those records that just didn't come easily, and by the time we had got it in the can we discovered we had only fifteen minutes left in which to record 'Miss You'. Once both sides were safely completed, we went into the control box to hear them back. We heard Norman's song first and then 'Miss You'. Seeking an independent opinion, I asked the studio engineer what he thought. He didn't know that one of them was Norman's, so we really did get his honest assessment: 'Well, I think the first song's a load of crap, but "Miss You" is fantastic.'

Fortunately Norman had the good grace to laugh. I don't think he agreed that his song was a load of crap, but he did agree that 'Miss You' should be the A-side. It went to number fifteen and stayed on the best-seller list for a total of thirteen weeks.

I thought it ironic that when I desperately needed a hit I couldn't get one, yet now, when it was no longer so important, there I was in the Top Twenty. I was immediately approached with offers to go back to the old routine of touring theatres while the record was still hot, but there was no way that I was going to take that backward step. My new career took first place, and that was what I was going to pursue.

It was at the end of 1963 that I took the first major step towards the *JY Programme*, which I launched in 1967 and which ran until the end of 2002 when the BBC axed it. The *Radio Times* said:

Radio and television personality Jimmy Young is bound to remember the last weekend of 1963 because that's when he takes the hot seat in a studio in the heart of Broadcasting House to introduce the first edition of *Saturday Special*. His job is to line up offbeat facts and fancies of the weekend from our regional correspondents, keep his ears glued to the line between us and BBC Sportsroom and cue the music of the BBC Northern Variety Orchestra and vocal stars on record.

It marked a sea change in my broadcasting career.

Up to that time, every programme I had done had been scripted. Whether singing or disc jockeying, I had to choose the items to be performed or played and then write a script around them. I then had to submit my script to a producer who would decide, 'Yes, you can say that', or, 'No, you can't say that.' The script was then typed up and copies sent to executives higher up the scale who would also either approve or disapprove. The script was then returned, amended or not as the case might be, and when the red light went on I read it. And woe betide me if I changed even a single approved word. That was BBC broadcasting as it had been, not just for me but for everyone else

70

too. However, all that was about to change.

There was absolutely no way that you could script the *Saturday Special*. Once the red light went on none of us was really sure what was going to happen next. We set out a running order, of course, but we had to do items or interviews as and when they became available. The programme was in the forefront of the new style of 'make-it-up-as-you-go-along' spontaneous broadcasting. Some broadcasters hated it. I was very fortunate. I loved it. In fact I took to it as a duck takes to water.

Alongside *Saturday Special* was another show helping to pave the way for the *JY Prog*. It was called *Through Till Two—TTT* for short—and it started in October 1964. I presented the first two hours, from 10pm to midnight, and Steve Race presented from midnight till 2am. However, we hadn't been running for very long when Steve suffered a heart attack and couldn't continue. I was asked if I could do the whole four hours, and that's what I did for the rest of the programme's run.

The format was simple. It was a record request programme with a difference. Listeners were invited to make telephone requests for records to be played during the show, and sixty operators sat at sixty telephones to deal with their calls. The listeners' requests were quickly typed on to slips of paper which were rushed in to the producer. Our studio was situated next door to the record library, and once the producer decided which record we were going to play next someone would run into the library and dig it out.

In those days I was not self-operated—in other words I didn't play the records myself. The turntables weren't even in my studio, but in the cubicle where the producer, Geoffrey Hayden, sat. So I sat in my studio in a kind of limbo. I could see, through the dividing glass window, my producer's head bobbing around as he and his assistants sorted out the mountains of paper—but that was all. Unless I was familiar with the record playing at the time I had no idea how long it was or how much playing time was left on it. In short, I was completely in the dark as to what the hell was going on.

From time to time I would put down the talkback key and say, 'What's coming up next, Geoff?'

He would invariably reply, 'I don't know. We haven't sorted it out yet. I'll let you know.'

Some time later a body would hurtle through my studio door and throw handfuls of requests at me while saying something like, 'The next record is Nat King Cole and you've got about fifteen seconds left on this one.'

We all did it in later years when we presented our stint on *Children in Need*, but in those days of scripted broadcasting it was unheard of. At about 2.30 one morning, after four hours of hard pounding, Geoff and I were talking outside Broadcasting House. I told him I was sure he knew what record was coming up next long before he told me, and I asked him why he didn't let me know until the very last moment.

Said Geoff, 'You work best under pressure.'

Of course he was absolutely right. If I was not at my best under pressure, I would never have lasted for twenty-nine years on the *JY Prog*.

Through Till Two became an enormous success. In fact we achieved the highest-ever listening figures for a late-night radio programme. Telephone calls came in not just from all over Britain but from all over Europe, and the longer the programme went on the more the calls increased. The sheer volume of them swamped the local Langham telephone exchange to such an extent that the GPO simply couldn't cope. Discreet words were exchanged between the Post Office and the BBC, which was always very reluctant to upset the Post Office, and at the end of 1965 we were taken off the air.

I know it sounds bizarre, but we had actually become too popular. We were victims of our own success.

CHAPTER SEVEN

PERSONAL FAILINGS

Over the next couple of years my professional life settled down to regular broadcasts for both Radio Luxembourg and the BBC. However, my personal life was, as ever, anything but settled.

Eve and I had been together for six years and for most of that time had been very happy, but the old familiar pattern of silence and edginess emerged and we broke up in 1966. Eve truly was a super girl, and six years is a big slice of life to throw away. I believe we both tried very hard to save our partnership, but it simply didn't work out.

I know one can argue that there are always two sides to the break-up of a relationship, but I really did feel that the fault was mine. With my track record, how could it be otherwise? Would I ever be able to find a woman with whom I could be really happy? Of course, the excuses were there and easy to identify.

Facts tell us that children of broken marriages often find close relationships difficult. I had not enjoyed a happy, secure home environment and had been forced to leave home at what, in the 1930s, was an early age. That was followed by the war and the years of being shunted around in the RAF. If I wanted to find excuses I didn't have to look very far. But deep down I felt that, in affairs of the heart, I was flawed.

It is certainly true that I found close relationships very claustrophobic. However happy in the short term, there came a time when I began to feel smothered, penned in. I remember one instance when I was appearing at the Birmingham Hippodrome. An ex-girlfriend phoned me to tell me the good news that she had got engaged. Could she meet me for lunch to tell me about it? We had a very pleasant lunch and I thought no more about it. That is, until I phoned my then wife in London, as I usually did, to find out if there were any messages or news for me.

'How did you enjoy your lunch with your girlfriend?' asked Sally.

Some kind friend had rung to tell her I had been lunching with another woman. If I really did feel claustrophobic—and even a bit paranoid—at the time it seemed well justified. Simple questions like, 'What time will you be home, dear?', a perfectly reasonable question if dinner was to be prepared, would begin to feel like checking up. If I was performing out of London and received a telephone call at my hotel to see if things had gone well, I would assume it meant, 'Who have you got in the hotel with you?' With my track record a perfectly reasonable assumption, I hear you cry. But it confirmed my fear that I was being pinned down.

Actually I am a very shy, introverted person. To this day I still find entering a crowded room or joining a party very difficult. If I'm obliged to attend a formal reception, I tend to find a corner and stay in it until the earliest moment at which I can decently leave. 'Working the room' is a social skill I should have acquired but I'm afraid I haven't. As Andy Williams once sang, 'I'm a Home Loving Man'. Testimonial dinners and the thought of having to make a speech are an absolute nightmare.

I've also always found it difficult to make a pass at a woman. 'So how is it that they appear to have come your way in considerable numbers?' I hear you ask. Well, could it be that my shyness has worked in my favour in that respect? Is it possible that attractive women who have men chasing them all the time find a man who doesn't chase them much more interesting? Perhaps even a bit of a challenge? In matters of romance men may appear to be the hunters, but it's often women who in the end do the choosing. If a woman really fancies you she will find a way of letting you know.

For many years I was never short of girlfriends but I shied away from settling down and I let it adversely affect my judgement, and especially my financial judgement, in the silliest ways. For instance, I resolutely declined to buy a house or a flat because I felt it would be a move towards making a commitment. So for years, while people I knew were buying houses, living in them for a while and then selling them on and making an enormous profit, I continued to throw away money by paying rent when, for roughly the same outlay on a mortgage, I could have been buying something. It's true that I have never been all that interested in material things—even now I live in a very modest house. But my feelings about buying property at that time were absolutely crazy.

All things considered, at this stage of my life a psychiatrist would have had a field day with me.

CHAPTER EIGHT

BROADCASTER LOYALTY

As we moved into 1967 a business crisis loomed. Let me explain. For almost fifty years the BBC had been allowed to maintain a virtual monopoly on broadcasting in Britain. The only real alternative was Radio Luxembourg, which, as I've already explained, had a very weak signal beyond mainland Europe. However, another alternative to the BBC had arrived in the mid-sixties with the so-called pirate ships, which were close enough to experience no problems with signal power.

Throughout the fifties and early sixties the BBC had clearly failed to respond to the growing demand for popular music. In his history of the BBC Asa Briggs writes that there was no interest in 'pop music' amongst most of its Governors, and some had disliked it intensely. At the time the term 'popular music' was deemed to include jazz, all Top Twenty material, dance music, folk music, concert music and even old-time dance music. Record request programmes like *Family Favourites* and *Housewives' Choice* were taken more seriously than the few outlets for pop music.

It was to fill the demand for more genuine pop music that on Good Friday 1964 Radio Caroline, the first pirate pop music station, began broadcasting from a ship moored just outside the three-mile limit, near Harwich. She had been named after the daughter of President Kennedy, who had been assassinated the previous year.

Because they were moored outside UK territorial waters the pirate stations could play unlimited numbers of records and their broadcasting largely consisted of disc jockey programmes. These were hugely popular with young people and, within a few months of coming on air, Caroline had an audience of 7 million. As one MP said at the time, 'The BBC has quite clearly failed to cater for this section of the public. If the BBC had met needs, the pirates would never have arisen.'

By September 1964 Radio Caroline had more listeners than the BBC. As you can imagine, the Corporation, although unwilling to admit it publicly, found Caroline and the other pirate stations that climbed on to the bandwagon extremely irritating. No doubt ears were whispered into, and at the beginning of 1967 the government announced that it was going to 'sink the pirates'. That year saw the passing of the Marine Offences Act, which effectively ended offshore broadcasting. This meant that all the pirate disc jockeys, whose very illegality seemed to make them more attractive and racy than us, would row ashore and attempt to pinch our jobs.

Our existence was precarious enough as it was. I was on a quarterly contract and the BBC never let you know until about week eight or nine whether or not your contract was going to be renewed. I often reflected that the public read in the press about the inflated fees performers are said to earn, but little is heard about the insecurity of an existence where you're given five weeks' notice of whether or not you're going to get another thirteen weeks in gainful employment. The public might well say that we chose to live that way, and they would be absolutely right. We did. Anyway, that was the situation at the BBC when Robin Scott arrived to shake things up.

I had never met Robin, but at least he knew something about the music business. He had co-written a song called 'Softly Softly', which Ruby Murray took to number one in the hit parade. In very short order his plans were announced. The Light Programme, the Home Service and some other programmes were going to disappear, and in their place we were to get Radios 1, 2, 3 and 4. There would be considerable effort put behind 'Wonderful Radio 1'.

Donald MacLean of the Popular Music Department sent for me and told me that he had nominated me for the ten-to-twelve weekday slot. Donald knew that I put bums on seats, but would his boss see it the same way? I waited in limbo for what seemed like an eternity and then, only six weeks before Radio 1 was due to launch, Donald called me to his office. He said, 'Well, you've got

78

the job on a three-month contract.' He then added, 'Under the new planning, if the show is a success it will probably run for a long time. By the same token, if it fails you are likely to be off for a very long time.' Had I needed something to spur me on to success, which I didn't, that would have been it.

However, there was a niggling worry at the back of my mind: 10am wasn't a good time for attracting a big audience. For many years the big attraction in the mornings had been the record request programme *Housewives' Choice*, running from 9 to 10am. The feeling was that a lot of listeners then switched their radios off and went out to do their shopping. But at least I had survived the big reshuffle. Without a doubt it was a make-or-break situation, but at least I was in with a chance.

Donald MacLean and his assistant Geoffrey Owen fought hard to get the right set-up for the show, and I can never thank them enough for that. The first step was choosing Doreen Davies as producer. I had known Doreen for many years, although I had never worked with her. Her reputation as a producer was excellent: she was tough but fair.

Initially, and fairly obviously, there were clashes. Doreen arrived wearing her BBC hat. The top brass had told her how they wanted the show to sound, in keeping with the new-look Radio 1, and she was there to follow official orders. I was there wearing my JY hat. The show had my name on it and I had already been warned what failure would mean, so I was going to fight for the show to be done my way. But having got those clashes out of the way, we became firm friends.

I had already come to the conclusion that, if

Radio 1 was going to consist of record shows followed by record shows, the personality of the presenter and of the programme itself would be the deciding factors where success and failure were concerned. Doreen agreed and, at a stroke, made my programme different from all the others in a way I would never have dreamed of. She came up with the idea of the recipe. Between us we invented a speeded up Bing Crosby singing 'Home Cooking' and a chipmunk voice saying, 'What's the recipe today, Jim?' We took the idea to Donald and Geoffrey, and I got the feeling that they were appalled. Recipes for suet puddings were not exactly what the planners of wonderful Radio 1 had in mind. However—prompted, I always suspected, by a good kicking from Doreen behind the scenes—they gave us the go-ahead.

The build-up to the launch of the new networks gathered pace. There were press conferences at which many of the other disc jockeys turned up with way-out clothes and beards. One even used to wear hairy boots. I, of course, was wearing what Dick Rowe at Decca Records used to describe as my bank manager suit. I felt so out of place that I rang Donald to ask him if he thought I should change my image. Perhaps get my floral shirt and hairy boots on.

'Not on your life,' said Donald. In fact he went much further, adding, 'I reckon that the sort of presentation you are going to do will be the salvation of this radio network.'

The new-look BBC launched on Saturday, 30 September. I made my first appearance on Monday, 2 October and there was a Roman-amphitheatre-blood-spilling feeling about the whole thing. The newspapers stoked the atmosphere. 'Sack your own DJ' was one headline. Another was 'Radio 1 jockeys face the axe'. One story was that the BBC was asking listeners to decide, via its Audience Research Department, which DJs should be fired. A newspaper asked me for a quote and I must have suffered a rush of blood to the head because I said, 'A basic rule of showbusiness is that if you don't draw audiences you don't eat.'

Actually there were lots of programmes on Radios 3 and 4 that didn't draw audiences, but their producers and presenters were still eating and drinking very well indeed. They would probably claim that, since they weren't in showbusiness, the rules didn't apply to them. Talk about blood sports. This was rapidly developing into one. All any of us could do was to go on air and do the best we could. The most difficult bit was waiting for the listening figures to come in. Normally this was a process that took several weeks, but there had been such a huge shake-up at the BBC that at this time it took no more than a few days.

We had been on the air for only about ten days when I received a message from Robin Scott to come and see him in his office. I thought I had done quite well, but I feared the worst. After all, I was very much the odd man out on Radio 1. Too old, too ordinary, too conservative in my dark suit. And then, of course, there was the recipe. Surely all those hip Radio 1 listeners would absolutely hate those.

When I walked into Robin's office he invited me to sit down and asked if I would like a drink. It felt rather like the condemned man being asked what he would like for his last meal. However, feeling that a little Dutch courage would be quite welcome, I asked for a scotch. Robin poured me a very large one. I figured that there were two possibilities. Either the large drink was a reward for a job well done, or it was to prepare me for the news that, at the end of my three months' contract, I was for the chop.

Robin fiddled with some charts on his desk for what seemed like an eternity. I sat with my scotch, waiting and wondering. Finally he looked up and called me to go round to his side of the desk. I saw that some of the figures on the chart were ringed with red ink. I wondered what was the significance of that. They were, in fact, the listening figures for my first day. The previous figures for the first hour of my slot had been around 3 million and, to be honest, all I was desperately hoping at that moment was that mine were no lower than that. But the figures ringed by Robin showed that my figures on my first day, far from slipping down from 3 million, had soared to an almost unbelievable 5 million.

'Enjoy your whisky, Jim,' said Robin. 'You've arrived.'

He did sound a cautionary note by suggesting that some people might have switched on purely out of curiosity, but in mid-October he was sounding very positive indeed. He told the *Daily Mirror*, 'The deepest impression is being made with Radio 1's morning programmes and the Jimmy Young programme is the biggest success story we have. It is a success because Jimmy communicates well. He is one of the old brigade but the audience has taken to him.' I knew I had arrived when people began to impersonate me on other shows, and especially when they began to use my catchphrases.

One day I came out of the front door of Broadcasting House and looked at the traffic which was, as usual, nose to tail. It included a very stationary, very large, double-decker red London bus. As I stood there the driver casually slid back the side window of his cab and called across to me, 'What's the recipe today, Jim?' On another occasion I was sitting in an aircraft at the end of the runway waiting to take off. We had received the usual lectures about safety drill and so on. Then the pilot came on the intercom. He said, 'We are now ready for take-off, so, since we have Mr Jimmy Young on board, I will say, "Orft we jolly well go."'

Catchphrases alone can't save a career, but if you've got a successful programme they can certainly provide the icing on the cake. However, one of life's irritations for anyone in the public eye is to be stuck with something that you never said, because once it's in print that's it. Every time a piece is written about you the writer will consult the records, up will come the misquote, and into the piece it will go. In my case the irritant is four initials that go TTFN.

Incidentally, everybody seems to believe that it was I who invented the concept of 'initial' or shorthand broadcasting expressions, but I didn't. That was done a long time ago. For the sake of my younger readers I should explain. Back in the 1940s the BBC used to broadcast a programme called *ITMA*, which stood for 'It's That Man Again'. The man in question was Tommy Handley, a huge star at the time, and Tommy's signing-off line was

'Ta Ta For Now', abbreviated to 'TTFN'.

Never in all my fifty-four years of broadcasting have I said, 'Ta Ta For Now'. The occasional 'BFN' I admit to. And 'Bye For Now' ended almost every *JY Prog*. TTFN? Never. But once something is in the press cuttings it's there for life. However, after life is another matter altogether. So I warn obituary writers in advance. Whatever else you write, do not head my Obit 'TTFN', because if you do your nights will be sleepless. You will be Numero Uno on my haunting target list.

But let's not worry about the future. Back in 1967 the BBC was so taken aback by what was happening to the *JY Prog* that they commissioned a survey to find out where I was getting my extra millions of listeners from at the unfashionable time of 10am. What the survey discovered was almost incredible. It reported that I had changed the routine in countless homes. It reported people saying that, whereas they used to listen to *Housewives' Choice* and then go out shopping, they were now doing their shopping before or after my programme so they wouldn't miss me. I had actually changed their shopping habits. This was something that neither I nor the BBC had envisaged happening. If it came as a shock to me, I wondered what the news was doing to Robin Scott.

Robin had been given the job of creating a Radio 1 that was so with it, so hip, so sharp that it could successfully replace the pirates. But his star had turned out to be a forty-six-year-old guy playing middle-of-the-road music and reading recipes. I knew I wouldn't turn Robin's hair white because it was famously white already, but I could imagine him tearing out handfuls of it in sheer frustration. He had wanted to create an overall youthful image for the station and had installed a host of young DJs to create it for him. The trouble was that the public didn't want them—they wanted me. I was very much an anachronism. I was the tail wagging the dog. But I was also the success story that Robin couldn't ignore.

Within a few weeks the press, including the heavyweight Sunday newspapers, had woken up to the story. I was featured in a two-page spread in the *Sunday Times* colour supplement which nominated me as holder of the office of Royal Microphone in Waiting. The *Observer* not only put me on the front cover but included interviews that took up almost half the supplement.

Robin Scott tried to stop the rot by making me take an enforced holiday. The BBC announced that I was being released to 'fulfil other commitments'. The truth was that the BBC had forced me out, but as usual it was putting its own spin on the news.

I was so much in demand at the time that I simply filled in the time by taking a well-paid part in a pantomime at the Golders Green Theatre.

Working on the principle that if at first you don't succeed try, try again, the BBC wondered if they could stop me in my tracks by making me switch channels. Accordingly it was decreed that I should broadcast on Radio 1 on Christmas Day and on Radio 2 on Boxing Day. Donald MacLean was in despair. 'They won't know where to find you,' he groaned.

Donald wasn't often wrong, but on this occasion he couldn't have been more so. On Christmas Day I got twice the audience of the person opposite me on Radio 2. And on Boxing Day I got two and a half times the audience of the person opposite me on Radio 1.

This made a complete nonsense of the theory of 'network identification' so beloved of radio planners. Their belief was that people identify with networks and will listen to their favourite network almost irrespective of who is broadcasting on it. Planners go away on 'brainstorming' sessions. These sessions do not encourage a hairshirt mentality to stimulate serious thinking. On the contrary, they almost always take place at extremely expensive hotels where, while consuming gourmet food and drinking fine wines, planners talk themselves into believing their favourite theories. Like 'network identification'. I had always known it to be a load of cobblers and I had just proved it.

There is no such thing as network loyalty. Look what happened to Radio 1 when it dramatically changed its policy. It lost half its listeners. Network loyalty is just another planner's fantasy. People don't have network loyalty. They have broadcaster loyalty. I can guarantee that if Terry Wogan left Radio 2 and went to another radio station which had the same signal strength and coverage as Radio 2 he would take most of his audience with him. Planners hate to admit this kind of thing, of course, because by doing so they would be admitting their own weakness and the strength of popular broadcasters. But they all know it to be true.

Meanwhile my own career was going from strength to strength. The Variety Club of Great Britain presented me with its Radio Personality award, and I burst into print with a weekly column in the *Daily Sketch*. I had always enjoyed writing, and my column led to invitations to write for *Woman's Own* and *Punch*.

And on the *JY Prog*, the recipes had developed a life of their own. It all began with a chance remark from me on the air. I had read out the recipe of the day, prepared of course by my excellent producer and cook, Doreen Davies. Then I added, purely as an afterthought, that if listeners had a recipe they should send it in and I would share it, on air, with our millions of listeners. The result was staggering.

Sack after sack after sack of mail deluged in, and parts of Broadcasting House looked like Christmas at the GPO. Special squads of helpers had to be drafted in and entire rooms set aside to cope with the influx. I remember well, typical of the old-fashioned, civil service-style BBC of that time, a lady executive ringing Doreen and saying, 'This Jimmy Young must be stopped. He's overwhelming us and he must be stopped.'

To which Doreen replied, 'But that's what he's there for, dear. That's what he's there for.'

Eventually even the BBC decided that if it couldn't beat 'em it might as well join 'em. It brought out a *Jimmy Young Cookbook* of listeners' recipes. I didn't think much about it at the time. I certainly didn't think of it as a major publishing venture. At the most I thought of it as a service for listeners. That was until I was reading the Sunday papers in bed one day. I turned over a page of the *Sunday Times* to discover that the first *Jimmy Young Cookbook* was number one in the non-fiction paperback best-sellers. What is more, it stayed in the *Sunday Times* best-seller list for three months. The BBC subsequently published several more JY

87

cookbooks and they were all extremely successful.

It was not until 1981 that we decided the recipe had outlived its usefulness and should be ditched. We took the decision in much the same spirit that motivated women in World War I to taunt young men who were still at home when the ladies thought they should be in the mud, blood and spilled guts of the trenches. The ladies serenaded them with a song that ran, 'We don't want to lose you, but we think you ought to go'. Easy for the ladies to say, of course. They weren't going.

The fact was that the recipe, which had helped enormously to launch the *JY Prog* in the first place, had become an embarrassment. I remember that when Mrs Thatcher came into my studio for the first time she actually brought a recipe with her to read out on the air. But that was in the days when getting a minister, let alone a party leader, on the programme was regarded as a huge achievement. That had long since ceased to be the case, and the recipe had no place any more. The time had long gone when we needed gimmicks to push up the ratings of the *JY Prog*.

*   *   *

Fearful that everything would change for the worse I was reluctant to admit, even to myself, that my career now seemed to be taking a turn for the better. But in my heart I knew that it was. I just prayed that it would continue that way. However, although my professional life was improving, my personal life was not. I still did not have the complete happiness that only true and lasting love can bring. But even that changed in June 1970.

Alicia was working as a secretary in Broadcasting House and I passed her in the corridors from time to time. She is a very attractive lady and, although it took some time for me to work up the courage, I eventually asked her out for a lunchtime drink. That meeting obviously went very well and I asked if she would like to have dinner with me the following evening. Neither of us is quite sure how what happened next came about—or perhaps Alicia is, but won't admit it. Anyway, she stood me up.

The result was that our relationship went on to the back burner for a long time. We saw each other from time to time but, according to Alicia, it took a few years before I saw sense and we began a love affair. We had actually been together for several years before we emerged in 1980, in an unwelcome blaze of publicity, as an 'item'. And this time I would not shrink from making a commitment. My relationship with Alicia is different from all the others that preceded it—not least because it's lasted for thirty-three years.

Happiness in my private life had eluded me for years, in spite of having several really smashing ladies pass in and out of my life. Clearly a lot of the trouble was with me. It took a long time to find the lady who could change me and do it so subtly that I didn't even realise it was happening. Now my friends tell me that I am a different person. There is a peace and tranquillity about my life which was never there before, and Alicia is the person who quietly brought about the change. What is it the song says? 'When he fancies he is past love, it is then he meets his last love, and he loves her as he's never loved before'.

CHAPTER NINE

GOING INTO EUROPE

The big debate in 1972 was whether Great Britain should join the six countries in what was then generally known as the Common Market—officially the European Economic Community or EEC, and nowadays the European Union or EU. It was a situation that would give me the opportunity to make the change of career I had been hoping for.

My producer Doreen Davies and I suggested to our BBC bosses that we could make some interesting programmes by asking our listeners to send in their queries, or worries, about joining, and then mounting programmes from the countries concerned to get their questions answered.

When I asked for questions on my programme the response was staggering, far greater than we had envisaged. The questions were predictable but important. Listeners wanted to know how joining the Common Market would affect vital areas of their lives like pensions, education, health services, housing, prices and working conditions. We asked the *Daily Mirror* if they would like to participate, and they enthusiastically agreed. They even sent one of their top reporters, Patrick Doncaster, on tour with us. I have to report, however, that the BBC top brass was not particularly enthusiastic. Perhaps because it wasn't on their all-important television service but only on radio. And Radio 2 at that.

And so, well aware that, lacking any kind of extra resources or encouragement from the BBC we might have bitten off more than we could chew, we set off. We opened in Belgium and after that, apart from a slight pause at the weekend, we were broadcasting from a different country every day. The batting order was Belgium, Germany, Luxembourg, Italy, Holland and France.

It was a tough tour by rail, road, air and sometimes even on foot, lugging all our equipment around with us. It seems bizarre in modern times that we were actually carrying around with us the records and tapes to do six two-hour programmes. But we were, and there were times when we despaired of ever making it to our next destination.

Our route from Cologne to Luxembourg was by rail through the beautiful Rhine valley via Bonn and Koblenz. In normal times it would probably have been an enjoyable journey—but not, I'm afraid, for us. For starters, it was winter and the whole route was covered in snow. It looked lovely but wasn't very helpful. We missed a connection, and as a result spent almost a whole day in trains or standing around on stations waiting for trains. To complicate matters, every porter in Germany seemed to be on strike. So although there were five of us in the party, all pulling our weight, handling the baggage became a big job of trundling, heaving and hauling. The grand finale of the day, having missed all our train connections, was a freezing two-hour wait on Koblenz station. That's something I would wholeheartedly recommend to someone I didn't like very much.

Eventually we arrived in Luxembourg, which I had visited many times before although wearing

91

a different hat as a recording artist. Radio Luxembourg was very important in terms of getting one's new record heard, so it was very much on the play list. Consequently artists and record company promotion staff were constantly flying to the Duchy to make personal appearances, to be interviewed by the Radio Luxembourg disc jockeys and to get their records played on 208 metres. This time things were different. I was broadcasting from the same studio that I had used before, but roles were reversed. Whereas in previous years I had been interviewed, this time I was doing the interviewing—including, ironically, a Radio Luxembourg disc jockey and his wife.

I had always enjoyed going to tiny but warm-hearted Luxembourg, and I knew that many of the British disc jockeys who lived there found the life very enjoyable indeed. Getting into and out of the place, however, could present problems, and we awoke on the morning of our departure to see the place covered in snow. 'No problem,' we thought. 'They're used to snow in Luxembourg.' Well, maybe they were—but not this much snow.

In due course we arrived at the airport and checked in to fly to Rome via Brussels. By this time the snow had become a blizzard and from the departure lounge we couldn't even see the runway. Then we heard the announcement that changed everything, including our schedule. We were to spend three hours travelling to Brussels by coach. Naturally by the time we got to Brussels our plane for Rome was long gone. Eventually we were informed that the only way we could get from Brussels to Rome was to fly via Geneva, so that we did, and after travelling around or across four countries we finally arrived in the Eternal City at 10pm. From Rome we flew to Holland and then, thankfully, to our last broadcast in Paris.

Hardly had the broadcast finished than there were encouraging noises on the telephone to our Paris studio from our bosses in London. The tour had been an obvious success and, somewhat belatedly, they wanted to be a part of it. As the saying goes, success has many fathers—but failure, alas, is an orphan. When I got home I was showered with praise. Listeners wrote their thanks to me. BBC bosses wrote and phoned congratulations.

One listener was so impressed that she suggested the *JY Programme* should now be even more adventurous. 'Why don't you broadcast the programme from Moscow?' she asked. My own thoughts went further. Why shouldn't we do the first-ever *live* broadcast from the Soviet Union to the outside world? The official reaction was that it was an outrageous idea to which the Russians would never agree. Being the determined little terrier that I am I decided to ignore such pessimism. My producer and I pursued the idea with tenacity and met with Russian officials over lunch. The negotiations were slow—very slow. But eventually it was agreed that the actual broadcasts would present no great technical difficulties, and, after major changes to the format of the programme, I did indeed do the first-ever live broadcasts from Moscow. But that was not until 1977, so more of that later.

Perhaps most satisfying of all when we returned from Europe in early 1972 was a personal letter from one of BBC Television's top executives. He wrote, 'Congratulations. You've just done in six days what I've been trying to do for six years.'

CHAPTER TEN

GOOD NEWS

By the beginning of 1973 my career had already experienced enough ups and downs and zigs and zags to satisfy the most enthusiastic roller-coaster rider. I had been a night-club pianist and singer and a bandleader in the early fifties; a pop singer and hit record-maker, the first British singer to have two consecutive number one hits in the mid-fifties; a DJ and radio presenter with an audience of millions in the sixties. And now I was about to make the most amazing change of all. Even when I was turning out the hit records I never forgot my recording mentor at Decca saying to me, 'You'll never be a really great pop star.' When I asked him why, he said, 'Because you're too bloody intelligent.' Was it possible that what had held me back in the past might now work to my advantage?

I had always been fascinated by the world of news and current affairs. I bought as many newspapers as I could afford and seldom missed the news on either radio or television. I was also convinced that most people were fascinated by, and eager to learn more about, what went on in the world around them, but were put off by the tone of many news and current affairs programmes. They felt they were being patronised, which quite often they were, and they didn't like it. The enormous success of the European broadcasts and the reaction to them both from my BBC bosses and from the public reinforced my strongly held beliefs. I longed for the opportunity to demonstrate a completely different approach to politics in the media. Little did I dream that I was about to get it.

I was still disc jockeying on Radio 1 when I received a telephone call from the Managing Director Radio, Ian (later Sir Ian) Trethowan. It was an invitation to join him in his office for a drink. On the face of it a very desirable offer, but in the BBC things are often not as straightforward as they seem. A social drink with one's leader can mean 'Thanks for all your good work, please keep on doing it', or it can mean, 'Thanks for all your good work but we feel we've squeezed every drop of creative juice out of you, so 'bye for now.'

Ever the pessimist, I expected the latter. And judging by Ian's opening remark it looked as though I was right. Having settled us both down with a large gin and tonic he said, 'I reckon we're only getting about 40 per cent effort out of you.'

I knew exactly what he meant, but I spluttered out a ritual protest that I didn't.

'You're so bored,' said Ian, 'that you put on the records and then sit back and read the papers.'

Clearly he had received reports from studio managers and producers who worked with me, so there was no point in trying to deny what was absolutely true.

Ian then asked why I didn't move to Radio 2 and mount the sort of programme that I really wanted to do.

It was now or never. I said that it would be a programme in which I could talk to anyone about

95

anything as long as my gut feeling told me that it would interest my listeners. The guests would include the Prime Minister, the Chancellor of the Exchequer or any other members of the great and good whom I deemed appropriate. It would be a programme in which my listeners got deeply involved. It would not be a boring, old-fashioned on-air phone-in but would involve the vital element of listeners' comments and reactions, phoned in and then read out by me.

It was a mind-boggling format to put on Radio 2, which had been set up to be a straightforward music channel, but to my amazement and delight Ian said, 'Well you've sold me. Now go and see Douglas Muggeridge, and if you can sell him you're on.'

Douglas, who was Director of Programmes, Radio, was enthusiastic, and that is how on 2 July 1973 I was able to set up the programme I'd always wanted to do. A programme that would reveal to millions of people the mysterious, remote, elitist world of current affairs and politics.

In terms of BBC politics I was uniquely blessed. BBC Radio subdivides into a series of powerful 'empires'. There are the news and current affairs empire, the sports empire, the Radios 1, 2, 3, 4 and now Radio 5 network empires. These subdivide further into empires headed by powerful, and often charismatic, individuals. The whole thing works on a sort of 'big fleas have smaller fleas upon their backs to bite 'em' basis. I say I was uniquely blessed because I didn't in 1973, nor for the next twenty-nine years, fall under the aegis of any empire other than Radio 2. Largely this was because in 1973 most of the BBC top brass, apart from Ian

Trethowan and Douglas Muggeridge, assumed I was going to fail, so they weren't interested in grabbing me for their empires anyway.

I have to say that Radio 2 wasn't exactly over the moon about having this new current affairs programme thrust upon it. The head of Radio 2 called me to his office to remind me that his was a music network and I must play fifteen minutes of music before doing my first interview. However, my success came so swiftly that it wasn't long before he called me to his office demanding to know why I played fifteen minutes of music before getting to the important stuff, namely my first interview. Ever the diplomat, I didn't remind him that kicking off with music was his idea. Instead I thanked him for his helpful suggestion and said I would now start my interviews right at the top of the programme.

From the very beginning I was trying to project considerably more confidence on the outside than I was feeling on the inside. To be honest, although Ian Trethowan had given me the go-ahead I wasn't absolutely certain where I was going. The matter was settled for me—as were most things in my life—by my gut feeling.

In the very early days one of our areas of interest was consumer affairs. We had been on the air only three days when I said to my researchers, 'Why don't we ask Geoffrey Howe if he would come on the programme to talk to me?' Geoffrey was the Minister for Trade and Consumer Affairs. To their, and my, surprise he said he would.

We talked about all sorts of consumer problems and our telephone lights began to flash. The reaction for which I had been hoping began to pour in. Listeners were firing in questions and I was firing them at Geoffrey. Accustomed to being interviewed in the more staid atmosphere of Radio 4, he'd never encountered anything like this and was thoroughly enjoying himself. Before the broadcast he had told my producer that he had to get away in time for a lunch appointment. However, I could see that he was having a really good time and so I wondered out loud whether he would consider cancelling his lunch and staying on to the end of the programme. Yes he would, and yes he did.

Meanwhile I asked whether, since I'd done him out of his lunch, I could organise some sandwiches for him from the BBC canteen. The sandwiches duly arrived but Geoffrey was far too busy to eat them. However, he was also far too hungry to leave them behind. They would, he said, be eaten in the ministerial car on the way back to the House of Commons. All this was happening within the context that at that time Radio 2 had no record of ministers coming in to appear on programmes. Geoffrey's visit was therefore a considerable event that demanded a suitable send-off committee, and various BBC high-ups were lined up in the foyer of Broadcasting House to bid him goodbye. The Minister for Trade and Consumer Affairs managed to maintain his dignity while shaking hands, a considerable achievement since he was still clutching his by now rather worse for wear BBC sandwiches.

*　　　*　　　*

From the very beginning my plan for the *JY Prog* was to be live on air and completely flexible, able to cover any subject at any time no matter where the interviewee was at the time. One morning when I was on the air our flexibility received its first test.

It was in the very early days of heart transplants, and a surgeon in this country had performed such an operation during which, unfortunately, the patient had died. Sir Keith Joseph, who was Minister of Health at the time, had issued a statement which suggested that surgeons should hold back from such operations until there was a greater chance of success. Charles Thompson, my researcher, asked if I would like to speak to the pioneer heart transplant surgeon Professor Christiaan Barnard about Sir Keith's statement. Assuming that Professor Barnard must be on a visit to Britain, I said I would.

A short time later Charles popped into the studio and said, 'I've tracked Professor Barnard down. Can you talk to him now because he's on the phone from Johannesburg?'

I read Sir Keith Joseph's statement to Professor Barnard and asked him to comment on it.

He paused for a moment and then said, 'What are the medical qualifications of the gentleman who made that statement?'

I replied that, as far as I knew, he had none.

'Then,' said Professor Barnard, 'I think he should keep his mouth shut.'

Our on-air exchange might not seem particularly startling in this day and age, but flexibility of that kind and instant comment from experts in countries as far away as South Africa was revolutionary in the 1970s for the music station Radio 2.

Flexibility, of course, means different things according to the context. Every broadcaster who has enjoyed a long career will have experienced less enjoyable moments when lines of communication go down and you lose touch with the person you are interviewing. It's par for the course when talking to someone in a far-off land. In fact, on one occasion I did most of the *JY Prog* from Israel on a telephone on the wall after more orthodox communication completely broke down.

Another such moment occurred much closer to home, and greatly amused both my guest and myself once it was over. I was interviewing former Conservative Arts Minister Norman St John Stevas on the telephone at his home on the delicate subject of whether handicapped babies should be allowed to live or die. Suddenly, to my horror, in the middle of a tense and emotional interview, I heard Norman's doorbell ring. There was a pause at his end before, stating the obvious, he said, 'Oh dear, there goes my doorbell.' Another pause and then, 'Do you mind awfully if I answer the door? You see, it's Harrods bringing back my curtains and if I don't answer the door I won't see them again for ages.' Away went Norman while I played a bit of music after which, curtains safely gathered in, we finished the interview.

Ironically, when my production team phoned Norman earlier in the morning to set up the interview he had asked, 'What happens if my doorbell rings during the interview?' My confident producer had simply laughed and said, 'Don't worry—that's never happened to us yet.' There's a first time for everything, they say.

Pre-recording is safer and some broadcasters pre-record their interviews—and in some cases their whole programmes—while pretending they're live. But pre-recording isn't half as much fun as the genuine article, live radio.

*   *   *

By this time other empires were casting envious eyes on my programme and wondering how they could seize control of it, but Radio 2 wasn't going to share its hit programme with anybody else thank you very much. The result of this was, as usual, good news and bad news.

The bad news was that, since I didn't officially belong to news and current affairs, I didn't have automatic access to their facilities. This meant that if we wanted phone lines to interview important people—especially if they happened to be overseas at the time—we only got them as a favour. It was purely due to the dogged persistence of my team, coupled with their charm and their knowledge of which BBC buttons to press, that in those vital early days when we were so vulnerable we managed to survive.

Given the swiftness of my success and the enormous surge in my listening figures, it was only natural that there would be some resistance. I well remember one incident in the infancy of the new-look *JY Prog*. I was interviewing a government minister down the line when I heard my studio manager's voice in my earphones. The message from 'news' was that if I didn't finish the interview within one minute they would take my line away

101

from me—which they were perfectly entitled to do. I ignored the threat, called their bluff and carried on with the interview. Nothing happened. Of course, as the programme escalated in importance such threats became less frequent, but for a long time any facilities that were given to us were only given reluctantly.

However, since my programme didn't officially fall within the control of the news and current affairs empire I never had someone telling me what items I could cover or how long interviews should run. This was the good news, and in my opinion it far outweighed the bad news.

CHAPTER ELEVEN

MORE CHAT AND LESS MUSIC

Right from its beginning in 1973, the *JY Programme* was a team effort. The best ideas are the simplest, and so was our routine. I started work at home at 7am. I'd always taken all the newspapers anyway, so going through them to see whether there were items which would be of interest to us was no problem. Following the news at 8am my producer would ring me from the office. He had the advantage of the overnight Press Association feed plus details of important meetings, government plans, events, announcements and so on that were happening that day or were imminent. By 8.10 we had compared our lists of possible subjects and agreed topics for discussion on the programme. Most of our telephone conferences took less than two minutes. They were considerably shorter than some of the marathon meetings conducted by some of our colleagues—or, as the *JY Prog* developed in stature, many would say competitors—on Radio 4.

Our research team then leaped into action. And how lucky I was; I was blessed with the best research back-up team, highly talented and experienced, that anyone could wish for. I simply cannot praise them enough. But over and above their sheer efficiency was the atmosphere in which we worked. We all shared a great friendship, so there was a feeling of 'family' about the *JY Prog*. It was this feeling that helped us through many a desperate situation.

Things don't always go smoothly, even in London's Broadcasting House. They quite often go badly awry in foreign parts, and that's when it would be all too easy for tempers to fray and voices to rise. I'm told that in some other programmes they often do, but I've never known that to happen with the *JY Prog*. I've taken it pretty well all around the world. All over Europe, to Egypt, Israel, America, Japan, Hong Kong, Russia, Australia (I got told off by the New Zealand Prime Minister for not taking the programme there at the same time) and Southern Rhodesia on the day that it became Zimbabwe. Whatever, and whenever, crises arose they were dealt with quietly, smoothly and efficiently. We were a team and we worked as a team, and this attitude always saw us through.

On any ordinary workday morning, while I was still at home we would agree who would be the ideal person for me to interview on a particular subject, and the team would then set about finding them. Almost always they would succeed.

103

Meanwhile I could simply relax and motor leisurely to Broadcasting House. For the final few years of its run the programme didn't go on air until midday, but I always aimed to be in the office by 9.30am. This gave me two and a half hours in which to ferret around in the research that my team had ready for me by that time and to prepare and finalise my questions.

Having said that, nothing was set in stone. Once we were on air, control of the programme was entirely in my hands. I decided the length of interviews, and whether an interview needed to be broken up by music or could be left to run to its end without any music at all. I could completely change the direction in mid-interview if I sensed that I was on to something that would particularly interest my listeners and the media. The whole thing ran purely on my gut instinct as to what my listeners wanted to hear. Fortunately it worked.

When pressed to explain it, I often likened it to the business of choosing songs to record in my singing days. As a reasonably successful recording artist in search of a hit record I would be shown various songs which were being pushed by their writers or publishers. They would assure me that their song was the big hit I was looking for. Almost all of them weren't, of course. All I had to do was pick the right one. The big one. The one that would lead me to the pot of gold. That was where the gut instinct came in. If it was in tune with what the public wanted to hear, I was in business. If it didn't, I would be out on my ear.

Exactly the same principle applied to the *JY Prog*. If my gut instincts were right about what interviews people wanted to hear and how long they would want to listen to them, I would be in business. If not, I would be out on my ear. And this time probably for ever. This last point greatly intrigued journalists who interviewed me for newspapers. They said that, in programme terms, they'd never come across anything like it before. That was quite simply explained. There hadn't been anything like it before.

For a start, there was the music. When we shot to instantaneous success, people who would have loved to see us brought down—the BBC Old Guard—tried to find points on which to criticise. The inclusion of music was an obvious one. A current affairs programme with music? What nonsense! How can it be serious? In other words, it doesn't conform to tradition so let's kill it off quickly in case it's a success and shows us up as old fuddy-duddies.

What they failed to realise was that not everybody can assimilate current affairs and politics. I regarded it as my mission to change that. I saw it as my job, initially, to feed my audience in bite-sized chunks, and music was the ingredient that enabled me to do that. I was lucky that the clock in my head and my gut feeling combined to tell me just how long I could run an interview without losing my listeners. Break for music. Then carry on with the interview. A spoonful of sugar helps the medicine go down. But that was only in the early days. Once the listeners got used to the format they loved it. They called for more chat and less music, and I was happy to oblige.

As I had told Ian Trethowan, I wanted listener participation on the programme but without doing it the boring old phone-in way. On commercial radio I had listened to too many boring Freds from Barking and Ethels from Bermondsey droning on every day as if they felt they were becoming radio stars in their own right, which they weren't. So I wanted listener participation, but I wanted it to be short, sharp and to the point. I had decided the answer was still to have comment and reaction phoned in, but not to put the phone calls on the air. Listeners would speak to a team answering telephones in the office or studio, and their comments would then be typed on to bits of paper which I would read out.

This developed into one of the most important features of the programme. My producer would rush into my studio and hurl handfuls of paper at me. I would then select the most interesting, entertaining or controversial and read them out. By making the final one the most outrageous I ensured a further deluge. Comment fuelled further comment and kept the programme rattling along.

It helped that I have a talent for picking up pieces of paper and reading them on sight. Long before the Radio 2 *JY Prog* I remember my Radio 1 producer Doreen Davies telling a journalist that I was the only broadcaster she had ever known who could pick up a piece of paper, sight-read it live on air and, she said, 'sub it three lines ahead of what he's sight-reading'. A very well-known broadcaster, now an equally successful journalist, told me that she had never been able to sight-read, even on a recording, and the thought of doing it live would absolutely terrify her. I suppose it's a talent you either have or don't have. Newsreaders have to have it, of course. I was lucky that I did.

It's a fact of broadcasting history that the *JY*

106

Programme became an enormous success very quickly. I was walking along a corridor in Broadcasting House one day when I met Douglas Muggeridge coming the other way. He had a huge bundle of files and tapes under his arm.

'Where are you off to, Douglas?' I said.

He replied, 'I'm off to the European Broadcasting Union to give a lecture on "multifaceted broadcasting".'

'What on earth is multifaceted broadcasting, Douglas?' I asked.

'You, dear boy,' he replied. 'You.'

In very similar circumstances—in other words in the corridor at Broadcasting House—I met Douglas on his return and asked him how he had got on. He said that his lecture had gone down extremely well to a packed house, adding that afterwards he asked whether his audience had any questions.

Commented Douglas, 'A forest of arms shot up, but their owners were asking only one question. It was "How do we do the *Jimmy Young Programme*?"' Douglas said he replied, 'First find your Jimmy Young.'

CHAPTER TWELVE

ASK A WOMAN

I've always been a keen follower of boxing and in my career I've closely followed the boxer's maxim, 'Train hard, fight easy.' Thus I prepared carefully and thoroughly for any interview. I was lucky in that I enjoyed both research and assimilating the results of research. I was particularly pleased, and I suppose flattered, when in the very early days of the 'new' *JY Prog* a cabinet minister who had not been on the programme before told me after his interview, 'A colleague said, "Do your homework thoroughly because Mr Young will certainly have done his."'

I certainly 'trained hard' and 'did my homework' between Geoffrey Howe's visit on 5 July and 14 August, because that was to be the *JY Prog*'s most important moment so far. I was to interview, for the first time, the then Education Minister Margaret Thatcher.

The news that this rapidly rising star of the Conservative Party was to appear on my programme caused a *frisson* of nervous excitement and anxiety in the upper regions—and physically, no doubt, also in the lower regions—of BBC Establishment figures. 'How will Jimmy Young cope with this formidable lady?' . . . 'What will she say to his vast Radio 2 audience?' . . . 'Jimmy Young is live on air, for goodness' sake! Is something going to be said that we shall live to regret?' I couldn't really see why they were worried. If something untoward was said, the only person who would regret it would be me. The BBC doesn't fire its top brass. It does fire broadcasters.

However, with hindsight it's easy to see why they were worried. I had only been on Radio 2 for six weeks, yet I had already secured interviews with the Minister for Trade and Consumer Affairs and the Minister for Education. Was I going too far too fast?

Anyway, Tuesday, 14 August 1973 was the date

of my first interview with the person who in later years would be dubbed 'The Iron Lady'. Broadcasting House was in a state of high excitement. Not only did the BBC's top brass clamour to witness the interview, but so many press photographers turned up that they could only be fitted into the small broadcasting studio in three separate shifts.

Even now, thirty years later, a question that gets asked in any interview I give is, 'What is Mrs Thatcher really like?' The answer is that I haven't the faintest idea, but more of that later. My first impression when she walked into my studio was that she was much more attractive than she appeared in pictures. She had a neat figure and very nice legs. She looked like a very feminine person indeed. Don't waste your time throwing things at me, feminists. We already knew about her formidable intellect—but aren't men allowed to admire powerful women for their looks as well?

We had decided that we would do this particular programme in the conventional phone-in format, allowing the listener to put his or her question directly to the minister. Mrs Thatcher was in charge of a large ministry and had to make decisions affecting every family in the country with children in the education system. Thus the range of questions was extremely wide, from primary to university level. She had no advance notice of the questions. She had to deal with them live, on air and spontaneously.

Like her or loathe her—and there is no doubt that she polarised opinion—watching Mrs Thatcher in action was to see a complete professional at work. She sat on the other side of

109

my desk, pen in hand and writing pad in front of her. As callers were put through I watched her work. She knew that my programme was conducted, whenever possible, on first name terms, so she was instantly on first name terms with her callers, even the bellicose ones. She listened to their questions. She chatted to them about where they lived. She smoothed ruffled feathers when that was necessary, and turned on the charm when it wasn't. She involved herself as a parent. All of which was designed to give her time to work out the answers to their questions. As she chatted she was writing, doing sums and making notes.

As an all-round, live, on-air performance covering a wide-ranging and difficult area it was worth paying good money to see. It was clear to see why Mrs Thatcher was rising rapidly through the Conservative ranks. She was indeed a formidable politician. Did I think that she would ever become Prime Minister? I can't honestly say that I thought about it. But in any event it's likely that you would have got long odds at that time against Britain having a woman Prime Minister.

Having listened to one of her answers, however, perhaps I should have had a bet. In reply to a question about getting things done Mrs Thatcher replied, 'In politics if you want anything ask a man, but if you want anything *done* ask a woman.'

*   *   *

Added to the sheer pleasure of doing my programme day after day was the bonus that I got to meet some legendary figures. No history of American politics could be written without several

110

chapters about the Kennedy family, and I was going to meet the matriarch. I didn't expect to see what I saw.

Into my studio walked the tiniest adult I had ever seen. My mother was a small lady but, standing next to Rose Kennedy, she would have been much the bigger of the two. Our 'interviewee chair' was fully adjustable and was usually capable of coping with any size of individual, but Mrs Kennedy defeated it. We searched for, and eventually found, a lower one, but even then assistance was necessary to get her seated on it. Not to put too fine a point on it, two of the prog's researchers stood one on each side of her and, tactfully putting their hands under her elbows, lifted her on to it.

She may have been small but in that fragile-looking body was a formidable lady. Rose Kennedy had the ability to reply to difficult questions with tough, aggressive, no-nonsense answers while still retaining the smile. It was a virtuoso performance on her part, and she made clear who had the final word in the Kennedy family. Yet during the whole of the interview the thought that fascinated me as I looked at her was that out of the womb of that tiny woman had come all those strapping Kennedy men.

*   *   *

Another formidable woman had become even stronger by the mid-seventies. In February 1975 Margaret Thatcher emerged triumphant in a battle with Ted Heath and other prominent contenders for the leadership of the Conservative Party, and I

111

asked her for her reaction. She replied that she'd had so much to do that she still hadn't fully realised that she was now the Leader of the Opposition. She said, 'Of course, I feel very sorry for Mr Heath, as obviously one would be for a person you've worked with for quite a time.'

It's often remarked that a political leader must be a good butcher. So, in terms of a reshuffle and forming her new shadow cabinet, I asked her whether she possessed that ruthless quality. She replied, 'I don't know whether I'm a good one. I'm a reluctant one, but I do recognise that it is one of the tests of leadership.'

I enquired what would happen to the people who would not be playing a part in the shadow cabinet. People like Geoffrey Rippon, Robert Carr and Peter Walker. Demonstrating that she would also have made a good diplomat, Mrs Thatcher responded, 'Well, you need a lot of talent on your back-benches in Parliament—people who have had experience of what it's like to be in office. Peter and the others will be great assets on the back-benches.'

In other words, the stiletto in the ribs is actually very good for you and for the party. Whether Geoffrey, Robert, Peter and others left out in the cold would see it in quite the same way is debatable.

*   *   *

In March 1975 I interviewed the delightful Shirley Williams. I mention the fact not because Shirley was a well-known MP but because there was another side to her about which she talked to me

112

on the programme.

In the mid-1940s Shirley happened to be in the United States, where she very nearly hit the jackpot as a film star. Names were being put forward to star in a film. It was to be about a girl who owns a horse which is destined for the knacker's yard but which can be saved if it wins a very important race. The girl had to be English, aged about twelve and, fairly obviously, a good rider. Shirley fulfilled all those criteria, and she got as far as a short list of seven. Unfortunately for Shirley another name on that short list was Elizabeth Taylor, and she it was who went on to star in the film, *National Velvet*.

Shirley also toured all over America playing Cordelia in *King Lear* and living, as she told me, 'from one hamburger stand to the next'. I asked her whether she had found her acting skills an asset in politics.

'Oh,' she replied, 'we've got some first-class actors in the House of Commons.' I think we'd all agree with that.

CHAPTER THIRTEEN

FINANCE, INFLATION AND OTHER WEIGHTY MATTERS

A firm indication that we had really arrived came just three months after our launch. The front cover of *Radio Times* is a much-coveted honour and, overwhelmingly, is reserved for television programmes. However, the week commencing 1 October 1973 saw the *JY Prog* occupying the front cover, and the accompanying article confirmed the welcome news that we had been accepted as a responsible forum on which to discuss serious issues. Which is not to say that we had turned our backs on the lighter side of life. From politicians, celebrities and members of the public came moments of wit, farce and sheer delight.

*　　*　　*

It is generally thought that the then unknown, although now world-famous, Uri Geller was introduced to a startled British public by BBC Television. Not true. Uri had already bent Britain's forks and stopped Britain's clocks on the *JY Prog* before he did it on television, as he makes clear in his book *My Story*.

Actually we very nearly didn't get Uri to bend anything. Good-looking and charming, he also has an abundance of nervous energy and, on occasions, can be very temperamental. Obviously, on 23 November 1973, since I was introducing Uri to Britain I had to get him to bend something. The trouble was that he was fed up with bending things and told me so in no uncertain fashion.

Shock horror. If I couldn't get him to bend anything, what was the point of him being there? True, it wouldn't be visible as it would on television, but I could at least describe it for my listeners. There followed ten minutes of on-air and off-air wheeling and dealing before, very grudgingly, he said, 'Oh, all right then. Give me a key.'

To this day I don't know why I then did what I did. Perhaps it was my instinct for self-preservation

114

subconsciously coming into play. Obviously I had my own door keys in my pocket but, turning to my chief researcher, Charles Thompson, I said, 'Could you lend Uri one of your keys, please?' Being a really hard-nosed journalist, Charles probably didn't believe the stories of Uri's powers anyway, so without hesitation he handed him the key to the front door of his flat.

I know there are people who still doubt Uri's ability to bend things, but I can only tell you what happened there and then, before our eyes. Uri rubbed Charles's key gently with his finger and it gradually began to bend. He then put the key down on my desk and said, 'There's no need for me to touch it any more. It will continue to bend.' Sure enough it did. And it kept right on doing so until it had bent to an angle of about thirty degrees.

It was next morning that we heard the fairly hilarious end of the story. Well, we thought it was hilarious. Charles didn't.

He went home to Chelsea, where he and his wife lived in a first-floor flat. He still hoped that he would be able to open his front door with his 'Uri'd' key, but lock and key proved incompatible. He wondered whether there was an alternative. There was. His apartment had French windows and they were open. Charles was a product of Millfield School, famous for its athletic and sporting prowess, and there was a bus stop sign immediately outside.

'Easy peasy,' thought Charles. And the first part of it was. Up the bus stop sign he shinned. Could Millfield have seen him, they would have been proud of him. He reached the top. In fact he had one hand and foot on the sign and one hand and foot on the balcony when he heard a voice from below.

' 'ello, ello, ello, what's all this, then? . . . Perhaps you would accompany me to the police station, sir.'

The ensuing scene in the Chelsea nick would have been worth seeing. Since Uri and his metal-bending exploits were unknown in Britain at the time you can imagine Charles attempting to explain: 'It's like this, officer. I work on the *JY Prog* and this morning this guy called Uri Geller bent my front door key by rubbing it with his finger.'

He stood no chance. In the nick he stayed until his worried wife tracked him down and got him released. And although I pleaded 'Nothing to do with me, guv', I wasn't very popular for a while.

*   *   *

The 'Charles incident' proved that we could still deal successfully and humorously with light-hearted material, but there was no doubt that the programme had changed enormously in just a few months. We had speedily moved our huge audience into the area of discussions on important and often complex topics. I was also able to announce that I would be dealing with the results of the forthcoming General Election in a 'Jimmy Young Election Special'.

Looking back from 2003, with my track record of having interviewed hundreds of MPs, foreign heads of state, and every British Prime Minister since Alec Douglas-Home who was at No. 10 in the early sixties, it seems incredible that the Jimmy Young Election Special was regarded as such a big deal. However, back in 1974 it was considered sensational for Radio 2 to be attempting anything of the kind. There were a few furrowed brows and sweaty palms among the senior BBC suits, and a lot of them made 'casual' visits to the studio to see that we weren't falling over the furniture.

As though we would. We chalked up another enormous success, and had one quite amusing moment when Left-inclined trades union leader Hugh Scanlon popped in to see me in the studio. I asked him if he would, as we say in the trade, 'give a bit for level'. That's broadcasting jargon meaning 'Would you say a few words so the engineer can get a proper balance on your voice?' This Hughie duly did, but he was a little off-mike so the studio manager put down his key on the other side of the soundproof glass and said, 'Could you move a little to the left, Mr Scanlon?'

'Any time, my boy,' boomed Hughie. 'Any time.'

*   *   *

In the early days I came in for a lot of stick for calling people by their first names. Actually it came about in the most innocent of ways. Right from the start of the new-format *JY Prog* we had attracted big names to be interviewed and I said to my producer, 'Would you ask them how they would prefer me to address them, please?' Whether it was because I worked in a small studio, or whether it was because of the very informal atmosphere of the programme, I don't know—but almost without exception they said they would prefer first names. So Margaret Thatcher was Margaret and Neil Kinnock was Neil, and so on.

Actually, and don't ask me to explain it because

117

I can't, my gut feeling told me that perhaps there should be a couple of exceptions to the first-name rule. One should be the Prime Minister and the other the Chancellor of the Exchequer. In 1974 Denis Healey was Chancellor, and I was due to interview him in September.

Now I had never met Mr Healey but I knew of his reputation as a bruiser. He was a war hero. A big man. The voice, the eyebrows, the extrovert personality, the sense of humour and the laugh that went with it. I didn't particularly like his approach to taxation. His statement that he would 'squeeze the rich till the pips squeak' was one thing. That didn't affect me, because I wasn't rich. But when he still threatened to take, as I remember, over 80 per cent of my salary in tax you could say that he got right up my hooter.

Anyway, on the appointed day into the studio walked the Chancellor and I was prepared for confrontation. But that was not what I got. I expected his first words to be about tax or his budgets, but they weren't. They were much closer to home than that. He said, 'I'll bet you didn't know that your mother used to accompany my mother-in-law's singing on the piano.'

He was right, I didn't. Denis had obviously done his homework before our meeting. What a way to disarm an interviewer. He told me that his mother-in-law, Rose Edmunds, sang in the particular Forest of Dean church choir that was accompanied by my mother on the piano or organ. Mrs Edmunds, who sang so beautifully that she was known as 'The Nightingale of the Forest', described my mother as 'a very talented pianist and organist and a delightful lady'. I couldn't have put it better myself, and after such an opening even the Chancellor of the Exchequer had to become Denis, didn't he?

Having said that, one always got the impression that the Chancellor was capable of becoming a bit physical if required. I concluded one burst of questioning by asking him something which verged on the very personal. I then played a record and, as the music was playing, said, 'Nothing personal intended by that question, Denis.'

Quick as a flash and still smiling he replied, 'If I thought there had been, I'd have come round there and knocked your block off.'

I *think* he was joking—although with Denis you could never be quite sure.

Jokes and personal reminiscences apart, next day's *Sun* commented: 'The Chancellor surprisingly chose Jimmy's Radio 2 show to make his first statement on his weekend secret meeting with world finance ministers.' Already the *JY Prog* was becoming a powerful political forum.

*　　　*　　　*

On another occasion I interviewed Joel Barnett, who had been Chief Secretary to the Treasury under the previous Labour Government. He is not only an extremely intelligent man but is also great company. Even when discussing heavyweight matters like the state of the nation's economy he has a fund of amusing stories, even if they are not all politically correct.

On air I asked Joel if he could define inflation in terms that everybody could understand.

Joel thought for a moment and then

119

pronounced.

He said, 'Well, there was the wife who asked her husband the very same question and her husband replied, 'Well dear, when we first married your measurements were 36-24-36. Now thirty years later they are 42-42-42. There's more of you but you're not worth as much—that's inflation.'

I waited for the telephone calls from outraged feminists and they weren't long in arriving.

*   *   *

The public were also not to be outdone in supplying moments of light relief. One senior citizen wrote to us about a very personal problem indeed. He had enjoyed a long, happy and fulfilled marriage. Unfortunately his wife had died and he sounded both lonely and depressed. He was obviously a fit, healthy, vigorous gentleman who was missing all the comforts formerly supplied by his wife. He hoped in time to feel in the mood to find another partner. However, we all have needs and so, as a temporary solution to the physical side of his problem, he decided, so to speak, to approach things from a different angle. Readers of a delicate disposition, or who have had a sheltered upbringing, would be best advised not to read the next few paragraphs.

He purchased by mail order an inflatable doll and, when the need eventually overwhelmed him, he sought to make her closer, indeed her intimate, acquaintance. Eagerly he inflated her but, although he was rising to the occasion, she didn't. Air rushed out through her ruptured seams. She remained wizened and lifeless. He remained frustrated.

120

A stiff letter was called for. He duly wrote one and posted it, along with her, back whence she came. The firm sent him a new one.

Three days later the urge again overcame him. He turned to his lover but she proved just as leaky as had the first one. Again he returned her, this time with an even stiffer letter. He awaited with increasing frustration the arrival of a replacement, brand-new, super-sealed, non-leaky lady.

What he actually got was doll number two returned along with a bicycle tube repair kit. Aggrieved, and no doubt pink-cheeked with frustration, he wrote to us demanding that we did a piece about manufacturing standards in the inflatable rubber doll industry.

I'm afraid that even the *JY Prog*'s experts couldn't tackle that one on air.

CHAPTER FOURTEEN

CONTROVERSY

Interest in the programme, as well as our listening figures, kept increasing by leaps and bounds. Hitherto Radio 2 had seldom merited a mention in the so-called 'heavy' papers, but we broke through that barrier. Highly respected writer Gillian Reynolds wrote in the *Guardian:* 'Educated consumers may laugh, sophisticated BBC planners may shudder, but I would bet a pound to a privet hedge that it's Jim's show the commercial boys will be listening to and learning from.'

I operated on the unwritten agreement from my

bosses that I could deal with anything that I thought would interest my listeners. And although there was no doubt that the *JY Prog* had become an important political forum, I didn't want my programme to be limited to that. Some of the topics we covered over the years were serious and controversial social issues. And so, when we received a request for help from a compulsive gambler, I interviewed him on the programme.

This man had lost three businesses and an additional £60,000 through gambling, and he spelt out vividly what a really serious problem it could become. He thought that, if he could set himself the target of coming back a year later to tell us how he was getting on, he just might be able to break the habit.

He came back in 1975 and 1976 to confirm that he had managed to last that long. However he had been beaten up, he alleged, by people employed by the bookies with whom he used to gamble. It seemed that his losses and their gains had turned into his gain and their loss, and they didn't like it.

*   *   *

Euthanasia is one of the subjects that you know, as soon as you utter the word, will produce a flood of telephone calls, emails and letters. It also polarises opinions. Pros and antis feel so strongly that one is unlikely to change their viewpoint. Nor would I ever try to do so on the programme, even though I myself have strong opinions on euthanasia.

It was on that subject that I found myself interviewing George Mair, a surgeon with a healthy, robust approach to life, a ready laugh and

122

a great sense of humour. George is also the man who wrote a book called *Confessions of a Surgeon*. He told me how he had been treating a woman in her forties, who was riddled with cancer and in almost unendurable pain. George was doing his ward rounds one day when she said to him, 'Will you help me out? I've had a hairdo and I've said goodbye to all the people I love. Will you bring me my favourite record of Beethoven's Ninth and give me a final injection while the record is playing?'

I quote George's words exactly as he spoke them to me on air: 'She held my hand and when she asked I gave her the injection. A little while later, as she was about to fall asleep—and at that stage I do mean fall asleep—she looked at me with real gratitude and real love.'

Understandably there was a massive and immediate phoned-in reaction to the interview, which, as expected, mostly divided into those speaking of blessed relief and those speaking of the evil flouting of God's will. The overwhelming majority, however, supported George's pro-euthanasia stand.

Given that euthanasia is illegal in Britain and George had publicly admitted that he had carried it out at least once, I wondered whether he might get arrested. I was very pleased that he didn't.

*   *   *

In May 1993, to quote the *Financial Times*, 'Radio 2's World of Faith week reached its peak on Wednesday with the appearance of the Archbishop of Canterbury on the Jimmy Young programme to discuss the Church of England.' Well, that's how

123

the Radio 2 bosses thought it was going to be. A bland discussion with the person described by David Sexton in the *Sunday Telegraph* as 'The Church of England's answer to John Major' (that was before we got to know about Edwina Currie, of course). I had other ideas.

While researching the Archbishop's background I discovered that he had a daughter who was divorced and a son who had separated from his wife. I decided that it would be interesting to ask him, as the leader of the Church of England, for his views on divorce.

One would have to award him full marks for courage because he must have known that what he was about to say would be extremely controversial. While denying that he was moving away from traditional thinking, he said, 'I am not among those who say divorce is bad, full stop. I have ministered to people in such distressing circumstances that when a divorce has happened it has led to a new and better relationship. We have got to look at divorce more positively.'

Some traditionalists, such as the then Archdeacon of York, reacted adversely but, overall, the press coverage of the interview was very favourable to the Archbishop for encouraging the Church to come to terms with things as they are rather than as, in an ideal world, it would like them to be.

*   *   *

Talk about from the sublime to the Gawdblimey! One week I was in discussion with the Archbishop of Canterbury. The following week I was in jail on

Dartmoor. The visit was part of a campaign by Dartmoor's governor to improve the prison's bad image. I suppose he'd decided that, given the background of my number one hit recording of 'Unchained Melody', I was the man to do it.

Hard as any governor might try to improve conditions inside the prison, nothing is going to alter Dartmoor's impact on anyone approaching it for the first time. Built in the early nineteenth century to accommodate captured French soldiers in the Napoleonic wars, the place looks every bit as intimidating as its reputation. It may or may not be Britain's toughest prison, but it surely has to be the most isolated. We were booked into a hotel very close to the prison, which we passed on our way there. With its towers and high security walls and its location in one of Britain's bleakest landscapes it looked forbidding enough as we drove past it on a sunny June afternoon. And we were going in knowing that tomorrow we would be coming out. What the impact must be on someone due to serve a lengthy stretch, arriving in the middle of winter in the biting cold with the notorious Dartmoor fog shrouding everything, God only knows.

Meanwhile, after our long journey down we were able to bath and change and then enjoy a really excellent meal in our hotel. But as we ate and drank I couldn't help reflecting that just up the road were some people eating very different fare, to whom I would be talking the next day.

And so, on 16 June 1993, after the predictable press pictures of me standing outside the prison gates, I became the first person, on either radio or television, to present a programme live from Dartmoor prison. Before we went on air the governor showed us around the gym and recreation areas, and we were all shocked to see so many posters warning of the dangers of HIV and sharing needles. Clearly, despite security precautions, hard drugs were available in prison—even one as strict as Dartmoor. A lot of the prisoners we passed greeted me, so they were obviously able to listen to the *JY Prog*. You would have thought being sent to Dartmoor was enough punishment.

I had not attempted to impose conditions about the type of prisoner I would talk to. However, I later received complaints from some of the really hard men that they had been looking forward to talking to me but had been refused permission to do so. Clearly the prison authorities had been selective about the prisoners I was allowed to interview, but I consoled myself by reflecting that even a soft-hearted hard man would still have to be pretty hard to end up in Dartmoor.

Most of the programme, including interviews with the prison governor, members of his staff and some prisoners, was done in front of a live audience in the prison chapel, but one interview I carried out with a prisoner in his cell. For the purpose of the programme we named him 'prisoner John'. It was not that prisoner John said anything particularly interesting or exciting—it was more my slight claustrophobia that makes me remember the interview to this day. As John and I sat opposite each other in his narrow cell, my imagination got the better of me. Although I tried my best to keep the thought out of my mind, I just couldn't help imagining how I would feel if I was sitting there with this tiny space as my home for the next twenty years.

I loved the job I was doing. But rarely have I been so relieved to get out of a place where I was conducting an interview.

CHAPTER FIFTEEN

THE POWER OF INTERACTIVE BROADCASTING

By 1975 the *JY Prog* had developed a considerable reputation for listener involvement—interactive broadcasting. While I would never allow it to be used for blatant political advertising, it was none the less becoming seen as the place to be if you wanted to get something done. For instance, the Manpower Services Commission asked if I would try to find employers who would be willing to take on an extra employee. In just five days I found two thousand employers who said they were willing. It was a result I found very rewarding—as, no doubt, did the Manpower Services Commission.

*   *   *

I'm not by nature a 'joiner', but if I'm going to do something I like to do it properly. So, as my job had moved decisively away from being a disc jockey and into the journalistic world of news and current affairs, I decided the right thing to do would be to join the National Union of Journalists. There was no obligation on me to join, it was just that I felt I should. And much good did it do me.

Just a few days after I joined the union the NUJ

called its first-ever journalists' strike at the BBC. And from the way my picture was plastered all over the front pages you would think I personally had called them out. For the first time in a twenty-six-year-long career, during which time I had been a member of three trades unions, I found myself on strike.

I asked various friends in the upper echelons of the BBC what I could do about my plight. Their reaction was pretty bleak. Summed up, it was, 'You shouldn't have joined, Jim.'

* * *

Using the media to provide help for people who really need it can be a very rewarding experience. In 1975 the BBC was planning a Literacy Referral Programme, aimed at adults who had not learned to read and write as children, and I was asked to help with an explanation of what it was all about on the *JY Prog*. A switchboard manned by eight people was set up to deal with incoming phone calls. 'More than enough to cope,' said the BBC bosses. I expressed my doubts, but was over-ruled. Yet again the BBC had underestimated the power of the *JY Prog*.

As soon as I mentioned the proposed scheme some six hundred calls jammed the switchboard. Six members of the team working on the series plus senior administrators and their secretaries had to be rushed over in taxis to cope. I know do-gooders can be a bit of a pain sometimes, but I was beginning to feel like one.

* * *

Thursday, 5 June 1975 was the date of the referendum on whether Britain should stay in the Common Market. I told my listeners that, if they sent in questions they would like asked, we would set up a special programme with various experts to get them answered. The response was immediate and enormous. In fact, far from mounting just one Common Market Referendum Special programme we decided to do three.

So it was that during May I interviewed anti-Market spokespeople Tony Benn MP; trade union leader Hugh Scanlon; and Mary Blakey, President of the British Housewives' League; as well as pro-market George Thompson MP; Sir Frederick Catherwood, Chairman of the British Institute of Management; and the President of the National Farmers' Union, Sir Henry Plumb. The phoned-in reaction was so great that once again it jammed the BBC switchboard, but by the end of the three programmes I felt we had achieved what we had set out to do. We had got both sides of the argument aired to the fullest extent possible. Now it was up to my listeners to make up their own minds based on the evidence they had heard. And that was what the *JY Prog* was all about.

CHAPTER SIXTEEN

INTERVIEWING THE ROYALS

In 1976 the *JY Prog* made its first visit to Buckingham Palace. I was to interview Prince

Philip in connection with the Queen's Award to Industry. We had, as is par for the course with royal interviews, to submit my list of questions in advance. This I did with a heavy heart, because I feared I was going to get bland answers to my questions.

Sure enough, Prince Philip arrived clutching my list of questions and his answers to them all neatly typed up. He settled himself comfortably with his script balanced on his knee. I fired question one. He immediately fired back his well-rehearsed answer.

Even as I fired question two I had decided that this just wasn't going to work. I seized on something that he had said in his answer, departed from the script and fired a supplementary. Question 2(a), you might say. Back came his answer, fluent and unrehearsed, so I asked him another question that wasn't in the script. As he answered it he removed the list of prepared questions from his knee and put it on the sofa beside him. He never glanced at it again for the rest of the interview. It seemed to me that, where interviews were concerned, he was being given protection that he didn't really need or want.

After we had finished he was very complimentary about the way I had conducted matters. He finished by saying, 'The thing I really like about your interviewing technique is that you actually listen to the answers.'

I replied, 'I thought you were supposed to.'

'You are,' said Prince Philip, 'but most people don't.'

Five years later I spoke to him again, in an interview that contained an unfortunate reference to leisure and unemployment. I am sure that Prince Philip was simply suggesting how to respond to leisure and take advantage of it—whether it was leisure brought about by unemployment or by new technology—but he was savagely attacked in the media.

However, the *Guardian* leaped to defend him, printing a leader which opened with these words: 'What the Duke of Edinburgh said to Jimmy Young about the jobless has been universally condemned, not least, after the event, by Prince Philip himself.' It then listed various incomparably worse royal indiscretions of the past, naming and shaming Charles II, George IV and James I. The leader concluded, 'The fact that, according to the admittedly imperfect records of the time, there was no "Jimmy Young Show" to record their various indiscretions does not necessarily prove that no indiscretions took place.'

* * *

In 1989 my team and I went to Sandringham to interview The Prince of Wales about the work of the Prince's Youth Business Trust. The Trust had been set up in response to the inner-city riots of 1981, with the purpose of giving start-up grants and loans to disadvantaged young people who wanted to set themselves up in business. Prince Charles told me that young people needed help, encouragement and a bit of organisation to get them going. He said there were a great many young people whose talent and ability were being wasted and whose self-confidence needed to be built up, because so often that had not happened to them at school.

When I asked him specifically what should be done about lager louts and hooliganism he said that in many ways he felt not enough was being done to help those people. Then, in a statement which, predictably, was picked up everywhere in the media, he confessed that he wouldn't have known what the hell to do with himself if he had left school at sixteen.

The interview with the Prince of Wales was fine, but my impression of Sandringham was anything but. It is set in beautiful countryside, but I thought the house itself really gloomy. In fact as I trudged, in search of the gents, along a corridor heavily hung with portraits of ancestors blackened by age, it seemed to me to merit Dame Edna Everage's favourite description of 'spooky'. Prince Charles seemed totally happy, relaxed and at home there but, if the reports I've read are true, I can easily believe that Princess Diana hated it.

*   *   *

In 1990 The Princess Royal, in her role as Patron of International Literacy Year, spoke to me about her crusade for a return to the traditional methods of teaching the 3 Rs in schools. Calling for a more competitive attitude in schools and criticising the reluctance to set attainment targets, she added, 'A continuation of the progressive attitude has been taking competition out of education on the basis that nobody should be seen to fail. But human beings have always required a challenge, and doing away with the competitive element has actually done away with quite a lot of those stepping stones that have allowed people to assess themselves and be assessed by their community. I think that has done them a disfavour.'

She called for a revival of emphasis on basic skills traditionally taught and her views struck a chord with my listeners, as I knew they would. Predictably, they were less popular with the teaching profession.

It was an interview that was of particular interest to me since twenty or more years earlier I had been responsible for launching the BBC's Literacy and Numeracy Campaigns on television. Once again, I felt privileged to be in a position to help ordinary people make more of their lives.

CHAPTER SEVENTEEN

A WHO'S WHO OF COMMUNICATORS

I had always intended the *JY Prog* to be in the best traditions of public service broadcasting. By which I meant that it should educate, inform and entertain. Our regular contributors, without mention of whom no history of the programme would be complete, did all three.

At least one commentator recorded that the programme had become a sort of club with 5.75 million members, and I wouldn't argue with that description. The 'club' had its own doctors, lawyers and a food expert who were always available. And in the 'specials' which we mounted we also called on experts in any other areas in which my listeners expressed an interest. In other words we were quite clearly there to serve the public and, as my audience expanded from 2.5 million to almost 6 million, it was equally clear that the public approved of what we were doing.

The BBC, of course, has a considerable track record in the area of broadcasting medical advice. Long before the *JY Programme* a distinguished broadcaster named Charles Hill made a great impact with his instructions to 'keep your bowels open'. So successful was he that he went on to become Chairman of the Board of Governors from 1967 to 1972, and Baron Hill of Luton.

When, in January 1977, we decided that we needed to be able to give medical advice and answer listeners' questions, we gave Dr Mike Smith a trial run as one of two regular doctors. Mike had appeared on the programme before in his role as Chief Medical Officer of the Family Planning Association, but this was his debut in a more general capacity. He was an immediate, and enormous, success. Mike is of medium height with sandy hair and bushy eyebrows. A dapper dresser and nicely extrovert, he loves public speaking and is also an author. His manner of answering listeners' questions could probably be accurately described as 'brightly brusque'. When presented with a listener's particularly scatty answer to a medical problem his nicely weighed, deadpan response was usually, 'Well, there you are then.' Which doesn't sound like much in print, but when delivered by Mike conveyed a much more significant message.

Bill Dolman, our other doctor early in the life of the programme, was the ideal complement to Mike. A much quieter person altogether, he studies because he enjoys it. In fact, not content with being a GP, he decided he would like to be a lawyer as well—so he became one. In due course he combined both talents as a coroner.

Gillian Rice became our third regular programme doctor. In addition to being a first-rate doctor, Gillian is an absolutely delightful person. Married, with a lovely family, she is a very attractive lady with a lively, happy presence and a wonderful sense of humour. Seated opposite me in my studio she was a joy to behold and a pleasure to listen to.

And last but by no means least we had Mark Porter. He was a fund of medical knowledge but, had he not decided to devote his talents to medicine, could easily have become a star of the silver screen. Mark is tall, broad-shouldered and blessed with rugged, masculine good looks—one could well imagine his bedside manner being much in demand. Perhaps I should add that he is a very happily married man.

Among the special guests who appeared on the *JY Prog* was Dr Ruth, the controversial author of a book called *The Encyclopaedia of Sex*, and she sometimes had to deal with questions from listeners who were anything but happily married. Her wonderfully infectious laugh enables her to deal easily with sexual problems and, occasionally, to offer unorthodox advice.

An anonymous gentleman told us that, because of dryness and a problem with cystitis, his wife refused to have penetrative sex. The question he posed for Dr Ruth was, 'Is the answer a younger woman for me and total abstinence for my wife?'

If he was hoping for Dr Ruth to open the door for a younger woman, he was about to be disappointed. 'The answer is certainly not a younger woman for you,' she said, then added, 'However, there are many different positions which can give satisfaction, and I am about to add a new one.'

The nation—and I—waited with bated breath.

'I would suggest,' Dr Ruth went on, 'that if you place your erect penis under her armpit that would be very enjoyable. Do try this new position, which you heard about for the very first time on the *Jimmy Young Programme*.'

I have to report that we never heard from anybody who actually tried the Dr Ruth 'erotic armpit' position.

Monday was medical day and Thursday was food day, presided over by Tony de Angeli. Tony was for many years editor of the influential trade magazine *The Grocer*. Witty and bespectacled, he has a great sense of humour and is extremely knowledgeable about not only his subject but much wider matters as well. In 1995 Tony chaired the MAFF (Ministry of Agriculture etc.) Nutrition Task Force, set up to pursue the government's dietary targets, and the following year he was awarded the OBE for services to journalism and the food industry. Our listeners used to write to him with the most obscure questions and he would go to endless trouble to sort out their problems for them. Food is always a good subject anyway—we all have to eat—and that, combined with Tony's irrepressible sense of humour, made him one of our most popular regular contributors.

In addition to our regulars we were also fortunate to have guests who would interest our listeners in ordinary subjects presented with their own particular, personal flavour. Thus Sarah-Jane Evans of the *BBC Food Magazine* might pop in to give her slightly upmarket suggestions. Then there was Beryl Tate, a wonderful cook with the most infectious laugh you could ever wish to hear, who presented her food tips in her delightful Yorkshire accent, chuckling and giggling with me as she did so.

The third main area in which we served our listeners on a regular weekly basis was the law and listeners' problems with it, of which there were many. Our longest-serving lawyer was Bill Thomas—our 'Legal Beagle', so called because he had a lovely beagle named Robinson. Robinson departed long ago for a well-deserved rest in his kennel in the sky, but Bill, I'm happy to say, is still with us. Bill possessed not only a thorough and comprehensive knowledge of the law but also a wonderful, dry sense of humour.

It was heard to full effect when one day, while Bill was on air, the air conditioning began to pump out thick smoke. Nevertheless we continued broadcasting. Bill gave a running commentary and continued to do so even when the smoke had filled the studio to such an extent that we could no longer see each other. Listeners adored him and so did we.

Bill's mode of dress was casual, unless he was off after the programme to address some august body on the intricacies of the law—by which you will understand that, despite his casual appearance, he is a first-rate lawyer. Andrew Phillips, by contrast, almost always appeared in a formal suit. He is a big man, tall and broad with an outgoing presence, a big, well-projected voice and a sense of humour to match. He is the senior partner in his own international law firm and an enthusiastic supporter of the Liberal Democrat Party, for which he has stood as a parliamentary candidate.

Like Bill an astute and able lawyer, Andrew didn't stand on his dignity in my studio. In fact, he retained his well-honed student sense of humour. When he got carried away in the heat of a discussion, had there been bread rolls handy he would have thrown them at me. Fortunately there weren't any, but that didn't deter him. He used to throw the windshield off the microphone or anything else not too hard that came to hand in the studio. In due course Andrew was elevated to the peerage and became Lord Phillips of Sudbury. I'm happy to say it didn't change him one little bit. He remained the happy, extrovert guy who was such a big asset to the programme.

As the years went on we acquired other lawyers as well. For instance we had Mark Stephens, who is sometimes referred to in the press as the 'media lawyer' and can often be heard on radio or seen on television explaining knotty legal problems, among others who brought their own particular area of expertise to the programme.

Our special gardening programmes were in the expert hands of Daphne Ledward. Quite early on in our association I called her 'Daffers' on air, and it was a name that stuck. But woe betide anyone else who called her Daffers—only I was allowed the privilege of doing that. Listeners' questions sometimes verged on the bizarre. One man wrote in asking about building a garden in his loft. He had already had a window installed in his roof and had built raised beds filled with soil together with a water feature, but he needed to know what kind of plants he could grow next to his water tank. The programme never offered advice on building and plumbing disasters. Perhaps we should have done.

Bruce Fogle was our 'pet vet'—and what a charming man he is. He is a tall, good-looking Canadian with a wonderful broadcasting talent. Sometimes, when answering a question, he would slip into the role of the animal. Thus a cocker spaniel or a labrador would find itself answering the listener's question from a personal point of view. He told so many interesting and occasionally very funny anecdotes that even people who didn't have pets enjoyed listening to him. Bruce is happily married to actress Julia Foster, who starred with Tommy Steele in the film *Half a Sixpence*, and talent runs in the family. Their handsome son Ben emerged as a heart-throb when he appeared in the television programme *Castaway*.

Our 'antique gentleman', as I sometimes referred to him, was Eric Knowles. Eric also appears on television's *Antiques Roadshow*, for which he invariably gave a couple of mentions on my programme—although I don't recall them ever mentioning me. Eric has an impeccable pedigree as a director of the auction house Bonham's, but he didn't allow that to interfere with his terrific sense of humour and anecdotes delivered in his wonderful Lancashire accent. He supports Burnley football club and I'm almost tempted to say that you need a sense of humour to do that. I won't, though, because I don't want abusive letters, and possibly worse, coming from Burnley.

Hugh Jolly, one of Britain's leading paediatricians and a big man in every sense of the

139

word, was a regular guest on the programme answering parents' problems concerning their babies and children. He had written a standard work on the subject and was well respected in the medical world. One of the letters we received involved parents who had adopted from Vietnam. The child apparently spent a lot of time gnawing chair and table legs. Dr Jolly gave his considered and learned opinion on what could be done to cure the problem. It was days later that we discovered that the letter had been written by Dr Jolly's students and they were referring to a Vietnamese pot-bellied pig.

All our contributors shared one particular asset. They were all great communicators. And they could all communicate, without sounding patronising, in language that everybody could understand. If that sounds easy, believe me when I say that many people find it very difficult to do.

Many years ago I was asked by Dr Jolly to talk to the West London Medico-Chirurgical Society. Flattered but puzzled, I asked what he wanted me to talk about—after all, he was the expert and I was just the interviewer. 'Communication,' he said. 'It's as big a problem in medicine as it is in many other areas in life, and it's something about which you know a great deal.'

In no way am I criticising the medical profession, but how many times have you come out of your GP's surgery not really knowing what he or she was talking about? It's often the sheer pressure of time. It's sometimes because the doctor uses medical terms that you don't understand or are too timid or embarrassed to ask about. Whatever the reason, as Hugh Jolly said all those years ago lack of communication skills was, and still is, a huge problem not only in medicine but in many other areas of life as well.

I've sometimes been criticised by other journalists and broadcasters for allowing my listeners to make up their own minds about issues. Because they seek to impose their own biased views on their readers and listeners, they assume that everybody else should do the same. They're wrong, of course—and arrogantly wrong at that. They're also rather stupid—I would never assume that I was so powerful that people would simply accept what I say or write. They, in their arrogance, patronise the British people as being too thick to think for themselves. And then there's their stupidity. If there is one thing the British public doesn't like it's being lectured. The more you lecture them, the less likely they are to take any notice of you.

We trust ordinary men and women to vote in elections that affect our future. We trust them to form juries that decide the future of people accused of serious crimes. In running my *JY Programme* I took the view that they were capable of having views on many issues, and I wanted to hear those views. I asked for them, and they gave them in large numbers. I am absolutely certain that I was right to do so.

CHAPTER EIGHTEEN

LIVE FROM MOSCOW

In the early 1970s the programme was poised to take another new and radical step. A breakthrough for broadcasting, in fact. Following our successful broadcasts from the Common Market countries, as I explained earlier, the idea of broadcasting live from the Soviet Union was beginning to take shape. The Russians had never allowed anybody to do so before, and we thought it extremely unlikely that they would agree to us doing so now. However, it was a challenge and we decided to give it a try.

To give an idea of the enormity of the task it is necessary to go back to a speech that Winston Churchill made on 5 March 1946 in Fulton, Missouri. World War II had ended ten months previously as the Red Army swept towards western Europe. In that famous speech Churchill declared that 'From Stettin in the Baltic to Trieste in the Adriatic an iron curtain has descended across the Continent.' Many people considered this moment to be the beginning of the Cold War, when Russia and the Western powers, until recently Allies against Hitler's Germany, turned against each other. Moscow was only two hours away from London by plane, but it seemed so alien that, as far as Westerners were concerned, it might have been on another planet.

It was against this background that we approached the Soviet Embassy in London and, after a long wait, were informed that someone would be sent to have a look at the *JY Prog* in action. The Russians were not exactly the fastest movers in the world, but eventually two gentlemen turned up at Broadcasting House. Predictably, they were the hard man and the soft man. The hard man was short, very wide and, we were told, spoke no English. We were never really convinced about that. The soft man came in the complete English kit: smart blazer, cavalry twill trousers and suede shoes. And he, of course, spoke perfect English.

They sat, stone-faced, through the whole of the *JY Prog* and then departed, clutching the tape-recordings we had made for them. They were never heard from, or seen, again. It was as though they and the whole 'live from Moscow' project had disappeared into some gigantic Siberian snowstorm.

All this happened in 1972. We waited patiently, but by late 1976 I thought we'd waited long enough and suggested we should have another try. Once again we approached the Soviet Embassy, and once again they agreed to come along and discuss our suggestion. Everything seemed to be going well apart from the fact that the programme was to be live. But we had no intention of settling for the sort of recorded broadcasts that had been done before, and so, politely but firmly, we dug our heels in.

With hindsight, a fly-on-the-wall observer would have found our discussions with the Russians very amusing. Every time we pointed out that all our broadcasts were done live, the Russians attempted to head us off.

'We quite understand,' they would say. 'You record the interviews and then transmit them live

143

the following day.'

Patiently I would reply, 'No, I sit in my studio with my guests and the interviews are broadcast as we are doing them. That's what we mean by live radio.'

One could see the problem from the Russians' point of view. The Iron Curtain was still firmly in place but, with the *JY Prog* going out live from Moscow, Russian citizens might take the opportunity to broadcast unapproved personal opinions to the rest of Europe. Which, of course, is exactly what happened, although none of us was to know that at the time.

Eventually, and somewhat reluctantly, the Russians decided to give us the go-ahead, and the broadcasts were set for 16 and 17 May 1977. The news was announced in the previous February, and the press had a field day. 'It's the Jimmy Young Showski', 'JY Prog Goes Red', 'Listen in to Comrade Jimmy', 'Orft We Jolly Well Goski' and 'The JY Prog Steppes into Radio History' were just some of the newspaper headlines. The BBC's approach was, as you would expect, rather more dignified. Our Controller merely said, 'This is a broadcasting scoop and naturally we are proud of that.'

Outwardly we presented a united and confident face. However, as the man who would be at the sharp end I felt some trepidation. A research team from our end would visit Moscow in advance to look at studios, equipment and technical facilities generally. None the less I knew only too well that things could go wrong even in my cosy little studio in London, so my mind boggled at what might happen in faraway Moscow.

Meanwhile the Russians seemed to be not only warming to the idea but becoming positively enthusiastic. They asked whether we would like to extend our trip from two days to four. In addition to the two live programmes from Moscow, would we also like to do two from Leningrad (nowadays known once more by its pre-revolutionary name of St Petersburg)? It sounded tempting. Two 'firsts' instead of one. However, we decided not to push our luck and settled for just the two programmes from Moscow.

We sent Alan Wilson, one of our engineering experts, and John Gurnett, my chief researcher, over to 'do a recce'. Alan reported that he was happy that it would work technically, while John said the broadcasting authorities were very helpful. He also said that he'd talked to our proposed guests on the programme, who seemed unworried about going live and appeared not to have been warned as to what they could or couldn't say. John had also discovered that you had to queue for everything, but he had found the answer to the problem. 'Tights, chewing gum and heavy rock records are what you need to get by in Moscow,' he said.

We were due to fly out on Friday the 13th, though I wasn't convinced that Friday the 13th and going up in a plane were a good combination. I'd never flown Aeroflot before, but I guessed that since everybody in the Soviet Union was supposed to be equal they would have only one class of accommodation on their passenger aircraft. Wrong. They have first class and the rest, just like everybody else.

Including the Controller and the head of Radio

145

2 we made up a party of nine. The BBC had decreed that the Controller, the head and myself should fly first and the other six should fly economy. The Russians had other ideas. We arrived at Heathrow at 2pm for a 2.50pm take-off and were met by the Aeroflot representative. She was not the commissar I expected but a delightful, charming north of England lady who had never been to Russia in her life, and she had a very pleasant surprise for us. Perhaps feeling pity for the hard-up BBC the Russians had, for no extra charge, upgraded the whole party to first class. The surprises were to continue.

As we sat at the end of the runway awaiting clearance for take-off the Russian flight attendant asked if we would like a drink.

'What do you suggest?' we asked.

'The champagne cocktails are excellent,' was her reply.

Here we were, on our way to do broadcasts which we hoped would expose some of the flaws in Russia's Communist society, and here were those same Communists upgrading us to first class and serving us champagne cocktails. Incidentally, when the champagne cocktails arrived they were indeed excellent.

Any delusions that Russia might in some incredible way have become capitalist were banished as soon as we touched down at Sheremetyevo airport. The magnificent hospitality ended when the flight ended. Getting through immigration was a nightmare. Our bags were not just inspected, they were practically taken apart. We had to produce all the currency we were taking into the country. And it was made clear to us that, until we could account for what we'd spent and made it balance with what we'd got left, we wouldn't get out again. As for the form-filling—well, I'd never seen anything like it. Since we were classed as an official visiting BBC party we had been allocated what the Russians euphemistically called a 'guide', but even so I began to think we'd never get everything sorted out. Eventually, of course, we did, but we were an absolutely exhausted and short-tempered team that set off for our Moscow hotel in a minibus.

Driving down the Leningradskoye Shosse, the motorway connecting Moscow with Leningrad, we passed a massive tank trap which had been left as a war memorial. It marked the spot that the Germans reached in their assault on Moscow in November 1941. From it you can see the centre of the city, revealing vividly how close the invaders were to reaching their objective.

We were in Moscow for only a short time, but it was depressing to see that the authorities appeared to place such importance on keeping war memories fresh in Russian minds. Indoctrination started early. Walking in Red Square, we saw parties of young schoolchildren being taken to view the tomb of the Unknown Soldier. We all formed the impression that, although the war had ended more than thirty years earlier, the Russian leadership was in no mood to let its younger citizens say, 'Isn't it time for forgiveness and working together to ensure a peaceful future?'

We duly arrived at the Rossia Hotel, about which I was told an anecdotal story. The hotel is quite different now, but in those days it was run by the Soviet state which had put it up in the first place. Apparently when the Russians were thinking of building the Rossia they asked the American hotelier Conrad Hilton for advice. When he was told the numbers they intended to accommodate, Mr Hilton advised them to build not one hotel but three. Fairly predictably the Russians, having asked for American advice, then ignored it and built just one. Thus the Rossia Hotel in its wonderful, historic location opposite the Kremlin on Red Square is enormous. One day when our party had been out for a walk we passed a side entrance to the hotel. Thinking we could avoid walking all the way round to the front by cutting through, we went in. But the place is so vast that we got hopelessly lost. We had to trace our way back to where we came in and go round to the front.

When we booked in we were each given a pass and Uri, our guide, stressed its importance. Never mind showing it to get in, in this hotel you had to show it to get out. And of course if, having got out, you then lost your pass you weren't allowed back in again. It was as simple as that.

Even when you were in the hotel your troubles were far from over. You were given a key to your hotel room. And with every key came a key lady.

Key ladies or babushkas are, as the Americans would put it, something else again. Every floor in the hotel had its key lady. They were stationed just before you came to the elevators and their purpose in life was simple. Going out, you showed her your pass and handed her your key. On returning, you showed her your pass and she handed you your key. No pass, no key. Life was simple in the Soviet Union. Physically, babushkas all appeared to come out of a one-size package. Almost without

148

exception they were short, fat, and wore the shortest of mini-skirts. Viewed from behind as they bent down to pick up a dropped key, they were not a pretty sight. We were also told that they listened in to your telephone conversations and, given the coolness between our two nations at the time, that seems entirely possible.

It was difficult not to be suspicious of some of the odd things that happened in Moscow. For instance, there were nine of us and we were an official BBC party invited by the Russian broadcasting authorities. Knowing, and they must, that we would have a great deal of work to do, you would think they would have arranged for our rooms to be close to each other. But you would be wrong. Every single one of us was booked into a room on a different floor of the hotel. Life couldn't have been made more difficult for us if it had been done intentionally—which, naturally, leads one to think that it had.

On our first day, feeling pretty tired after our journey, we all arranged to meet downstairs in the dining room, have an early dinner and go to bed. On our way to the dining room we heard music playing and realised we had stumbled on a Russian dinner dance. A dance band, playing rather badly, was accompanying a blonde lady who had seen better days singing standard songs in an American accent off-key. 'Well intentioned but badly executed' would probably have been a judging panel's verdict. The same could be said of dinner. We were handed large menus that we carefully perused. We shouldn't have bothered. Almost everything was 'off'. Aeroflot, champagne cocktails and cheerful flight attendants were long gone.

You'd have thought we were in a different country now. Waiters bustled by but ignored us. Any attempt to attract their attention was greeted with a brusque '*Niet*'.

As we made our way to our rooms afterwards we were agreed that, if we were going to survive in Moscow, we would need plenty of the records, chewing gum and tights that John had advised. And what rooms they were! I was allocated one with an en-suite bathroom. The trouble was I only had one light bulb, and repeated phone calls failed to produce another. So, if I needed to see what I was doing when visiting the bathroom—as with having a shave, for instance—I had to take the light bulb with me.

The next morning we visited the radio station to have a look at the studio, and to say I was shocked would be the understatement of the year. Instead of my tiny, intimate, homely studio in London I was going to have to work in a great barn of a place complete with a grand piano standing in one corner. Clearly, getting the kind of atmosphere I was able to create in London was going to be all down to me, and it wasn't going to be easy.

Meanwhile, what could be done about getting us something decent to eat? I was wandering about the hotel wondering how we could use John Gurnett's assets to our advantage, but the trouble was that nobody spoke English. I had almost given up when I saw a lady cleaning up the tables in one of the hotel's restaurants. She was blonde and in her younger days had clearly been very attractive. Like most things in Moscow she was rather faded, but she was to be the answer to our food problems.

For the umpteenth time, and not very hopefully,

I asked, 'Excuse me, do you speak English?'

'Only a little,' she replied. I thought that, just at this time, only a little would do for me.

I said, 'I have some tights and chewing gum if you would like them.' For both of us it was like coming up on the lottery.

'I would very much like, please,' she said. 'My son loves chewing gum and I need tights.'

I said, 'We would like a table for nine for breakfast tomorrow, please, and if we could have bacon and eggs that would be lovely.'

I hadn't the faintest idea how tomorrow's breakfast would work out, but I figured that it couldn't be worse than what we'd endured so far.

That evening John Gurnett and I were going to have a meal with a man who sounded very interesting and whom I was due to interview. His name was Vladimir Pozner. Vladimir's father had gone to work in America when Vladimir was very young, and he spent the first twenty years of his life over there. Indeed, when he spoke you could be forgiven for thinking that he was an American. I needed to keep in mind, though, that he also spoke fluent Russian, and would think like both an American and a Russian. He would almost certainly be an excellent broadcaster—and a formidable opponent if that was the way our interview went.

We already knew that, contrary to the mistaken beliefs of Communists in Britain, not all Russians were equal. And Vladimir was more equal than most. Before we left London it had been impressed on us that status was of the utmost importance in Russia. We were told very forcefully, 'It is vitally important that the Russians respect you.' It was immediately obvious that the authorities respected Vladimir and that he had status. For a start he had a four-room apartment, which was not easily come by in Moscow. Next, as he offered us a wide range of drinks, hard-to-obtain Western records played in the background. We spent a very pleasant evening in Vladimir's apartment, and I formed the view that he was very much a regular player in Moscow's first team.

At breakfast the following morning our blonde waitress friend was waiting for us. We waited, hopefully, for the promised bacon and eggs. I cannot honestly say that what we got was the best bacon and eggs I had ever tasted. Actually it was a skillet full of something yellow in which were tiny flecks of something that looked vaguely like bacon. However, it was hot, and we filled up with the excellent Russian bread.

As we were tucking in, someone waved a hand at me from a table halfway down the vast restaurant. Wondering who in Moscow could possibly know me, I waved back. The man immediately came over. He wasn't a Russian, he was a Brit with a delegation to Moscow from the tractor manufacturer Massey Ferguson. They were trying, and failing, to get something to eat. He said, 'I don't know how you've done it, Jim, but could we join your table, please?' Next day we had a similar request from Girling Brakes. 'Train hard, fight easy,' I thought as I thanked the good Lord for John Gurnett's research.

The highlight of our Moscow Sunday morning was a visit to the British Embassy, where we received a warm welcome from the British Ambassador and the Cultural Attaché who had

152

done so much to smooth our visit. However, getting invited to the British Embassy in Moscow had been one thing, and getting in quite another. British soil it might have been, but it was guarded by very large, gun-toting Russian soldiers who marched— did the good old German goose-step, actually—up and down in front of the entrance. Having got by the goose-steppers, we then had to negotiate the pass-examiners. Just as at the airport, it wasn't sufficient for them to give your pass a cursory once over. Oh no, they read the print as though it was the first time they'd ever seen one. Then came the picture examination. This involved first looking at your passport picture and then conducting a close-up examination of your face to be sure the two matched.

Having passed all the tests, we were allowed to go in. We were shown over the Embassy, including the basement which, we were told, was the only room in the entire building in which you could be sure of having an unbugged conversation. Given the atmosphere in Moscow at the time, I don't think we were convinced that even that was certain. There was always a lot of joking about bugs. On going into a room people would speak to potted plants or into lamps or chandeliers along the lines of 'Can you hear me, Ivan?' It was all James Bond stuff, of course, done amid much nervous laughter, but I was never quite sure where the joking ended and reality began.

We took drinks with the Ambassador on the Embassy terrace, which provided an excellent view of the Kremlin. Apparently in slightly earlier times this used to infuriate Stalin, who for years applied various kinds of pressure to persuade the British o move to another building. Clearly he didn't understand the British sense of humour. The more he showed that their presence was annoying him, the more determined they became to stay where they were. 'Uncle Joe' Stalin was never the benevolent uncle portrayed by the Russian PR machine. In fact he was completely ruthless, and one can imagine the Brits quite enjoying seeing the steam coming out of his ears.

The first of our two history-making programmes was on Monday, 16 May. We were to cover housing, women's role in Russian society, young people, juvenile crime, sport, dissidents, human rights and emigration. The next morning *The Times* reported, 'Yesterday Jimmy Young sat in a red-carpeted studio in central Moscow and conducted the first live radio programme to be transmitted from East to West. For the Soviet State radio and television committee it was an unprecedented experiment.'

The *Guardian* said,

The Iron Curtain turned briefly into a sieve yesterday as a jolly Russian journalist called Vladimir Pozner chatted to Jimmy Young for all the world as though the KGB was asleep. He galloped into the controversial fields where Jim was tip-toeing and launched into a carefree admission of Russian social problems. Did Soviet teenagers engage in truancy, alcoholism, vandalism, the generation gap and living together, asked Jim. 'Of course they do,' said Vladimir. 'Of course there is truancy and of course we have a Soviet alcoholic problem.'

And in the *Daily Mirror*, 'There were plenty of sniggers when it was announced that Jimmy Young would present the first live radio programmes from Moscow. What could he do? But, in a Russian word, yesterday's programme was *"Khorosho"*— excellent. Jimmy put some straight questions to Vladimir Pozner, a smooth-talking Moscow broadcaster, and pinned him down to admitting that there is Anti-Semitism in Russia.'

I was delighted that the first programme had been judged an unqualified success. I was also delighted that we had thrown back in their faces the sneers of those who had said the Russians would use me to put over their propaganda. The message from Broadcasting House in London was that the programme was viewed as an enormous achievement and there had been a 'tremendous response from listeners'.

The mood in Moscow was excellent. Our hosts had laid on a modest reception for us, and we were due to do the same for them after the second programme the next day. Champagne cocktails were offered and accepted. Then Mr Lev Korolev, the head of the Foreign Relations Department at the Soviet State Committee for Broadcasting, whose face looked as though it had been carved from granite, addressed me personally.

He said, 'You are an excellent broadcaster. If tomorrow's broadcast goes as well as today's I would like you to come back and do some broadcasts from Siberia. We will send you to Siberia, but not for ever.'

Russian joke, but when uttered by Mr Korolev it also sounded like a threat.

Naturally, after all the accolades from both home and Moscow we slept well and, on Tuesday morning, set off for the radio station in confident mood. Yet on arrival we were greeted by sullen faces. No one spoke to us, and for the life of us we couldn't understand why. We were left in ignorance until Vladimir Pozner arrived. His face was white and drawn and he had dark circles under his eyes. He looked ghastly.

I said, 'You look bloody terrible. What's the matter?'

He replied, 'I've been on the carpet about the broadcast.'

'But your people loved the broadcast,' I said, 'they told us so yesterday.'

Vladimir shook his head. 'They're not talking about *that* broadcast. They're talking about the one the BBC beamed back to the Soviet Union last night.'

The BBC knew perfectly well that my broadcasts from Moscow, although being transmitted live to Europe, were not being transmitted within the Soviet Union. They also knew that the Russians, having reluctantly agreed to allow me to broadcast live to Europe for the very first time, would not be very happy if those broadcasts were heard at home in Russia. Despite knowing all that, and despite knowing that they would risk damaging the breakthrough I had managed with the Russians, not to mention the risk to my team and myself still in Moscow, the BBC External Services decided otherwise. Without warning us, they recorded my Monday morning transmission from Moscow. They then selected the bits they knew would most antagonise the Russians and transmitted them back

156

Young Jim with unidentified object

Mum and Dad

Camera-shy Jim nuzzles
up to Mum, 1926

Hello sailor—but I
joined the RAF

Lesley, aged 3

Leading
aircraftsman
Young—
Bexhill-on-Sea

Me in my first
long-trousered
suit

Convalescing up
a Swiss mountain
after one of my
bouts of chest
problems

With the Egyptian President Sadat at his
Summer Palace, 1978

With Alicia on our first visit to Florida, 1980

With Australian Prime Minister Bob Hawke in the
VIP lounge at Sydney Airport, 1988

With Tony Benn—a formidable MP who has
become a formidable theatre performer

into the Soviet Union on the Monday night. Not much BBC brotherly love visible there.

What was even worse from our point of view was that, even before leaving London, we had decided that, although the Monday programme would be hard, Tuesday's should be even harder. By this time we had all grown rather fond of Vladimir and rated him as one of the good guys. Nevertheless, when he arrived for Tuesday's broadcast I warned him that I had to carry through the firm, probing, questioning programme I had gone there to do. To his eternal credit—especially since I had no doubt that being 'on the carpet' in the Soviet Union was a very much rougher experience than it would have been in Britain—Vladimir said, 'Don't worry about me. I'll be OK. You just carry on doing your job.'

The *Sun* newspaper's retrospective verdict on the two programmes was, 'Jim's radio shows start Cold War again', and after Tuesday's show it certainly felt like it. At the small reception we had arranged for the Tuesday I had the misfortune to be the first of our party to arrive, and as I walked in I could see a group of very agitated Russians at the bar. Possibly the most agitated was Mr Korolev. When I went over to get a drink he poked me in the chest with a very large, very stiff, Russian forefinger. He didn't speak English, but he didn't need to. I knew perfectly well what was wrong, and it was confirmed as the interpreter translated his words. Sure enough, it was the broadcast the previous night by the BBC External Services which had by now engulfed the British Embassy in Moscow and the Foreign Office in London and was escalating into a major diplomatic row.

I tried to explain that the BBC External Services

163

were an entirely different and independent arm of the BBC from the domestic service for which we worked. Explaining that in Britain is difficult enough. Trying to explain it to a non-English-speaking Russian through an interpreter, I stood no chance.

I decided to try smoothing ruffled Russian feathers, and said to the interpreter, 'Tell Mr Korolev that I'm sure all will be well when we come back to do our broadcasts from Siberia.'

A lot of very angry-sounding Russian language came from Mr Korolev, and his arm moved energetically backwards and forwards horizontally.

The interpreter translated, 'Mr Korolev says any more broadcasts like last night and today and we shall all be in Siberia, sawing.'

The bad news was that we were still in Moscow and, in the Cold War climate, feeling very vulnerable. The good news was, as I said, the discrediting of all the people who had predicted that I would be exploited by the Russians for propaganda purposes—and before my departure there had been banner-waving protests outside Broadcasting House. Far from being discredited, we had been praised in the media for getting brave people like Vladimir Pozner to talk openly, and at some risk to themselves, about the shortcomings of the Soviet Union.

Vladimir's name cropped up again in 1990 with a review of a book he had written called *Parting with Illusions*. Chaim Bermant, the reviewer, described him as 'Far and away the most brilliant commentator on Russian affairs in any medium, fluent without being glib, informed without being pedantic, and with a voice and presence which

164

carry their own authority.' He then added, 'Pozner was largely unknown in Russia or abroad and possibly owes his fame to Jimmy Young who came to Moscow in 1977 for a series of live broadcasts from the Soviet Union. Pozner was among those interviewed and turned out to be the star of the show. As a result other interviews followed and he was invited to appear on radio and television in Canada, Britain and America years before glasnost.'

On our programme Vladimir had talked at length about social problems such as prostitution and alcoholism. Until that time the Soviet authorities had always denied the existence of such flaws in their Communist paradise, and in his book Vladimir revealed that a planned trip to America was abruptly cancelled by the Russian government as a direct result of his remarks on our programme.

However, back in Moscow in 1977 there was still one hard-line Russian surprise coming our way. The next day we were waiting in the hotel foyer for the airport bus when a very agitated key lady headed for our party. Her face was distorted and her arms flailed wildly. Pointing to John Gurnett, she shouted at our guide, Uri.

Said Uri to John, 'Would you open your luggage, please? This lady says you have one of the hotel's coat hangers in your case.'

John had little choice. To this day he swears it was an accident. He had simply swept up his own hangers into a heap and, by mistake, one of the hotel's with them, and dumped the lot in his case. Having seen the hanger in question you would have to agree with him. It was the cheapest, nastiest, white plastic coat hanger you would ever wish not

165

to see in your wardrobe. However, to the babushka it was clear evidence of a deep-laid capitalist plot to steal Russian coat hangers. She seized it triumphantly and proceeded to poke John in the chest with it until made to desist by Uri.

Now all this was happening in the middle of a crowded foyer and everyone was gaping. What could John do to save British honour? He played his ace. He whipped out his very last pair of tights and, with a beaming smile, presented them to her. Pink-faced and flustered, but extremely happy, she fled.

Uri explained to us that key ladies are ordered to count the hangers in your room before you leave the hotel. If there's one missing you don't get out, as John had just discovered.

As we boarded the plane I reflected that we had done two successful programmes and made broadcasting history. Nevertheless a little later, when I heard the thud as the landing gear came up, I felt greatly relieved to be going home.

The end of the story was supplied for me a couple of years later when I was interviewed by Tony Lewis at Pebble Mill in Birmingham. Tony said, 'I did the second live broadcast from Moscow about a month after you left. As I was shown the studio from which I was to broadcast, our Russian guide said proudly, "This is it, Mr Lewis. This is the 'Jimmy Young studio.'"

CHAPTER NINETEEN

HAPPY ANNIVERSARY (FROM AN OIL RIG)

Clearly our broadcasts from abroad had gone down very well and we were going to be directed to do more. Not all, however, were from distant or exotic locations. Friday, 30 September 1977 was the tenth anniversary of Radio 2, and our bosses were keen that we should be seen to celebrate the fact. My part in the overall scheme was to broadcast from the oil rig *BP Forties Alpha*, 120 miles out in the North Sea off the east coast of Scotland.

We awoke in Aberdeen on the Friday morning to very high, almost gale force winds and were convinced there was no way we would be allowed to travel by helicopter in such conditions. However, we were eventually allowed to take off and headed out to sea.

The landing area on an oil rig is painted rather like an archery target, and from the air it looks about the size of a very small pocket handkerchief. As a matter of fact it doesn't look all that big even when you're immediately above it and about to land. The pilot manoeuvred the helicopter around to the lee side of the rig, and then lost height so that we were hovering just below the landing platform. He explained to me, seated beside him, that he was still quite worried about the very high wind and therefore he was getting as much shelter as possible. He also said that what he intended to do, when a suitable moment arrived, was to shoot the helicopter up and over the landing area and then plonk it down. We hovered for what seemed like an eternity and then he said to me, 'Right, then! This is where we find out whether I can fly the bloody thing.' Having said which, up we zoomed and down we plopped.

It was bitterly cold on the rig and we speedily and gratefully hurried below. We were handed mugs of hot coffee, and as we began to thaw out started to remove our heavy outer clothing. I didn't get far with my disrobing, however. The gentleman in charge of the rig said, 'Keep yours on, Jim. I thought to get some background for your broadcast you'd like to be shown around the rig.' Back out into the wild arctic conditions went my guide and I.

Oil rigs may look tiny from the air, but I can assure you they're pretty damned big when you're standing on one. Also, standing on one of the outside gantry walkways in close to gale force winds is an uncanny and slightly unnerving experience. For a start you're completely out of sight of land. You're standing in the middle of the ocean on what feels like a very large Meccano structure. It's just you on a large lump of metal in the middle of nowhere. The wind shrieks and howls as though it's trying to blow you away and, as you look through the holes beneath you, you can see the sea lashing away at the very foundations of the rig. You know it's safe because it was there before you arrived and will still be there after you've gone. Nevertheless I was very glad to get back to the comfort, warmth and security below deck.

Ariel, the BBC's in-house magazine, also celebrated the first ten years of Radios 1 and 2. In a full-page article headed 'Growth of the JY

168

Politics Show' it said, 'Radios 1 and 2 have come a long way in ten years but few programmes have developed like the Jimmy Young Show.' It continued, 'The *JY Prog* has changed style yet remains one of the most popular shows on Radio.'

There were lots of other live outside broadcasts, though none from venues quite as windy and scary as *Forties Alpha*. BBC management had us visiting many places around Britain, mainly to boost audiences in areas where there was more competition from commercial radio. The Isle of Man, when it rained for most of our stay, and Jersey were two memorable places. On Jersey we toured the island and we were invited into the home of Sir Billy Butlin, the founder of the Butlin holiday camps. His mansion, filled with seaside knick-knacks and ornaments, was set in a large, ornate garden with an aviary. Inside, the main living room was designed like a 1930s' set. His belief was that if he gave the customers a fair deal, a roof over their heads and amusements they would flock in. It worked, to judge by the opulence of his house.

On one occasion we went down to the seaside at Brixham in Devon, where we broadcast from the deck of the unmistakable and unique replica of Sir Francis Drake's *Golden Hind*. As the broadcast continued, crowds gathered on the quay and I began to wonder whether they, and we, were safe. When the programme closed and we gathered ourselves to leave there was a crush of holidaymakers at the bottom of the gangplank. As usual they wanted autographed pictures, and I was struggling to keep up. Eventually I became separated from the rest of the team and they had to come back to rescue me, laughing at my predicament. If that's the price of fame and a huge listening audience, then so be it.

And just to keep us on our toes, towards the end of 1977 our masters decided to change the programme's time slot. We were to start ninety minutes earlier, at 10am instead of 11.30am. It was a better time slot in terms of increasing the size of our audience, but it also increased the pressure on us. Following my telephone conference with John Gurnett after the 8am news, he and his research team and I would have only two hours to prepare for the programme rather than the three and a half hours that we had had previously. It was a formidable task, but we coped.

CHAPTER TWENTY

MIDDLE EAST INITIATIVE

Following the success of our live broadcasts from Moscow in 1977 we were encouraged to mount similar ones elsewhere, and the troubled Middle East seemed an obvious place to go. We suggested doing two programmes, one from Egypt and one from Israel.

Since 1947 there have been three regional wars and two Palestinian uprisings against Israeli occupation. The Arabs' desire to destroy the State of Israel, founded in 1948, and on the other hand Israel's wish to extend its boundaries, have been at the heart of the conflict. Arab states launched a major initiative in late 1976 and early 1977, with the aim of resuming the Geneva Middle East peace conference. After months of diplomatic activity, in November 1977 President Sadat of Egypt made a historic visit to Jerusalem, and the following month Israeli Prime Minister Menahem Begin visited Ismailia in Egypt for discussions with Sadat. But this peace initiative, like the others, eventually failed. This was the background to our visit to the Middle East in 1978.

As soon as we had received permission to go ahead with our projected broadcasts, my producer, Harry Walters, set about arranging them. He wrote the necessary diplomatic letters, and on 30 May we were able to announce that I would be broadcasting from Cairo and Jerusalem. The icing on the Cairo cake was that, in addition to discussing the Egyptian economy, press freedom and British business interests, I had been given provisional permission to interview President Sadat. Sadat was under criticism for cracking down on some sections of the Egyptian press. Sixty journalists were under investigation for 'defaming their country abroad', so, if I was granted an interview, it looked like being interesting, and possibly quite lively.

We duly boarded our British Airways flight at Heathrow and set off for Egypt, but we didn't get very far. We were about halfway across the English Channel when the captain announced, 'Don't worry, folks, but our radar's packed up and we'll have to go back to London to get it fixed.' He added another 'Don't worry, folks' before saying, 'Just to be on the safe side I'm dumping most of our fuel before landing at Heathrow.' As I watched the fuel streaming out of the tanks I thanked the

Lord that I'm not a nervous flyer.

Because of the delay we arrived in Cairo very late, very tired and longing to get to bed. We were booked into the legendary Shepheard's Hotel, and I went to my room dreaming of clean sheets and long hours of beautiful sleep. What I actually got was the biggest pile-driver in the world at work on the road right outside my bedroom window, and it thudded away every minute of every hour of every day and every night that we were there.

Sleep or no sleep, as usual I had done my homework. I knew that at the time when his predecessor, Colonel Nasser, was overthrown Sadat had taken over the radio and television networks to announce the revolution to the Egyptian people. He was elected President in October 1970, and re-elected in 1976. In between, he had led the 1973 Yom Kippur War against Israel, in which the Egyptian Army had managed to cross the Suez Canal into Israeli territory, but, as in the Six-Day War of 1967, was ultimately defeated. Subsequently Sadat had vigorously intensified his efforts to establish a peace settlement with Israel.

Thursday, 8 June was to be President Sadat day for us. We had still not received confirmation that I would be allowed to interview him, but we had been told that, if we cared to present ourselves at the Summer Palace at 10.30 on Thursday morning, it was just possible that I would be allowed to record an interview. Accordingly we presented ourselves at the appointed hour hoping for the best.

Included in our party was a charming Egyptian lady named Sana el Saed who had, she hoped, arranged the interview. She walked across to the

172

guard on the gate to ask him to telephone the Palace and let the President know that we had arrived. It should have been a very short conversation, but it wasn't. As a matter of fact it developed into a very long and quite heated conversation with much waving of arms.

Sana walked back to us looking very flushed and angry. She said, 'The guard says the President is giving no interviews at all today.'

By now it was 11am, and Egypt at 11am in June is baking. We groaned and collapsed on the ground in our individual pools of sweat. But Sana didn't collapse. On the contrary, she was furious and raring to go. Her professional pride was at stake. As far as she was concerned she had fixed for me to interview President Sadat and, come Hell or high water, she was going to make it happen.

She commanded, 'Stay exactly where you are. Do not move until I get back.' Then she jumped into her car and roared off in a huge cloud of Egyptian dust. Running down the middle of the road outside the Palace at Ismailia is a grassy bank with palm trees growing up from it. We sat down there in whatever shade we could find to await Sana's return, whenever that might be. At 2pm we had just about given up hope when Sana skidded to a halt in the now expected cloud of dust. Jumping out of her car, she said, 'Quick, into Ismailia town for some lunch, then we come back and do the interview.'

Since we were by now starving, we gratefully piled into the car and headed for town. When we got to the restaurant we ordered lunch, but it took ages to arrive. It had just been put on the table when Sana's phone rang. There followed a brief conversation and then she said, 'Right, that's it, we leave for the Palace now.' We never did have lunch.

On our return to the Palace, Sana was admitted first. Then the rest of us were escorted around the building and behind it on to the Palace lawn. As we turned the corner we walked into the most breathtakingly beautiful scene. The rich, green lawn runs right down to the Suez Canal. There are trees, brightly coloured flowers, shrubs and bushes and, in the background, ships ploughing their way through the Canal. Seated close to the water's edge was President Sadat. Standing next to him and in earnest conversation with him was Sana. She said she would fix it, and she had. Professional pride was restored. She had fought for us and won. Well done, Sana.

Turning away from the President, she ran back to where we were standing. 'We have to do the interview now,' she said. 'And we have only thirty minutes in which to do it.'

It was now 4pm, and after almost a whole day in the sun we were all exhausted. But for me the day was just about to begin, and the next thirty minutes were all-important. Despite the fact that the sun was still blazing down, there was quite a strong breeze blowing. On a normal day this would have been a wonderful blessing, but if I had to interview Sadat out in the open it would prove a nightmare for our technical expert, Alan Wilson.

Alan said, 'We've got to get him inside, Jim. You'll never get an interview of broadcast quality out here.'

I explained the technical problem to Sana, who didn't look too happy about having to explain it to the President. Nevertheless she said she would try.

174

I don't speak Arabic, but I didn't need to. The expression on the President's face and the tone of his voice conveyed his message to all of us loud and clear. It was, 'There is no way I am moving inside. You either record the interview here or we don't do it at all.'

Spotting a hedge about thirty feet from where the President was sitting, Alan said to me, 'Let's see if we can get him behind that, Jim. At least that would give us some kind of shelter from the wind.'

I whispered to Sana, Sana whispered to the President and, reluctantly, he agreed to make the move. We tried again.

But 'It's still no good, Jim,' said Alan. 'You must get him to move inside the Palace.'

By this time tempers were getting a little frayed. I told Alan, 'If you think I'm going to risk losing an interview with an already bad-tempered President of Egypt by telling him he's got to move twice in one day against his will, you've got another think coming. We do it here.' By this time my precious, and reluctantly granted, thirty minutes was down to twenty minutes and I could wait no longer.

I had divided the interview, roughly, into two parts. The first half would be about Middle East problems, with special reference to Egypt and Israel. The second half would be about President Sadat's problems at home.

The first part went relatively smoothly. The President made the expected references to being disappointed by Israel's reaction to his Jerusalem initiative. He said he was 'stunned' by Israel's proposals to retain its settlements in the Sinai desert under Israeli Army protection. He stated that Israel must withdraw to its pre-1967 borders.

I asked the President about attacks on his government from within Egypt, and went on to enquire about the referendum he had recently held to decide what measures should be taken against the most vocal of his critics. How did this square with his statement that he had created for Egypt a liberalised parliamentary system?

According to the *Guardian*'s report of this part of the interview, 'President Sadat, his voice rising in volume, replied, "I was very furious with your Radio when you took their part in the doubt campaign." He continued, "I told them, either convey to British public opinion the real picture, or not at all. I'm only asking for the truth and nothing but the truth."'

Certainly the *Guardian* was accurate in stating that the President's voice rose, and continued to rise. What they couldn't know, of course, was that he was leaning forward around the microphone and shaking his forefinger at me. I pressed the President further on the allegations that he was suppressing criticism. His voice became even louder, and he continued to be very agitated and angry. And then, quite suddenly, the most extraordinary thing happened. He broke off in mid-sentence, returned to being the charming, charismatic man he really was, and said, 'I must apologise, my friend, if I was sharp. I know I was, and I am sorry. But I must explain that Thursday is my fast day, and I have not eaten or drunk anything since last night. Even worse than that, on fast day I cannot even smoke my pipe, and *that* makes me *very* irritable.'

It also, I thought, made that great man very human. His assassination three years later, by

176

Islamic fundamentalists opposed to his policy of rapprochement, deprived the world of a sane, clear-sighted statesman.

Over the weekend we flew to Israel where we were due to broadcast from Jerusalem on 12 June. Put like that, it sounds fairly simple. However, at that time relations between Egypt and Israel were so strained that it was anything but simple. We couldn't fly direct—it was necessary for there to be seen to be a complete break. Accordingly, having worked our way through three sets of security checks at Cairo airport we flew Egyptian Airlines to Athens. This was a particularly tiresome and irritating journey. Not so much because it was a long distance, but because we were conscious that we were heading, roughly speaking, in the opposite direction to that in which we wanted to travel. Eventually we arrived at Athens where, just to put a little icing on the cake, we lost our luggage. Having finally retrieved it, all that remained was to negotiate the second leg, which was to fly TWA to Ben Gurion airport in Israel.

It's odd how often it's the little things in life that stick in the mind. One such event occurred as we came in to land. The aircraft was crowded with American Jews taking a holiday, and at the same time making a pilgrimage, to Israel. As we landed they all applauded. Many of them wept. It was a first-hand demonstration of the depth of feeling of the Jewish people for Israel. Even to a non-Jew it was an extremely moving moment.

As we were driven from the airport to Jerusalem we noticed the ruins of burned-out lorries which seemed to have been preserved. When we asked why, we were told that they had been destroyed during the most recent war and were now retained as war memorials. Russia last year with its tank trap, now Israel with its burned out lorries. I wondered why people had such a fascination with keeping alive the memories of past wars.

Eventually we arrived at our hotel, the Jerusalem Plaza. All modern chrome and glass, sleek, sophisticated and Americanised, it has none of the history or ambience of Shepheard's in Cairo. On the other hand, nor did it have a pile driver, I was pleased to note. One thing it had was a wonderful view. From our balconies we could see clearly across Jerusalem to the Old City and the Mount of Olives. We all hoped that we might have time to see at least a little of the Holy City. Little did we know that, for once in our lives, we were going to have almost a whole day to spare.

Things seldom go as planned in the broadcasting business, and this trip was to be no exception. One of the most important areas to cover while in Israel was President Sadat's courageous peace initiative, and I was to talk to Israel's Deputy Prime Minister, Yigael Yadin, about it. However, we discovered that during the course of our circuitous flight from Egypt to Israel the Israeli cabinet had been called to a crucial meeting, which meant that Professor Yadin would not be available for the broadcast. My producer, Harry Walters, described what happened next as 'demonstrating the flexibility of both the *Jimmy Young Programme* and Radio 2'. It also demonstrated the good luck of having the Controller of Radios 1 and 2 with us, because Charles McLelland took an on-the-spot decision to postpone the broadcast by a day and transmit on 13 June instead.

I find it difficult to sum up what I felt about Jerusalem. True, we visited all the legendary places, and I was glad that I had seen them, and would never forget doing so. But somehow, for me, the Bible didn't come alive. Perhaps I expected too much. Perhaps I was too put off by what seemed blatant, and at times extreme, commercialism.

The only other thing of interest that happened that day was that I broke a rib when I managed to fall down a flight of stairs at the hotel. And should you be thinking what I think you're thinking, I wasn't. I was rushed off to a doctor who strapped up my ribs tighter than anyone had done since my rugby-playing days, and I realised then that my Jerusalem broadcasts were going to be conducted in the classic bent-over-holding-my-side-does-it-hurt-only-when-I-breathe style.

On the morning of 13 June we had a recording to do. For a programme which boasted that it always broadcast live, we seemed to be doing a lot of pre-recording. The fact was, although the Deputy Prime Minister was most happy to be interviewed, he could not be with us for the actual transmission. So, once again, it was pre-record or nothing. Accordingly we presented ourselves at a very ordinary-looking house not too far from our hotel, where we were shown up to the first floor and into a rather dark, very quiet room.

I started by putting it to Professor Yadin that President Sadat had given his peace initiative a further two months to succeed, and that he had accused the Israeli government of being intransigent. How did he feel about that?

The Deputy Prime Minister answered, 'I think it is naïve of President Sadat to think that one can

179

solve a very deep conflict of many years within two months, like an instant coffee solution.' He went on, 'President Sadat, who I think is a great man, and whose courage I admire, is making a mistake by setting these dates.' When I reminded Professor Yadin that the whole Israeli Parliament had applauded Sadat when he spoke there on his peace initiative, Yadin replied, 'The Parliament only applauded him because he said what he said in Jerusalem and not somewhere else. But they still disagree with him.'

It seemed that President Sadat had presented the Israelis with what he saw as his conditions. The Israelis had interpreted them as Sadat's opening offer, and subject to negotiation. Since then, it appeared, no dialogue had taken place between the two sides. I told Professor Yadin that I found this terribly depressing, even frightening. I was even more depressed when I heard his reply, 'I regret that it appears the only way I can talk to President Sadat is through Jimmy Young. If only I could talk to him direct I am sure we could find a solution.'

It hadn't taken very long, that hot morning in 1978, to see why Middle East negotiations wore out good men very quickly. Now, twenty-five years later, the situation is sadly still with us. Personalities come and go (and there have been many, from both within and beyond the Middle East, who have been involved), but the gap still seems unbridgeable. The last peace initiative, the Oslo process, began in 1992 with negotiations between the then Israeli Prime Minister, Yitzhak Rabin, and Yasser Arafat on behalf of the Palestine Liberation Organisation. That too collapsed—in fact each peace initiative has failed. And, despite the support of the USA, the UN, Russia and the European Union, the latest initiative, the so-called road map, shows little sign of bringing the two sides together. But if, as happened in Northern Ireland, the militant groups could bring themselves to make a truce with Israel, then perhaps for the first time in over fifty years a stable agreement might yet be achieved. In the meantime the suicide bombers, some of them women, continue to strike in Israeli areas, and the Israeli Army continues its attempts to wipe out the leaders of the terror movement.

The views of ordinary people matter as much as those of politicians, of course. One of the most fascinating moments in our live broadcast later that day in Jerusalem came when I found myself interviewing an Arab Israeli. This may seem like a contradiction in terms but, of course, it isn't. In 1978, when we were in Israel, there were 1.7 million Arabs living under Israeli control, and talking to me was one of them, Zaiden Atashi. When I asked him to describe the relationship between the Israeli Jews and the minorities he bridled instantly. 'To start with I don't like to use the term "minority",' he told me. 'I am Israeli and I am equal. All the Israeli Arabs who stayed after the Independence War have been granted Israeli status and equal rights.' The further we probed into this troubled country, the more complicated it became. Now I was hearing about Arab Israelis who were almost more proudly Israeli than the Jews themselves.

Were the Arabs inside Israel looking to the PLO for leadership? Zaiden gave his opinion that in recent years some Arab individuals, mainly of the younger generation, had been claiming the right to

Palestinian determination, a phenomenon that had not existed before and which he regarded as unfortunate. 'But,' he said, 'we are a democratic society, so everyone has the right to say whatever he wants.'

When I asked Zaiden whether he accepted President Sadat's accusation that the Israeli government was intransigent, I was confronted with the unusual situation of an Arab not only denying that that government was intransigent but transferring the accusation to certain Arab states—Syria, Jordan, Algeria, South Yemen and Libya. 'What about *their* intransigence? They do not want even the *existence* of the State of Israel in the Middle East. Why do you always ask this question of the Israelis?'

There was one other interesting point that Zaiden raised. I had mentioned that the Arab birth rate in Israel was much higher than the Jewish one. He agreed, and added that well within his lifetime he could see there being at least as many, and quite possibly more, Arabs in Israel than there were Jews. When I asked how he saw the political implications of that eventuality the staunch Israeli surfaced immediately: 'I do not want to see the Israeli Knesset [Parliament] represented by 50 per cent Jews and 50 per cent Arabs—that would create more problems than it would solve. We are moderate Arabs, and I do not want it to come to an unfortunate civil war. I want to keep the State of Israel the way it was envisaged by the Jewish Zionist leaders.'

Economist and political analyst Dan Bavly then spoke to me about Israel's internal problems. The Israeli government was apparently trying to move towards encouraging free enterprise, freeing up foreign currency controls, and tackling a high inflation rate caused by government overspending and the trades unions trying to negotiate big wage increases in order to keep up with inflation. Shades of things to come in Britain!

The rights and freedoms of Israeli women was a subject I discussed with Ora Namir, a Labour member of the Knesset and former Chairwoman of the State Commission on the Status of Women. In a country in which women are by law equal to men, and which had had, in Golda Meir, one of the first women Prime Ministers in the world, I expected to hear that women participated fully and actively in all areas. However, when I asked about the role of Israeli women in the armed forces Ora replied, 'We are not pleased with the status of women in the Army. Women can contribute much more than they do today. Women are less and less involved in most fields of work in the Army, and are not used in combat.' I knew Ora had recommended that women in the forces should be allowed to train as pilots, and I asked her about it. 'Nothing came of that,' she said. 'The Ministry of Defence refused to accept it.'

In spite of equality by law, a few facts emerged very clearly. There were fewer women in the Knesset than ever before, fewer women were showing an active interest in politics, and Israeli women were, more than ever, wrapped up in their families. When I asked Ora why she thought this was, she replied, 'There is hardly a family in Israel which didn't lose a son, a husband, or a relative in one of the wars.' She went on, 'At times like these, women want to devote more and more time to

183

their family.'

The day had certainly had its surprises. First we had learnt of the possibility of there being, in the not too distant future, more Arabs than Jews in the Jewish National State. Then the news that the nation's women, many of whom had received military training, were feeling the urge to return to the role of homemaker and earth mother. But then, the Middle East is such an extraordinary place that perhaps nothing should have surprised us. Whatever, we felt we had fulfilled our task, and on our arrival back home it was gratifying to be commended for making some interesting, informative and entertaining broadcasts in difficult conditions.

*   *   *

A postscript. The *JY Prog* has always owed a lot to its listeners—a huge audience of ordinary, everyday people. In 1990 I interviewed Queen Noor of Jordan, the American-born wife of King Hussein. She told me that thousands of ordinary, everyday people were facing death and disease in appalling conditions in refugee camps because of the Gulf crisis, and she urged Britain to give more aid. My warm-hearted listeners phoned in large numbers, offering as much as they could.

In 1981 that wonderful audience had responded to another situation, in a different part of the Middle East and involving just one man, not thousands. The Archbishop of Canterbury's special adviser, Terry Waite, had talked to me about the prospects for Jean Waddell, Dr John Coleman and his wife Andrea, and Andrew Pyke, all of whom were detained in prison in Iran. Terry was trying to negotiate their release and in the case of the first three seemed to be making good progress. Indeed, they were released shortly after we talked. However, he seemed to be getting nowhere in the case of Andrew Pyke.

The Ayatollah Khomeni's regime had originally accused Andrew of spying, but those accusations had been dropped. Instead he was now accused of 'financial irregularities' and, despite his protestation of innocence, was still held prisoner without even the prospect of being brought to trial. Our listeners were interested, concerned and sympathetic. However, exactly how sympathetic we were not to discover until the New Year.

On 27 January 1982 the JY team was busy opening and sorting our customary huge quantity of mail. The address at the head of one letter read 'Ghezel Hesar Prison, Karaj, R.I. Iran'. It had been written by the incarcerated and still untried Andrew Pyke. As I read the letter out on the air I reflected yet again on the brightness, intelligence and warmth of the people who listen to the *JY Programme* and are such an important part of it. When they feel something needs doing they don't just sit there, they get up and do something about it. This is the letter.

Dear Mr Young
    A request for your assistance, if I may?
    My somewhat unusual circumstances have resulted in my being inundated with thousands of Christmas cards and letters of encouragement from all over the UK. 99.9% of these are from people who are strangers to

185

me, and I have no way to thank them all, other than through you.

If you are able, please say I have been overwhelmed, cheered and strengthened enormously by the flood of kindness and goodwill I've received. In a situation such as mine, you have no idea what one Christmas card can mean, let alone thousands!

My gratitude to everyone is endless. I'm glad to say I'm in pretty good shape here; I truly have no complaints regarding my present living conditions—yet naturally I am eager to be home, which I hope will not be long forthcoming.

My treatment by the revolutionary authorities has always been good and courteous, which is surely confirmed by the fact that they have authorised the mailing of this, and other letters.

With thanks for your anticipated assistance, and regards,
Andrew Pyke

PS—why not play a quick blast of something that makes you smile?

In recent years it's become fashionable among a certain type of person to sneer at national pride. Well, I'm certainly proud to be part of a nation that, without even being asked, sent ten thousand Christmas cards to someone they didn't even know in an Iranian jail.

CHAPTER TWENTY-ONE

REWARDS AND HONOURS

If you're in the public eye, you get asked to do things. In 1978 I received an invitation to return to my roots. Cinderford in Gloucestershire, where I was born, was about to get its first-ever Mayor, and I was invited to invest him with the title and regalia. I was delighted to accept. Accordingly on 5 August in a crowded town centre I installed Councillor Frank Beard, who in return presented me with a scroll and the symbolic key to Cinderford town. As I stood there I reflected that, if my dear old mum had still been alive, she would have been a very proud mum indeed.

More rewards were to come. The following year, 1979, I was awarded the OBE in the Queen's Birthday Honours List. It was an honour I was delighted to receive, not just for myself but for my wonderful team and my loyal listeners, all of whom had helped to make the programme the huge success it had become. Some newspapers expressed the view that I'd got it because I was the favourite interviewer of new Prime Minister Mrs Thatcher, although as far as I was aware she had never actually said that. In any event, whatever the reason it was a significant honour and I was significantly chuffed to get it.

On 4 December I went to Buckingham Palace to collect my award. As she hung it on the little hook provided on my lapel for the purpose the Queen said, 'Mr Young, I quite like that little argument you have with Mr Wogan in the mornings.' Surely the royal wireless couldn't be tuned in to us in the mornings, could it? Or was it simply that HM had been very well briefed?

The ceremony was to be followed by lunch with my BBC bosses at Broadcasting House. A very nice gesture, but unfortunately the Beeb's basic research on timing hadn't been done too well. I had already been told that it was unlikely I would be away from Buckingham Palace before, at the earliest, 12.30pm. So when the invitation arrived saying '12.30 for 1pm' I protested that I would almost inevitably be late. I was wasting my breath, of course. Once the Corporate BBC has made up its mind on something, it is not easily moved. The timing stayed as it was.

At 12.30pm I was still having my picture taken in the Palace yard for the next day's newspapers. Then followed an interview for television news. I eventually arrived in the BBC Governors' dining room at 1.30 p.m. They, urbane and charming as ever, greeted me warmly—but Mrs Kitty Smith BEM, who was in charge of the catering, was certainly not best pleased. She was worried that lunch would be spoiled, and she made that clear. Getting my priorities right I apologised, first to Mrs Smith and then to the top brass, and all was well.

*   *   *

A less regal occasion, though a memory I particularly treasure, is of a lunch at the Savoy Hotel in London, where I received an award of which I am very proud. I was one of twelve people named 'Men of the Year' in 1979 by RADAR, the Royal Association for Disability and Rehabilitation. Two other 'names' among the twelve were Sebastian Coe and J. P. R. Williams. But what really made the occasion for me was meeting people who had performed the most astonishing acts of courage and endurance, without any thought whatsoever for their own safety. People who had triumphed over the most severe physical and mental handicaps and come through to lead rewarding lives.

One of the twelve was a young army officer who had only recently suffered the most appalling injuries in Northern Ireland. He had lost an arm and a leg, but he was clearly going to walk, unaided, from his table to the rostrum to collect his award, no matter what the pain. Agonisingly slowly, he made his way from his seat. He almost fell several times and we all held our breath, but he made it there and back. As he reached his seat we sighed with relief, and every single person in the room leaped to their feet to applaud his magnificent courage.

JPR, a man who has demonstrated his courage on the rugby field often enough, turned to me and said, 'Doesn't that make you feel bloody humble?'

Yes, indeed it did.

*   *   *

I was back at the Palace in 1993. My first inkling of what it was about arrived in a rather unusual way.

In November 1992 we were on holiday in Florida. I was enjoying a nice leisurely soak in the bath when my wife rushed in to say, 'The Prime

189

Minister's office is on the phone.' At first I thought someone was pulling my leg. However, you don't hang about when a message like that arrives so, dripping water everywhere, I rushed to the living room to take the call.

Needless to say it wasn't actually John Major on the phone personally, but a lady from his office to inform me that I was to be honoured with the CBE. Then came the tricky bit. I was told that I must keep it secret until the honour was announced officially. Easier said than done. Hardly had I put the telephone down before it rang again. It was my producer. 'OK—so why did the Prime Minister want to talk to you?' he asked. Obviously the PM's office had contacted my BBC office to get my Florida phone number. What a buzz of excitement there must have been in the office as they tried to work out why the Prime Minister should want to talk to me so urgently that only calling me in Florida would do!

You cannot imagine how difficult it is to keep something like that secret from a team as worldly-wise and knowledgeable as mine. Prime Ministers don't call you from across the Atlantic just to pass the time of day or enquire about the weather. And since I'm a terrible liar anyway, the team accurately guessed that it was some kind of honour. The only thing they got wrong was which honour. They told me later that they were convinced it was to be a knighthood. But that was to come much later.

When I went to collect my award on 16 March 1993 it was in the company of the late, great actor John Thaw, who had also been awarded a CBE. When asked how the irascible Morse might have reacted to the honour, John replied, 'I think he would have been rather chuffed—like I am.' However, on the basis of 'Set 'em up to knock 'em down', what the press really wanted to ask him was how, after the enormous success of *Inspector Morse*, he had allowed himself to get involved in the comparative failure of his television series called *A Year in Provence*. John gave a typically blunt, robust reply: 'I don't want to talk about *A Year in Provence*—and what's more, I don't give a damn what the press say about it.' We ordinary artistes have to be very careful what we say to, and about, our friends in the press. It must be wonderful to be a superstar, able to say what you like and, frankly, my dear, not give a damn.

*   *   *

So there I was, Jimmy Young CBE. A couple of years later I was appearing on Michael Parkinson's show on BBC Television. Michael asked me whether I had found things difficult at the beginning of my career. I replied that I had auditioned for, and had been turned down by, just about everyone in showbusiness. One eminent agent, I added, a lovely lady named Lillian Aza, had personally turned me down more than once.

The day after my appearance on *Parkinson* my telephone rang. It was Lillian, now in semi-retirement. She told me how much she had enjoyed seeing me again and how, as I was telling the story of my rejection slips, memories of 1949 came back to her. She said, 'I shall never forget the letter I received from the BBC after I sent you to audition for them. It read, "Dear Mrs Aza, we regret to have to inform you that, in our opinion, Mr Young will never be broadcasting material."'

I hadn't done too badly, all things considered, had I?

CHAPTER TWENTY-TWO

BY GOD, I WILL CONFRONT THEM

From its beginning in 1973 the new-style JY politics and current affairs programme had consistently made headline news, and we were doing so again at the start of 1978 during Jim Callaghan's Labour government. Speaking of immigration on the programme Margaret Thatcher, now Leader of the Opposition after ousting Edward Heath in 1975, said, 'We shall have better race relations if we don't have these vast numbers coming in and the prospect of them coming in indefinitely. We just cannot go on taking in people at the rate of forty to fifty thousand a year. What most of us want is to live in perfect harmony with the people who are here. And those who are here must have equal rights and responsibilities.' She condemned the right-wing National Front and said of her critics, 'What these people are saying is that we, in politics, cannot discuss the issues that really concern people.' The newspapers responded with 'Maggie in attack on absurd critics', 'Race row—Maggie hits back', 'Callaghan in race attack on Maggie' and 'Maggie stands firm'.

In July that year Edward Heath, now a back-bencher, came in to talk about youth and unemployment, an interview which I thought would be interesting but low-profile. However, while participating in a by-election campaign in the constituency of Penistone Ted had made a speech the previous evening in which he had said he would fight alongside Mrs Thatcher in the next General Election 'just as hard as I have ever done'. Now, given the fierceness with which the party leadership struggle had been fought three years earlier, and their differences in policy and leadership styles, the two were not exactly friends. I therefore decided that I would start by asking him about what seemed like a conciliatory gesture.

On entering my studio Ted asked me, as many guests do, what I was leading with. When I told him he reacted angrily, saying that he would on no account talk about his speech. I protested that it was the big news of the day, to which Ted, looking furious enough to walk out on me, replied, 'Exactly. So we're not going to get any more out of it.'

Not wishing to lose such an important guest, or at least not wishing to lose him right there and then, I led in with the problems of young people facing unemployment. I had no intention of dropping my questions about his speech, and while carrying on with the main thrust of the interview I was seeking a suitable opportunity to introduce them. Eventually I decided that, since there never was going to be a suitable opportunity, I might as well ask them anyway.

I began, 'I know that you said under no circumstances would you talk about your speech last night, but if I don't ask you about it I shall get shot by my listeners.'

To which Ted replied, 'And if you do ask, you

may well get shot by me.'

Since the interview was live I went on, 'Well, I'll work on the basis that the worst thing that can happen providing you don't shoot me is that you walk out on me.'

He didn't, of course. He's far too professional for that. As a final question I asked whether he would accept a cabinet post if the Conservatives won the next election. Ted, always the consummate politician, answered, but then again didn't answer, the question: 'I think we'd better concentrate on winning the election first, don't you?'

*　　　*　　　*

A few years later, when Mrs Thatcher was in Downing Street, we had more fireworks from Mr Heath.

Ted had been ill and out of the limelight for a while in 1981, but he certainly made up for lost time as he laid about him on the *JY Prog*. The front page of *The Times* the following day carried his message. It read, 'In another astonishing outburst against the Government's approach on many issues Edward Heath continued his onslaught yesterday by telling Margaret Thatcher in the bluntest language that neither she nor anyone else in the Conservative Party would stop him from speaking out.'

At various times during the interview he called the Thatcher government's political style and strategy 'childish', 'stupid', 'ridiculous'. He told me that, in his experience, businessmen found the government's economic policy incomprehensible and were baffled by its contradictions. In a very

194

determined voice he declared, 'I am not going to be intimidated by anybody, whether it be by the Press, or the battling brigadiers who send me stinking letters. I do not mind. There is no need to write. I am going to tell the country plain home truths which the great majority of people recognise. I am not going to stop. I shall not be stopped in the House. I shall not be stopped by anybody in No.10. I shall go on doing it.'

I again asked him whether he might quit the Conservative Party and join the Social Democrats. Said he, 'I have absolutely no intention of getting out.' It was one of his strongest and most outspoken interviews and, plagued as she was by unemployment, a troubled economy and rioting in the streets, I wondered what Mrs Thatcher would make of it.

*　　　*　　　*

In the autumn of 1978 we commissioned the first National Opinion Poll report ever produced specially for the *Jimmy Young Programme*. Fairly predictably, it was called *The Young Report*—not just after the programme but also because it dealt with the attitudes and concerns of young people.

The results surprised many people, especially those who were expecting revolutionary ideals.

On 26 September the *Daily Mirror* reported, 'Kids today are a jolly good bunch. They favour the traditional values that Mum and Dad cherish. As for being more liberal and way out—forget it.' On the same day the leading article in the *Daily Express* ran:

Youth is conservative with a small 'c'. A public opinion poll commissioned for the *Jimmy Young Show* reveals overwhelming support among the 15–21 age group for law and order (including the return of hanging). They also favour fair treatment for minorities and the institution of marriage: in short stability, tranquillity, authority and toleration. Which must make some of our middle-aged trendies, still dreaming of their fun revolution of the Sixties, wonder what has happened.

In fact 90 per cent of young people surveyed wanted tough punishment for vandals, and 64 per cent supported capital punishment for all murderers. Most were against the legalisation of cannabis, and most believed that if teenagers wanted to take drugs older people should try to stop them. A majority agreed that homosexuals should be treated like everybody else, and a similar proportion disagreed with a suggestion that coloured immigrants should be sent home. The vast majority agreed that the family was tops and their heroes were Mum and Dad.

However, not everything was peace and light: 24 per cent thought life had become more difficult, and very many said that unemployment was by far the most serious political issue for young people. The last finding was particularly relevant and showed how close *Jimmy Young Programme* listeners were to the mood and state of the nation, because we were just four months away from a particularly nasty crisis.

January 1979 saw Britain in the grip of a big freeze and also in the middle of what became known as the Winter of Discontent. Strikes were called all over the place, and things became so bad that there were reports of panic buying of food and other essentials. At one stage 220 bodies had to be stored in a Merseyside warehouse—they couldn't be buried because the grave-diggers were on strike.

Apart from mass picketing of strike-bound premises by union members there was a sinister new development—the arrival of secondary pickets, also called flying pickets. The title meant what it said. These were people who were not connected with the place of employment they were picketing but were 'flown', or more accurately bussed, to locations where they were likely to cause maximum disruption to the employer. This led to ugly confrontations. Not only did pickets fly, but fists as well. And when asked where some of these flying pickets were coming from one militant shop steward said, 'I don't care if they come from bloody Bertram Mills Circus.' The situation was out of control and spelled big trouble for the Labour government.

At the end of January I talked to the Conservative leader, Margaret Thatcher, again. It was a wide-ranging interview in which we talked about the closed shop, picketing and trades union power. Specifically, I asked her what she would do if she became Prime Minister and unions not only refused to co-operate with her but actually confronted her. In what became one of the quotes of the year she replied, 'If someone is confronting our essential liberties and inflicting injury and hardship on the sick, the elderly, and children then I will confront them. By God, I will confront them.' Looking at the expression on her face as she leaned

197

across the desk I had no doubt whatsoever that she meant every word of it.

The date of the General Election was set for 3 May and on the day I presented two Election Special programmes. The first ran from 10am to midday. The second started at 11pm and was scheduled to run for as long as was necessary.

We actually ran from 11pm to 3.45am, although, as far as determining the result of the election was concerned, we knew very early in the morning of 4 May 1979 that the country was heading for its first-ever woman Prime Minister.

CHAPTER TWENTY-THREE

INTO AFRICA

Our overseas broadcasts in 1977 and 1978 had been so successful that the following year we were once again under pressure to do more. We put our thinking caps on and decided that Southern Rhodesia, which was very much in the news as it moved closer to becoming Zimbabwe, would be the place to go. We therefore decided to broadcast from there on 9 and 10 August.

Much of the blame for the present chaotic internal state of Zimbabwe lies in the failure of the white residents of what, in the 1960s, was the British colony of Southern Rhodesia to pay heed to Harold Macmillan's statement that in that decade a wind of change was blowing through Africa. They also never had a political leader of the stature of Nelson Mandela, who could have brought about change without conflict. When independence from Britain was sought, it was offered on condition that there should be economic and political power-sharing with the black population. This proved unacceptable to the white-controlled government and in 1965 the Prime Minister, Ian Smith, emphasised the intransigence of the whites by making a Unilateral Declaration of Independence or UDI.

In the 1970s the black nationalists began a war of liberation. Until 1976 Ian Smith had successfully held out against black majority rule, but when South Africa withdrew its military aid he began negotiations with Bishop Abel Muzorewa's moderate element among the nationalists. The resultant agreement was, however, not accepted either by the majority of the black population or internationally, and the war dragged on. At the time of our visit it was still being waged by the Patriotic Front, an alliance of two groups led respectively by Joshua Nkomo and Robert Mugabe.

The political situation and the vast distance involved made it a daunting prospect, and John Gurnett bravely volunteered to undertake the first research trip. There were several spanners in this particular works, and John was about to discover the first one. Because of the economic sanctions imposed after UDI we would not be able to fly direct to Southern Rhodesia. We would have to fly to Johannesburg in South Africa first, and then fly back to the capital, Salisbury (now Harare). Thirteen hours flying to Johannesburg plus two to Salisbury. And of course John would have the doubtful pleasure of doing the whole journey twice.

John returned from his research trip with the beginning of what was to be a very impressive guest list. Among others who had agreed to talk to me was a former high-ranking official in Joshua Nkomo's ZAPU (Zimbabwe African People's Union) Party, General Walls, the commander of the security forces, the Foreign Minister, and the Prime Minister, Bishop Abel Muzorewa.

Our exhausting schedule began on 6 August when we flew the thirteen-hour overnight trip to Johannesburg and then rested for three hours in a hotel. Then we re-embarked for the last leg to Salisbury. The 707 was absolutely packed. It was very hot, and it looked like being a most uncomfortable two hours. However, apart from the smell of bodies, there was also the smell of nervous tension in the air. It was to be about one hour and forty minutes before I discovered why.

There was a great deal of bantering from some of the Brits aboard who knew who I was. 'Is your insurance paid up, Jim?' was one remark. 'What are you doing over here, then, Jim? Don't you know there's a war on?' was another. Of course we knew there was a war on. After all, we'd known that when we'd volunteered to do the broadcast. However, the noise level of the backchat and ribaldry in the cabin had those few extra decibels that you notice when people are doing a bit of whistling in the dark. And I suddenly remembered that an Air Rhodesia plane flying between Johannesburg and Salisbury had been shot down by a ground-to-air missile not all that long ago.

Anyway, there we were, sealed in, and there wasn't an awful lot we could do about it. What slightly brought the pains on, however, was the announcement we heard when we were about twenty minutes' flying time from Salisbury. The voice said, 'This is your captain speaking, and this is just to warn you that we are about to make what we call a "security approach".'

'Oh, that's interesting,' I thought. 'What's a security approach?' Well, a security approach means that the steward pulls down all the blinds on the windows at the side of the cabin and then, just to be on the safe side, turns out all the lights as well. Quite suddenly we were sitting in what seemed very much like a cramped, flying, blacked-out potential coffin. The war was immediately incredibly real, and very, very close. Suddenly there was a loud, angry cry from one of the cabin crew. The gentleman sitting behind me had lifted up his blind to see where we were. The stewardess raced down the gangway and I quite thought she was going to punch him. Instead she contented herself with swearing at him and snatching the blind down again. I began to think that I'd be glad to get my feet on the ground. On a more practical note, I reflected that there wasn't anything in my contract about the BBC paying me danger money!

Our traditional luck with the timing of important broadcasts had worked again. However, it had thrown up, so to speak, the good news and the bad news. The good news was that a very important Commonwealth conference, to be attended by Britain's new Prime Minister, Mrs Thatcher, had been arranged to take place in neighbouring Lusaka, Zambia during the week immediately prior to our visit. This would make our broadcasts even more topical. The bad news was that the discussions taking place and decisions being made

201

there would render out-of-date a lot of the research over which we had sweated so long at home. It was obvious that we would have to begin re-researching the first of our two broadcasts the following morning. I had the feeling that all I was going to see of Zimbabwe was my hotel room and the broadcasting studio, and that is exactly how it turned out for the whole of the team.

Wednesday, 8 August dawned hot and clear, with none of the heavy humidity which had characterised Johannesburg. It was the sort of day which made me reflect that it would be quite nice to enjoy a bit of sunshine—but I would return to London as pale as on the day I left. The free copy of the *Salisbury Herald* thrust under my hotel room door informed me on the front page that back in London the BBC was being picketed by the 'Campaign Against Racism in the Media' protesting against 'The Young Programmes'. The BBC's Director General, Ian Trethowan, had stated that he would ignore the protests and that the broadcasts would go ahead as planned, being no different from others that I had done from such places as Russia and the Middle East. We might be out of sight but we certainly weren't out of mind.

First we went to see the studio which I would be using. Broadcasting House in Salisbury was in a very pleasant setting indeed. Surrounded by fields, it was a far cry from London's Broadcasting House with the nose-to-tail traffic of Portland Place outside. The Rhodesian staff were very courteous and helpful. They were also very suspicious, something of which we were conscious the whole time we were in Salisbury. The whites' attitude seemed to be that we had gone there specifically to attack them. In fact all we wanted was to present two balanced and fair-minded broadcasts.

We returned to our hotel to begin work, where we were joined by the BBC man in Salisbury, Ian Mills. As the sun poured down invitingly outside we spent the day slaving over hot typewriters in my room. It was the early hours of the following morning before we decided we could do no more.

As I sat in the studio waiting to begin our first broadcast, I reflected that 9 August was a significant date for me. Exactly thirty years earlier I had been sitting in the BBC's studios near Piccadilly Circus in London waiting to begin a very different kind of broadcast. It was my first ever, in which I was to play the piano and sing four songs. Had anyone told me then that, thirty years on to the day, I would be sitting in a studio in an African capital city waiting to interview, among others, the Prime Minister, I would never have believed them.

Bearing in mind that there was a bitter, savage civil war going on only a few miles away, I asked Lieutenant General Peter Walls, the man responsible for the security forces, how far one could go out of Salisbury in absolute safety. He speedily brought the conflict into very close focus: 'Well, I would say you can't go anywhere in this country in absolute safety.' He admitted that he was fighting a war which he could possibly contain, but which he knew he could never win.

The main thrust of argument from the white people I interviewed was that they realised that something should have been done for the blacks years ago, but that at least something was being done now. Yet even as they spoke to me their fear of the future was obvious. They knew that anything being done was far too little and years too late. The blacks to whom I talked made it clear that, whatever happened, it would be many years before life really got any better for them. A white educationalist told me, 'As black aspirations have grown they have been met', while in almost the same breath he admitted that only one in five black Africans received a secondary education, and that a whole generation of Africans had grown up without an education at all.

I asked a white farmer about the imbalance between black and white in land ownership. Said he, 'There is no racial barrier in the ownership of commercial land.' But, I protested, 'Presumably in order to buy land you have to have the money with which to buy it.' Quick as a flash he answered, 'Ah, that's an economic barrier!' I felt rather like a passenger bandying words with the captain on the bridge of the *Titanic*.

When it came to the turn of Mr Mwamuka, a black businessman, I asked him how difficult it was for an African to start out in business. How did he raise capital? 'Raising finance is one of the biggest difficulties in the African community,' he admitted. 'Finance houses will not let an African have money unless he can produce collateral, and he cannot get collateral until he has some money.'

Mrs Esther Rauson was a leading member of the confusingly named coloured community. This section of the population consists of the descendants of intermarriages between indigenous tribespeople, white settlers and imported slaves from Asia. Effectively, the term means anyone of mixed race. Arbitrary and meaningless tests to differentiate black from coloured, particularly in apartheid-bedevilled South Africa, resulted in tragic cases where members of the same family were classified differently depending on whether they had a lighter or darker complexion.

Mrs Rauson had been a candidate in the elections held the previous April, and I asked her how the electoral system worked. Was it in fact a case of white MPs for white people and black MPs for black people? She agreed that that was the way it worked out in practice so I asked her where, as a coloured woman, that put her. 'Ah,' said she, 'according to the Rhodesian constitution, for voting purposes I'm white.'

'I see,' said I, not really seeing at all. 'So blacks are black but coloureds are white.'

'Yes,' said Esther. 'I wasn't allowed to stand in a black constituency, so I had to stand in a white constituency. Naturally I didn't get any whites voting for me, so that did rather put me in the middle of nowhere.' I felt that, had I been Eric Morecambe, I might well have said, 'There's no answer to that.'

My final guest on the first day's programme was the Prime Minister, Bishop Abel Muzorewa, and I had already been told that the studio would first have to be inspected by one of his security guards. The door opened and in came a short, slightly built, almost delicate-looking young black man. He was carrying what looked like a Ken Dodd tickling stick and was presumably looking for explosives, although I've made a lifelong habit of not blowing myself up. He moved around the studio flicking things with his tickling stick, and eventually arrived at my desk. He never spoke a word, but had a good look at me. Then, even as I continued broadcasting, he flicked around my feet, around the legs of my trousers and under my chair. Seemingly satisfied, he exited.

After the programme I said to my producer, 'He didn't seem heavy enough to be a security guard.'

His reply was, 'You should have seen the ones next door. About fifteen of them and all built like bloody brick outhouses.'

Bishop Muzorewa was polite and reasonable until I moved on to the suggestions and statements coming out of the ongoing Commonwealth conference in Lusaka. I asked him what his feelings would be if the British Prime Minister, Mrs Thatcher, were to suggest new elections. This would be, he said, 'an insult to the electorate who braved strongly the threat of death as they went to vote for their Government'. And when I persisted he retorted at one stage, 'I am getting sick and tired of talking about what she said and what you said. I am now waiting to see, in black and white, exactly what is required of us.' I felt we all knew that what would be required would be new elections which the Bishop would lose.

A man called Cephas Msipa, who had been the assistant editor of the *Zimbabwe Times* until he was arrested and detained, was an interviewee on the second day. I asked him why he had been arrested. He said, 'I don't know why. They never give reasons. All I know is that I was detained.' I had introduced Mr Msipa as 'a former official of Joshua Nkomo's ZAPU Party'. Only after the broadcast was I told that at the very mention of the words 'Nkomo' and 'ZAPU' on air all the white Rhodesians in the control box gasped out loud.

Such was the overpowering air of fear and

suspicion that we were all glad to come to the end of the second broadcast. I remember thinking that the atmosphere in the studio during the two days was rather like being present at a death, with every member of the family blaming every other member for causing it. No sooner had my signature tune died away than we were delighted to hear the voice of the then Managing Director, Radio—later boss of BBC Television—Aubrey Singer, booming down the line from London. He said, 'You dodged all the pitfalls and avoided all the booby traps. Well done and warmest congratulations from everyone at all levels here.'

On our return to the hotel after two days of very heavy, serious, and sometimes downright gloomy broadcasting, we were rewarded with a moment of almost classic Goon-type humour. As we walked up the steps and then across the hotel foyer the loudspeakers boomed out, 'Will Mr Young please telephone his butcher immediately.' I said, 'Well, I know I haven't paid last week's bill, but this is ridiculous!' When I went over to the reception desk I discovered that, by the most extraordinary coincidence, my butcher from London just happened to be in Salisbury at the same time as us.

Come departure time we were carefully briefed by John Gurnett, drawing on the experience of his 'recce' trip, about take-off from Salisbury. John said their pilot had warned them that immediately after take-off there would be a very sharp banking manoeuvre followed by a steep climb at full power. 'If we don't do that,' said the captain, 'we stand a good chance of getting shot down.' Actually we flew out of Salisbury in a Viscount which was so ancient that, if you'd suggested anything like a sharp bank and full power climb to the captain, he'd have fallen about laughing. Instead, we did a gentle take-off and then climbed in what seemed like never-ending circles until we reached sixteen thousand feet. Considered then to be out of range of ground-to-air missiles, we set course for Johannesburg.

Only later did the captain conversationally tell us that the guerillas below needed only one vital piece of equipment to make their missiles operational up to twenty thousand feet. He went on to express the opinion that 'one of these days some airline captain is going to have a rather nasty surprise'. He did have the decency to wait until we were well on our way to Johannesburg before he told us!

I cannot say that the Zimbabwe broadcasts had been enjoyable to do, but we had no doubt that they had been well worthwhile. The struggle for majority rule ended with the Lancaster House accord, which paved the way for elections in 1980. It was then that Joshua Nkomo's ambition of becoming first black President of his country was dashed, as his party only gained twenty-seven seats to Robert Mugabe's fifty-seven in the new hundred-seat Parliament.

My abiding memory of Rhodesia at that time is being told by one of the white farmers' leaders that the country was rich and fertile enough to provide sufficient food for the whole of central and southern Africa. Yet today, almost a quarter of a century later, there are growing queues for bread. This is largely the result of the evictions of white farmers by Robert Mugabe's one-party state, ostensibly to resettle blacks. However, in practice many of the farms have just been abandoned and the blacks formerly employed on them have been forced into the cities in search of food. Yet the rising price of maize and bread means that few can afford to eat and many families are starving.

Indeed, one report in early 2003 claimed that a member of Mugabe's family, three cabinet members, some provincial governors and leading businessmen had illegally seized farms intended for the resettlement of blacks. It was also reported that a Chinese company had been awarded a contract to grow food on farms taken from white farmers but lying derelict after new black owners had failed to take them up. Unless Mugabe is removed from his position of power, the prospect of famine in Zimbabwe is likely to grow.

*   *   *

On our way to and from Salisbury we passed briefly through South Africa, another country that has been beset by political traumas. At the time of our visit it was still under white rule and the odious apartheid system. In my time as a broadcaster I have had the privilege of interviewing many distinguished figures, but among my great regrets is that I never had the opportunity of interviewing Nelson Mandela, one of the giants of the twentieth century.

CHAPTER TWENTY-FOUR

THE SUNSHINE STATE

February 1980 brought one of the most extraordinary and bizarre happenings of my entire life. In fact, the purchase of our Florida apartment is an interesting little story in itself.

Starting as long ago as the 1950s, when I was able to afford it I had taken my holidays in the South of France and, occasionally, in southern Spain. Several of my colleagues had purchased second homes in those areas and frequently attempted to persuade me to do the same. Over the years I had looked at properties and plots of land, but somehow had never felt the urge to buy. It was probably the very different Continental lifestyle plus the different language that put me off. Anyway, whatever the reason, by the beginning of 1980 I hadn't bought a second home overseas. But all that was about to change.

I was walking out of Broadcasting House one day when I bumped into a friend in the music business whom I hadn't seen for a very long time. He asked me what I was doing and I replied that Alicia and I were about to go on holiday. He asked where we were going and I replied that that was the problem currently exercising my mind. We hadn't decided where to go.

'Well,' said he helpfully, 'I have an apartment in Florida which is empty at the moment and you're welcome to use that for a couple of weeks if you like.'

Neither Alicia nor I had ever been to Florida, so it seemed an ideal opportunity to explore somewhere new. I gratefully accepted his offer. And so, in February 1980, we flew out there.

After a nine-and-a-half-hour flight we arrived at the condominium block absolutely exhausted. We could see as we drove up that it was situated right on the waterfront, but as we entered the building the deserted front lobby looked very ordinary. Shaded from the blazing sun outside, it even looked a little gloomy. We went up in the elevator and got out into a very ordinary, rather dull-looking corridor. We walked along it to the front door of the apartment. We opened the door—and in a split second everything changed.

Through the open door the view hit us. I cannot adequately describe the impact it made. Immediately ahead of us was a big picture window and through it we could see the sea beyond. We walked straight across the living room and through the door which led out on to the balcony. There we stood in the brilliant sunshine, cooled by a breeze coming in from the Atlantic. We thrilled at the sight of the open sea to the east, of the shoreline stretching away to the south, and all the little and not so little boats making their way out to or in from the ocean. Instantly, and I mean that literally, I knew I need look no further for my second home. This was it. I had found it.

Alicia agreed. I asked my friend Derek if he would sell. He said he would, since he also owned the apartment next door. We agreed a price, and I bought it. It was as simple as that. I just knew it was right for us, and it was one of the wisest decisions I have ever made. For the last twenty-three years

Florida has been much more than a second home. It has been a haven in times of pressure and stress—and there have been many of those, I can assure you. In fact, when a larger apartment became available we bought it and sold the smaller one. It will never be home to us in the same way as our home in London. We are Brits and will never be, nor want to be, anything else. But Alicia and I both love the relaxed, easy-going but efficient American lifestyle, and know that we were blessed beyond belief when we were first given the opportunity of coming to Florida in 1980.

So the long-term results of our two weeks' holiday were excellent and we're still enjoying them. However, the immediate results were not so pleasant.

The first week was blissful. It was in the second week that it all happened. Derek, who was staying in his other apartment, received a telephone call from the New York office of an English newspaper, asking if he knew where I was. Quite unthinkingly he said, 'Yes, he's next door.' The caller then told him that he had received a cable from his head office in London that read, 'Great interest here in JY and girlfriend sunning themselves in Florida.'

You could have knocked us over with the proverbial feather. Alicia and I had been together for years, attending official dinners and functions. We lived a quiet, normal, suburban life in west London, going to work, coming home, watching telly, eating dinner and going to bed. Derek said to me, 'Come in and use my phone. We'll speak to him and I'm sure it will quietly go away.'

I was not so sure. However, I agreed to give it a go. I explained the situation and, sure enough,

Derek seemed to be right. Indeed, later in the day he received another call from the journalist saying, 'What a nice man Mr Young is. Will you thank him for phoning and explaining?'

Said Derek, 'See, I told you so.' I still had my doubts.

We were to fly back overnight. Derek and his wife Siv drove us to Miami airport, and while Derek went to park the car Siv, Alicia and I walked on into the airport.

Suddenly all Hell broke loose. As we approached the checking-in queue a photographer jumped out from behind a pillar. He whizzed round and round us like a whirling dervish, taking pictures. Siv and Alicia ran to the ladies' loo and, looking in that direction, I could see two worried faces peering round the partially opened door.

A huge Englishman detached himself from the front of the checking-in queue. 'Having problems, Jim?' he asked.

'Not really,' said I.

He walked up to the cameraman. 'If you don't stop this right now,' he said, 'I'll bloody flatten you.' The cameraman took the hint, and Alicia and I were escorted through to Customs by three large Brits plus Derek and Siv.

Looking back, it's possible to see the funny side—but at the time it was anything but funny. Our flight home, too, completed a thoroughly bad day. We hit some of the worst turbulence I have ever encountered. Crockery flew everywhere. There were moans, groans, the occasional shriek and the sounds of people being ill. In the middle of it the captain spoke in an attempt to calm us down. 'I'm sorry about this extreme turbulence, but I

213

would just like to assure you that you are flying in a very safe aircraft.' That was just about all we needed. Everybody was now absolutely convinced that the wings were going to fall off.

A day or so later the 'Jim and Alicia Miami love story' was in banner headlines in one national newspaper. BBC Radio's senior publicity officer immediately advised me that, much though we didn't want to do so, the only way to stop the story from dragging on for ever was to call a midday press conference. This we did, and I've never seen so many reporters and photographers in one place at the same time as were gathered in the St George's Hotel in London that day. I pointed out that there had never been any secrecy about Alicia and myself, and that all our friends had known of our feelings for each other for many, many years. The writers scribbled, the photographers snapped, and everybody went away happy. The story had suddenly ceased to be news.

As an example of what constituted 'excitement' in our lives (as opposed to the 'love nest' scenario the tabloids had dreamed up), let me tell you a little story. In the early eighties Alicia and I were living high up on Putney Heath. It was a delightful spot. In fact when I was driving home from work up congested Putney Hill and turned right at the Green Man pub I always felt I was entering another world. On thundered the traffic, but I drove into a quiet road bordered by overhanging trees. At one end of our road there was a good pub, and immediately opposite our block of flats was the local cricket ground. It was so quiet you could hardly believe you were living just a few miles from central London.

Alicia used to complain that we were a bit too far from the shops, but at the end of a busy and often fraught day I thought it was as nice a place to live as one could wish for. It was certainly not an area in which one would expect murder to raise its ugly head. But that is exactly what happened on a September evening in 1984.

I was doing my research for an important interview next day when our doorbell rang. Alicia answered it and found herself facing two gentlemen who identified themselves as police officers. Could they speak to Mr Leslie Ronald Young, please? She explained that I was also Mr Jimmy Young, and that I was hard at work. Could she help? No, unfortunately she couldn't, but would she please ask me to telephone Putney police station as soon as possible?

When I did so I was informed that this was an extremely delicate matter which they were sure I would prefer not to discuss in front of my wife. Could I please come down to the station as soon as possible? I made arrangements to do so the following day.

I appreciated that the police were doing their very best to be tactful, although how they thought this 'delicate matter' could be kept from a perfectly normally inquisitive wife I didn't know. As soon as I had put the phone down Alicia addressed herself to wondering out loud what this matter could be which was so delicate that it required me to attend the police station rather than discuss it in front of my wife. I had to confess that I hadn't the faintest idea. But, as you can imagine, I didn't sleep too well that night.

As it happened, the matter was simple—but, yes,

215

delicate. I owned a BMW which I had bought in Brighton at a garage which also serviced it for me. The arrangement was that they sent a car up to London and left it with me temporarily, drove my own car back to Brighton, kept it for a couple of days to be serviced and then returned it. This all worked a treat except for the service in September 1984 which triggered my visit from the police.

It appears that while my car was in the Brighton garage for servicing someone had 'borrowed' it for an evening. Unfortunately he had parked my car right outside the front door of a prostitute who was murdered that evening.

It was all cleared up very quickly in the police station, of course, but it was the sort of experience one could well do without just the same. And, despite what the papers wanted to believe about our Florida trip, that was as close to the whiff of scandal as we ever got.

*　　　*　　　*

In 1989 Alicia and I were on holiday in Florida again when we received an invitation to take drinks with the captain and crew of HMS *Invincible*, which had arrived in our local harbour. A large number of people had been invited and we stood around talking in small groups. In Alicia's group was a submarine captain and, knowing that it had always been my ambition to look over a submarine, Alicia asked him if that would be possible. He replied that it would be a pleasure, and we arranged a date for us to visit.

I should explain that the harbour which our Florida apartment overlooks is a very busy one, and in addition to lots of merchant shipping and the occasional battleship we frequently see nuclear-powered submarines entering and leaving port. Naturally I assumed it was one of those. Surprise surprise. When we turned up at the docks it was the tiny *Ocelot*, a decidedly pre-nuclear submarine.

We clambered aboard, and for both of us it was an educational experience. Forget Sean Connery and *Red October*. This was no comfortable, medium ship-size, modern nuclear job—this was the real McCoy. At the bottom of the conning tower was the room, not much larger than a couple of good-sized wardrobes, in which eight men slept. Don't ask me how. Then as we made our way aft—and there wasn't far to go from stem to stern, I may say—we walked carefully across a very narrow plank beneath which were two enormous engines. Fortunately, since *Ocelot* was moored at the time they weren't working, but I can imagine the noise in that tiny space when they were.

By dint of ducking, indeed almost crawling, past the torpedoes and through a small porthole-type opening we moved towards the stern of the boat and saw, right at the end, a sailor writing a letter. The captain told us that he lived down there. From the description he gave us I would imagine that nobody else wanted to. The captain explained that a submarine is rather like a cigar tube and has no keel such as surface craft have to keep them stable. Thus, he said, it tends to move about a lot even in relatively smooth conditions. And, speaking of the letter-writing seaman's living quarters, he said that because of the action of the propeller the stern end of the boat, in addition to rolling from side to side and pitching up and down, performed a continuous

217

figure-of-eight movement as well. Gesturing to the seaman he said, 'You need a strong stomach to live where he lives.'

Alicia climbed up the ladder to the periscope and we have a lovely picture of her at home sitting up there as to the manner born. I tried to do the same thing but, with a foretaste of hip trouble to come, I couldn't because I wasn't able to—if you'll pardon the expression—get my leg over.

*   *   *

My time in America wasn't all fun in the Florida sunshine. In October 1983 the *JY Prog* went to America, and among my interviewees was Margaret Thatcher, in Washington DC. She had just been presented with the Winston Churchill Foundation Award, and seized the opportunity to deliver a blistering attack on what she described as 'Soviet tyranny'. On the same programme I interviewed the legendary Ben Bradlee of the *Washington Post*. Under Bradlee's guidance this was the paper that took the lead in uncovering the Watergate scandal, coverage for which it won a prestigious Pulitzer Prize.

The following day I spoke to Senator Nancy Kassebaum, a Republican Senator from Kansas and the first woman to chair a major US Senate committee. I also had a conversation with Ambassador Vernon Walters, whose distinguished diplomatic career was no doubt helped by the fact that, apart from his native English, he was also fluent in German, French, Italian, Spanish, Portuguese, Dutch and Russian. Patrick Murphy, a veteran police chief and an outspoken proponent of drug policy reform, was another guest, and Morton Halperin talked about American national security. We rounded off the week with an interview with the British Ambassador, Sir Oliver Wright.

I got a smashing write-up and picture in the *Washington Post* headlined, 'Live from London, BBC's Top Chap Jimmy Young chats up America'. Which I didn't, of course, because the broadcast was being transmitted only to the UK and they couldn't hear me. I very much wished they could have. It would have been interesting to see what reaction we got from an American audience.

CHAPTER TWENTY-FIVE

SUFFICIENT PROBLEMS IN TOKYO

The latter half of 1980 saw Radio 2 acquiring a new Controller. Four hundred years ago Lord Falkland said, 'When it is not necessary to make a decision, it is necessary not to make a decision', but that advice doesn't apply to the BBC. New Controllers mean new shake-ups. They have to do something drastic even if it's not necessary, to let you know they've arrived. And this one would certainly shake things up.

His name was David Hatch. He was only in his early forties, but he had already had enormous and widely varied experience of showbusiness and broadcasting. At Cambridge University he had been in the Footlights, along with John Cleese, Graham Chapman, Bill Oddie and Tim Brooke-

Taylor. He had worked as a radio actor and a researcher and at *Radio Times*. He eventually became a producer, and we were in no doubt that he would produce changes at Radio 2. Newspaper headlines braced us for the worst. 'Major Shake-up for Radio 2', 'Massive Shake-up', 'All Change at the Beeb', 'New Chief Shakes Up Radio 2'.

When the dust settled, just about the only two bottoms still sitting on their original chairs were Wogan's and mine. The headline in the *Edinburgh Evening News* summed it up perfectly: 'Wogan and J.Y. Survive'.

*   *   *

By the spring of 1981 we were under pressure from our new Controller to mount another of our successful overseas broadcasts and, providing that we were able to do them live, Japan seemed to hold many possibilities.

There was the motor industry for a start, given the problems of British Leyland as compared with the success of the Japanese. Incidentally, trying to be seen to be fair, we suggested to British Leyland that we should broadcast from their factory at Longbridge on our return. They declined to let us do so.

But the programmes in Japan would be about far more than just the motor industry. The Japanese had achieved a dominant role in electronics as well, so we would want to talk about that. Also, on behalf of my listeners, I wanted to find out about Japanese culture, housing, education, the role of women in society, crime, law and order, and Japanese foreign policy. In fact

220

there was so much ground to cover that we aimed to do three days of broadcasting instead of our usual two.

My only previous experience of people from the Far East had been at a party in honour of a group of Chinese radio and television officials who were visiting the BBC, at which I was given an example of subtle Chinese humour delivered by a non-English-speaking Chinese gentleman. Through an interpreter he enquired whether I was married. I replied that I had been married but at present was single.

He thought for a moment, then out came another flurry of Chinese. Through the interpreter he asked whether I had any girlfriends. I replied that I had quite a few girlfriends and wondered what was coming next.

There was another pause for thought, then his face lit up with a huge smile. He literally bounced up and down with excitement as he rattled out a Chinese joke. I waited, spellbound, for it to arrive. The interpreter said. 'He's just thought of the perfect title for your next book. You should call it *The Current Affairs of Jimmy Young*.' When I roared with laughter it was clear that I had made his day. As a matter of fact I thought that even for an Englishman it would have been quite a nice play on words but for a non-English-speaking Chinese it was absolutely brilliant.

Would the Japanese be anything like the Chinese? Only time would tell.

The BBC's representative in Tokyo was Bob Friend, a fine journalist, and although I had spoken to him many times down the line or on the phone on my programme I had never met him. He turned

221

out to be a large, outgoing man with a great sense of humour. He had recruited a 'fixer' for us whose name was Fuyoko Nishisato. Inevitably she invited comparison with Sana el Saed of, by now, legendary President Sadat fame. Would Fuyoko be as good as Sana? We needn't have worried. She was.

We were flying to Japan on 22 May, and my bosses decided it would be quite dramatic if I did the first hour of my programme as usual. Then, at 11am, I would leap out of the studio and into a waiting car which would rush me to Heathrow to catch the British Airways flight to Tokyo via Anchorage in Alaska. The 11am to midday part of my broadcast in London would be done by my friend Colin Berry, an excellent broadcaster in his own right.

It took about eight hours to fly from London to Anchorage, which is to international air travel roughly what Clapham Junction is to southern England. Nobody who's there really wants to be there. Everybody's flown for hours but knows they're still only about halfway towards their destination, so it's full of half-asleep, jet-lagged people wandering aimlessly about and bumping into each other.

And then there's the bear. He's about nine feet tall. He's white, with huge claws and vicious-looking teeth. Fortunately he's stuffed and in a glass case. Once you've seen the bear, that's it. You've done Anchorage.

Eventually we arrived at Tokyo's Narita airport and I, used to the fifteen-minute journey from my home to Heathrow, thought, 'Thank God for that. Now for a bath, a drink, and bed.' Little did I realise that, although it's called Tokyo's Narita airport, it's actually nowhere near Tokyo. In fact it's sixty kilometres from Tokyo. And that's just for starters. If you think you've seen traffic jams, forget it. Until you've seen Tokyo you ain't seen nothing. When, during our stay, I asked how long it usually took to get from Tokyo to Narita airport I was told, 'There's no such thing as usual. It can take an hour and a half, but on the other hand it has been known to take four and a half hours.' In fact we hadn't been in Tokyo very long before a local resident gave us this advice: 'Don't worry if you're late for an appointment because nobody else does. With Tokyo's traffic it's impossible to estimate how long any journey's going to take.'

So at 3.30pm local time we set out from Narita airport for Tokyo. Eighteen hours in an aeroplane is bad enough, but to follow that with two and a quarter hours in nose-to-tail traffic just about finishes you off. Suffice it to say that by the time we arrived at the New Otani Hotel at 5.45pm we were all absolutely knackered. We dumped our bags, had a shower and a snack, and headed for bed.

The studio from which I was to broadcast for three days in Tokyo was the smallest in which I have ever worked. It was also very, very hot and nobody could find a fan. However, the excellent BBC engineers John Ford and Alan Wilson, part of our outside broadcast team, were on hand to sort it out. We had worked together in foreign parts for many years, and they knew instinctively how to create studio conditions in which I would feel comfortable and confident. Don't ask me how, but they had the ability to go into a broadcasting studio anywhere, be it in the Soviet Union, Egypt, Israel,

223

Zimbabwe, Japan or Europe, and, whatever the language difficulties, have the local technicians eating out of their hands within a few minutes. I always knew they would set up the best possible conditions for me to work in, and as a man who finds it difficult to mend a fuse I have the greatest admiration for them.

In programme terms we were lucky with our timing. The EEC and Japan had just arranged to hold a conference in Brussels to discuss the controversial question of restricting the penetration of the European car market by Japanese cars. It was therefore extremely topical that I was able to record an interview with Mr Hashira Amaya, the Vice Minister for International Affairs, who was about to leave for the conference. But two minutes into the interview I felt I could have saved the EEC ministers the trouble of attending.

First, I asked whether Japan would be willing to lower the level of its car imports into Europe to equate with the lower proportion it had just agreed with the United States of America. Mr Amaya used a lot of words to say no, but that was his answer and he never moved from that position. I then suggested that, instead of simply forcing into Europe product made totally in Japan, a less controversial method would be to build product on a partnership basis. He agreed, and that is what eventually happened. In fact it was rather ironic that, years later, the Nissan factory in England turned out to be more efficient than some Nissan factories in Japan.

Mr Amaya was also fascinating on the way industry works in Japan, which is not at all in the totally capitalist way that an outsider might think.

In fact, Japanese government ministers are very much involved in forward planning. It is no accident that the motor and electronics industries are such important areas for the Japanese. They are for the simple reason that government and industry, the banks and the unions, sat down together and jointly decided that they should be. Apparently they meet and plan, in some cases, up to twenty-five years ahead. They decide which industries they are going to concentrate on and, having decided their priorities, pressure—ruthless if necessary—is brought to give those areas every possible assistance.

The Chairman of the British Chamber of Commerce in Tokyo, Norman McCloud, later confirmed and expanded on this. 'In Japan last year,' he told me, 'government and industry got together and produced what they called *A Vision for the Eighties*, spelling out where Japan is going in the next ten years. That is what we should be doing in Britain. The Confederation of British Industry, government, unions and banks should get together and think more positively. Study the Japanese vision, and then decide what the counter-attack is going to be.'

But perhaps we shouldn't follow the Japanese example too closely. In our interview Mr Amaya said that government tried to 'persuade' people to co-operate, begging the question that I asked next.

'If companies don't co-operate with the government's persuasion, do you cause them aggravation?'

'Yes,' said Mr Amaya. He didn't elaborate, nor did he need to.

Later that day I interviewed the fascinating

Mr Akio Morita, and I use the word 'fascinating' deliberately. It's not very often you get to meet someone who has started from scratch an organisation as vast and successful as the Sony Corporation. And this was where I had my first experience of the Japanese tradition of offering gifts. Mr Morita spoke rapidly to one of his minions, who disappeared and then reappeared carrying a radio. But this wasn't just any old radio, as Mr Morita explained. This was the very latest result of Sony technology. Very small but, said Mr Morita, it covers the whole world. He was right. It's an excellent radio, and still performs really well on a shelf in our kitchen at home.

Something that emerged very strongly from all the industrialists I interviewed in Japan was the concept of the 'Family'. Mr Morita told me that when a new employee joins Sony he is said to have joined the 'Sony Family', which sounds nice and cosy but is something of a two-edged sword. There are numerous stories of Japanese husbands ending up married to the firm, staggering home clutching their briefcases at midnight and getting up at 6am to begin a new working day. Indeed, I saw a quote from one Japanese husband who, when asked what were his priorities, listed them as No. 1 the firm, No. 2 his colleagues at work, No. 3 the quality of the firm's products, and No. 4 his wife and family. I don't think many British wives would be happy to put up with that.

The same ideas cropped up when we visited the Nissan Motor Company, where I interviewed Mr Mitsuya Goto, the General Manager of their International Division. I put it to him that in the Nissan Motor Company trades union officials and management seemed interchangeable. He agreed, saying that some employees might be asked to serve as full-time union officials and then, at some stage in the future, might be made managers or deputy general managers. I couldn't help thinking how different it all was from the way we understand trades unions in the West.

I'd been reading about something called the 'Quality Control Circle' concept, and asked him how it worked. Said Mr Goto, 'This is a grouping of ten to fifteen of our ordinary employees who monitor the quality of the product. In addition, however, once or twice a month they would stay on after their normal working hours had ended to discuss ways in which they could improve the quality of the product, or perhaps improve the production processes.' When I asked whether they would get paid for the extra time I was told that they would get a little money but were basically volunteers. 'You see,' explained Mr Goto, 'when you join a company you feel you are a member of a family.'

'Here we go again,' I thought, and I decided to ask Mr Goto to enlarge a bit on family relationships at Nissan.

'Well,' he said, 'a company like ours would provide housing, whether bachelor quarters or a family apartment, at minimal rent. A bachelor, for instance, would pay rent of about £3.50 per month. Fifty per cent of the cost of meals in the company dining room would be paid for by the company. The company also pays 60 per cent of our health insurance and medical care.'

I had heard an extraordinary story that employees tended not to take their holidays at all, or if they did only in single days, because they did not want the company to suffer. Mr Goto agreed that this indeed used to be the case, but added, 'That is beginning to change with the younger generation of employees. However,' he said, 'most of us in managerial positions are reluctant to take paid holidays. In fact I have accumulated thirty-six days' paid holiday.'

'Are you going to take it?' I asked.

'No, I'm much too busy,' he replied.

Another of my guests was Dr Saburo Okita, a former Foreign Minister who was now Chief Trade Negotiator at the Defence Ministry. It had not occurred to me that there could be a link between defence spending and economic achievement, but there was, it seemed. Ironically, Japan was under pressure from the USA to spend more money on defence. There was a feeling that, because Japan was sheltering behind America and its military power, it was able to spend more money on its super-efficient industrial capability that was causing America so many problems at home.

From industry we moved on to social issues. The assistant Managing Editor of the *Mainichi* newspaper came in to talk about Tokyo housing, which to our eyes was absolutely incredible. It's true that the whole city had to be rebuilt in 1923–4 after a disastrous earthquake, and again after World War II, but on both occasions it was done without proper planning in the rush to get the economy moving again. The result is one of the ugliest housing scenes you would ever wish not to see. Big factories, little houses and medium-sized office blocks are all crammed together in one terrible mess. In fact while we were there we heard a story, probably apocryphal, that the government was seriously considering a plan to move the capital somewhere else and start all over again.

One thing I had learned from our research before we came to Tokyo (and was confirmed to me constantly after we arrived) was that Japan is an intensely competitive nation. Once government and industry have taken the decision to concentrate on a certain area, let's say motor cars, that will not prevent individual Japanese motor manufacturers being as competitive with each other as they would be with foreign firms. But nowhere is competition harder, and in some cases more lethal, than in the field of education. It seems a constant fight, first to get to the best pre-nursery school, then the best nursery school, the best elementary, the best junior high and so on.

When I asked Mr Michio Nagai, a former Minister of Education and now an adviser to the United Nations University, whether the pressure on young children really was enormous, he answered: 'Tokyo University is the educational Mount Fuji of Japan and every Japanese wants to climb Mount Fuji, so the pressure is very great.'

I had in front of me a clipping from *The Times* that laid out the day of a Japanese fourteen-year-old. He left home for school at 7.45am, returned home at 4pm and went straight to bed. His parents woke him at 9pm when he had dinner. He then studied through the night until 4am, when he went back to bed for a couple of hours before getting ready for that day's school. In addition, he received private tuition in mathematics for an extra four hours a week. Was that typical of the pressure?

Mr Nagai thought that 'typical' might not be

absolutely the correct word. 'However, I am sure that many people, especially in city areas, are doing exactly the same thing, for the purpose of getting into a better university and having better employment.'

I quoted an American resident in the country who said his son had complained that he couldn't play with any of his Japanese school friends because they were all studying until midnight. 'That would be true,' said Mr Nagai. 'In most countries today there is a thing called the Diploma Disease, but in Japan the disease is more acute than anywhere else.'

I knew that there was a high suicide rate among young Japanese. Were these intense pressures the cause? 'Yes,' admitted Mr Nagai, 'and not only suicide. They are under so much pressure that some of them become psychologically disturbed.' While he was sure that the Japanese went to school or college to obtain a better diploma, he was not convinced that they actually received a better education.

Knowing that the Japanese seem prepared to accept much more authority, discipline and supervision than might be tolerated elsewhere in the world, I asked Mr Shikita, Director of the Asia/Far East Crime Prevention Institute, what effect, if any, it had on the very low level of crime in the country. He started by explaining how Japanese policing works. Officers are deployed in small 'patches', so they get to know the people in their area particularly well. They take turns to check on all the flats, houses and shops in their area, and the number of occupants in each building. Every householder fills in a 'green card' with details of the family's jobs, schools, cars, and whether they have any lodgers.

I wondered whether the Tokyo public resented this, pointing out that in many Western communities it would be called an invasion of privacy. But Mr Shikita told me that in general there was no objection because people knew the police would use the information only for their protection. He went on, 'It is more difficult to commit crime in Japan, because people who notice suspicious happenings report them to the police immediately, and the police react very quickly.' Juvenile crime, he told me, had increased slowly over the past twenty years, but on the other hand adult crime had been decreasing for the last thirty. In the previous ten years the incidence of violent crimes like rape and murder had gone down to one quarter of what it had been, while the number of assaults and burglaries had decreased to one third. 'However,' insisted Mr Shikita finally, 'we still have sufficient problems to keep ourselves employed.' I felt that the police in New York or Miami or some British cities would be very happy to settle for Mr Shikita's 'sufficient problems'.

The next topic I wanted to examine was the role of Japanese women in modern society, and I introduced the item by reading part of the lyric of a popular song which had been top of the Japanese hit parade. Called 'Declaration of an Overbearing Husband', it laid down certain guidelines for Japanese wives. 'Do not go to bed before I do. Do not get up after I do. Cook good meals. Always look pretty. Keep quiet. Follow me. And if I have a little affair, well, just put up with it.'

I asked Mrs Fukawo, the Associate Editor for

231

Women's Affairs on one of Japan's biggest newspapers, whether wives really behaved like that. She gave a qualified yes—'Well, there are not so many women nowadays who do that.' But she agreed that the song had provoked many letters in the press, and the odd thing was that most of them agreed with the sentiments expressed in it. So in Japan men would seem to be very much the dominant sex.

However, when it comes to running the home and controlling the finances, the opposite is true. Said Mrs Fukawo, 'At the end of the week the majority of husbands hand the whole of their pay packet to the wife, and she then hands them back their allowance.' She went on to explain something about the Japanese sense of humour: 'The equivalent of the British mother-in-law joke is the Japanese mean wife who keeps her husband short of pocket money joke.'

It was, incidentally, after this programme that Fuyoko, our Japanese researcher, told us what must be the definitive story about Japanese marriages. She said, 'As with most Japanese husbands, my old man's pet name for me is "Oi". Morning to night he just says, "Oi, breakfast. Oi, lunch. Oi, the newspaper. Oi, a beer." '

My last two guests were not Japanese but British: the Commercial Counsellor at the British Embassy in Tokyo, Merrick Baker-Bates, and the Chairman of the British Chamber of Commerce, Norman McCloud. I wanted to balance the Japanese view of themselves with that of some experienced outsiders, and see if there were any lessons that we British could learn. First, I asked Merrick whether the Japanese really were, as they were often portrayed, supermen, conquering all before them.

'No,' he answered. 'They are not. They've had a lot of successes, but they've also had their difficulties. There are, in this market, a good many niches which British exporters could fill. The name of the game is to find those niches, and we can help them.'

Norman McCloud spoke up. He said, 'Japan is a desperately poor country when it comes to energy, in that every ton of oil has to be shipped in. So they have a great weakness there. We must think harder to find the niches of which Merrick has spoken.' He slipped into a football comparison. 'If you're playing a very, very good team, you don't just pack the goal and defend. That isn't a goal-scoring, winning strategy. Defence, yes, but you must also think your way through to attack.'

We had just a couple of minutes of broadcasting time left and I wanted a final comment from each of my British guests. Merrick compared the interest shown by British companies towards Japan and China. He said, 'Recently we had an energy-saving seminar here which attracted eight British companies. I couldn't help remembering that, a couple of years ago, 350 British companies went to China on exactly the same theme. Nobody can tell me that the prospects for British exports to Japan in that field aren't better than they are to China, given the immense attention to energy-saving here.'

The final word came from Norman. I asked him what he had found to be his biggest problem when he came to live and work in Japan. He said, 'My biggest problem was the language. I was desperately enthusiastic to learn it, so I went to a shop and bought a book called *Japanese in Six Months*. I then saw *Japanese in Three Months* followed by *Japanese in Three Weeks*. And when I saw *Instant Japanese*, I got really excited. Six years later I'm still trying to make myself understood by taxi drivers!'

CHAPTER TWENTY-SIX

MAGGIE IN FIGHTING FORM

Contrary to the snide comments in some sections of the press that Margaret Thatcher was on my programme 'every five minutes', my major interviews with her occurred at intervals of, on average, about fifteen months. There is one left-wing Labour MP who can never be interviewed by me without making a reference to 'your friend Mrs Thatcher'. So far I've bitten my tongue in the interest of getting a good interview, but this would seem a suitable time to nail that lie. I only ever met the Thatchers socially on one occasion, and that was nearly thirty years ago. There is an impression that we are great friends but that is simply not true. In fact, other than at our meetings in my studio I never saw, or indeed spoke to, Mrs Thatcher.

But then, neither do I meet Tony Blair or Charles Kennedy socially. Even-handed at all times.

*　　　　*　　　　*

In 1982 long-running verbal battles over the

sovereignty of the Falkland Islands, a tiny British possession in the South Atlantic, had escalated into military action when the islands were invaded by the armed forces of Argentina on 2 April. Three days later a British naval task force set out from Portsmouth on its long journey to the tip of South America. A meeting of the British war cabinet on the 20th ordered the repossession of the islands, and in a big naval action which began on 1 May the Argentine warship *General Belgrano* was controversially sunk. On 17 May the United Nations initiated attempts to find a peaceful solution, and it was against this background that Margaret Thatcher arrived at my studio to be interviewed on the morning of the 19th.

The Prime Minister had come straight from a meeting of the war cabinet in what the *Guardian* newspaper described as 'characteristically belligerent form, especially when Mr Young persistently put to her over and over again that giving the Falkland Islanders an overriding say in any long term settlement for the Falklands was giving the islanders a veto'. The most the Prime Minister could manage in reply was, 'I don't like the use of the word "veto". It's a right.' She described the Argentinian reply to the UN peace proposals as, 'Not very encouraging. The gap looks big.'

While war had not actually been declared on the *JY Programme* we had come pretty damned close to it, and the next day's newspaper headlines agreed. In addition to 'It's not very encouraging' and 'The gap looks big' there were 'Thatcher set for battle' and 'Maggie signals invasion'.

The action itself was brief, brutal and bloody. By

235

the middle of June it was all over. On the 14th the Argentine forces surrendered and on the 25th Governor Rex Hunt returned as Commissioner of the Falklands.

Some two years later the Prime Minister's critics attacked the sinking of the *General Belgrano*, on the grounds that at the time the cruiser was heading away from the Falklands and towards home. Appearing on my programme again, Mrs Thatcher offered no excuses and made no pleas for special understanding. On the contrary, she mounted an aggressive counter-attack.

Putting the matter in the starkest and most personal terms, she said the task force had not gone to the South Atlantic for a cruise. It had been engaged in an operation to take back the Falkland Islands from a military junta that had seized them by force. The British fleet would have been seriously threatened had any of its key ships been sunk by the Argentine Navy and, in those circumstances, the sinking of the *General Belgrano* had been fully justified.

Mrs Thatcher pointed out that a warship that has changed course once can do so again, and then said, 'My goodness—suppose she'd done that and then got the *Invincible* or the *Hermes*. My decision was right and I would do it again. My job', insisted the Prime Minister, 'is to protect our boys.'

Even the most rabid Thatcher-haters found it difficult to torpedo that argument, and our listener reaction was overwhelmingly in her favour.

* * *

July 1988 saw the return of the Prime Minister to

the *JY Prog* to give a real Maggie 'handbagging' to the President of the European Commission (the law-making body of what was then the European Community, now the European Union), Jacques Delors. Monsieur Delors, who you may remember was nicknamed '*Frère Jacques*' when he came over to Britain to give support to militant trade unionists, said he envisaged a massive transfer of power from sovereign European governments to Brussels. He added that within ten years 80 per cent of decisions at present taken nationally would be taken by the European Community.

When I asked Mrs Thatcher if she would ever cede the majority of social and economic decisions to the European Community, her reply was immediate and emphatic: 'There are no circumstances in which I would do that.' In what was widely reported as a public dressing down of Monsieur Delors she said he had 'gone over the top'. His vision of a United States of Europe she denigrated as 'airy-fairy' and added, 'Europe has a history of many different cultures and many different languages. It is not possible to have a United States of Europe.'

Right on cue, the left-wing press leaped into action. The *Guardian* referred to 'Mrs Thatcher's decision to run up the Union Jack on the Jimmy Young Show'. The *Observer* rather sniffily observed, 'Mrs Thatcher chose not to say these things to Parliament, which might be thought to have some interest in the matter, but to the audience of the Jimmy Young Show on Radio Two'. But some would argue that, because the *Jimmy Young Programme* had millions of listeners, many of whom expressed fears at what they saw as

237

a drift towards a United States of Europe, it was exactly the right place for the Prime Minister to make her views clear.

Europe was again on the agenda in our next big interview, in June 1990. But first Mrs Thatcher savaged her old antagonist Ted Heath who, she said, had performed the biggest U-turn of all time and cost the Tories the 1974 election. In fact, she said, the only thing he had done right was to give her her first job in the cabinet.

When I asked her about her views on joining a single European currency, she replied, 'We are not prepared to go for a single currency, that is drop the pound sterling.' She added, 'Britain is not prepared to surrender the degree of financial control over its budget and finances that a single currency implies. I am not prepared to see the pound sterling go.' Having said which, Mrs Thatcher conceded that Europe would 'one day' have a single currency. Which sort of brings us to the Euro-debate that is raging today.

*   *   *

When, way back in 1975, the British people were asked to vote in a referendum on continued membership of the then European Economic Community, few of us had any inkling that the Community would become a political and economic experiment. The debate on the future of Europe has raised the question of whether it should be a federated United States of Europe, or a federation of nation states, or a union with federal powers. The British people were never asked to approve the Maastricht Treaty, signed by

238

John Major, which resulted in the present European Union. Maastricht became the blueprint for the next big change: economic and monetary union. A major decision about our constitutional framework was taken without consultation.

The contents of former French President Giscard d'Estaing's proposed new constitution for the European Union came as no surprise to me. I have long believed that the intention of France and Germany has always been to work towards a single European state. A United States of Europe seen, certainly by France, as a rival to the United States of America.

How many people would have voted yes in the 1975 referendum on whether to stay in the EEC had they known that, in this new millennium, the EU would be seeking to define our cherished freedoms? The new constitution will have primacy over the law of the member states. It sets out the areas in which we would hand over control to Brussels: foreign affairs, economic policy, trade, agriculture, immigration and asylum, employment policy, industrial policy, defence, environmental protection, justice and home affairs.

The Prime Minister, Tony Blair, has so far refused to consult the British people by calling a referendum, despite the fact that half of the other member states have indicated that they will seek a mandate from their electorates. His reason seems clear: he knows that the vast majority of the British people would reject it out of hand.

As I write this in 2003, Chancellor Gordon Brown has given a yes/no fudged answer to the probability of our joining the Euro and the possibility of a referendum on the issue. Our government knows that the likelihood of obtaining the 'yes' vote it wants is remote. Once again the British people know what they want, but the politicians don't want to let them have their say.

CHAPTER TWENTY-SEVEN

A WAY WITH WORDS

In the 1970s and again between 1984 and 1986 I did some very successful television series. Beginning in 1974, I did several series of *Jim's World* for ITV. Originally designed to be a light entertainment programme, its scope broadened to include current affairs as well. As with my BBC radio programme, it ranged from Uri Geller entertaining us with examples of the paranormal to serious discussions on capital punishment and battered babies.

Although piloted as an afternoon programme, it ended up going out at lunchtime. I was therefore on Radio 2 and ITV at the same time. Obviously I had to give up one or the other and, since I had just signed my first three-year contract with the BBC, there was only one choice.

Later, during the mid-1980s, I did an annual series called *The Jimmy Young Programme* for Yorkshire Television. I had a studio audience and the subjects we covered included child abuse, the Moors Murderers, spiritualism, human embryo research, field sports and unemployment. In other words, the sort of things that daytime television is doing today, nearly twenty years on. The TV

240

programmes were so successful that I was under a lot of pressure to transfer my radio programme to television. I thought very seriously about it but in the end decided that, although radio paid considerably less well, that was where the programme worked best.

Television, especially at that time, was not as flexible a medium as radio—on radio you don't have to worry about getting pictures! And on radio I could break up a particularly serious interview by playing a record—I couldn't do that on television. Radio is a more immediate medium even than live television. Listener reaction to controversial items is incredibly fast, which I can then complement by picking up huge bundles of phoned-in reaction and sight-reading them. Morning television programmes try to do the same thing but the result often seems clumsy and fumbled (as the actress said to the bishop). I think that is possibly because television somehow seems slower than radio.

At the end of 1984 many people thought they were hearing the last of Terry Wogan on radio as, after many years presenting his hugely successful early morning show, he embarked on a thrice-weekly television chat show. Terry said he was sad to be leaving radio, but added, 'Television is the only thing left for me to do—apart from becoming Pope. And I don't think I'm going to become Pope.' With his unique and often way-out brand of whimsy, fantasy and humour Terry had spun a magic spell on radio. But would it translate successfully to another medium? While wishing him well, I doubted the wisdom of what he was doing. In fact his new show ran for seven years, but three programmes a week on television eventually tried the critics' patience. It was described by one as 'dear old Terry, over-exposed and ill at ease in his thrice-weekly television borathon'. And, although Terry continues to delight us on television, I'm still convinced that his natural medium is radio.

Eventually Terry was to return to what I always felt was his proper home, Radio 2's early morning show, but in the meantime my programme was retimed to run from 10.30am to 1pm, with Ken Bruce coming down from Scotland to take over the programme before me. By this time the Wogan/Young hand-over chat had become something of a legend, often developing into a mini-programme all of its own. The Queen herself had remarked on it, if you recall, when she awarded me my OBE in 1979. Not only did the listeners enjoy it but Terry and I thoroughly enjoyed it as well, as you will gather by the departing Terry's final compliment to me: 'I shall miss the old fool.'

The question on everyone's lips around 'Headquarters' was, 'Can Bruce possibly emulate Wogan in the hand-over chat?' Ken, being a very experienced broadcaster and nobody's fool, didn't even try, but in a very short time we built up a double act of our own with which our listeners seemed very happy indeed. Yet less than one year after taking over the Radio 2 breakfast show from Terry Wogan, Ken was dropped from the morning slot. Said a BBC spokeswoman, 'Mr Bruce has certainly not been axed—this is simply part of a rescheduling of programmes.'

The BBC suits decided that the man to take over the Radio 2 flagship breakfast show was Derek

Jameson, the former editor of the *Daily Express*, *Daily Star* and *News of the World*. When Derek sat in as a holiday replacement for me some listeners complained about his abrasive manner, but Bryant Marriott, then Controller of Radio 2, said, 'Derek's East End breeziness and know-how is just what we've been looking for to pep up the *Breakfast Show*.'

A very different personality indeed. At any rate, Derek has long since moved on and Terry is still there. Maybe Terry is just irreplaceable.

CHAPTER TWENTY-EIGHT

A NEW FUTURE FOR THE OLD COMMONWEALTH

In February 1985 the *JY Prog* dropped in on Gibraltar. This was at the time when the frontier gates to Spain, closed by General Franco in June 1968, had just been reopened.

For many years Gibraltar was a British fortress guarding the entrance to the Mediterranean, but with the withdrawal of our military forces it became a free port with duty-free shopping and has attracted tourists from elsewhere in Europe, especially Britain. Indeed to the visitor it is rather like a British seaside resort in the 1950s, with fish and chip shops and kiss-me-quick hats.

Spain has claimed sovereignty over the Rock, but the residents reaffirmed their ties with Britain in a UN-supervised referendum in 1967. The border with Gibraltar was then closed, although pedestrian traffic was permitted across in 1982.

In February 1985 Sir Geoffrey Howe, the then Foreign Secretary, committed the British government to examining Spanish claims. Eighteen years on those claims have not been agreed simply because the Gibraltarians wish to remain British. At the time of our visit the Union Flag was flying from almost every building. From my interview with the Chief Minister of Gibraltar it was clear that any move to change the status of the Rock would be met with strong resistance by the residents, and that position hasn't changed since.

It is difficult to imagine that any senior Spanish official who has visited the Rock can believe, hand on heart, that the Gibraltarians are ever going to give up their allegiance to Britain in favour of some sort of accommodation with Spain. Of course we may, and probably will, treacherously desert and double-cross the Gibraltarians, using so-called 'European Unity' as an excuse. I suspect they believe that in the end we shall rat on them and sell them out. It will be interesting to see what happens if we do.

*   *   *

Australia's bicentenary celebrations were to take place in 1988, and we flew out there to report on the build-up. Because of the timing we had to spend Christmas in Australia. Sad for members of the team with families, and sad for Alicia and me—it was our first Christmas apart. But the Australians did their best to make us welcome and the hotel set up a special table for us, despite being fully booked, to have our festive dinner.

On Christmas Day I interviewed two of the stars from *Neighbours*, Anne Charleston and Anne Haddy, also the Australian actor and comedian Bill Kerr, and TV presenter Clive James who happened to be staying in the same hotel as the JY team. Then we went to the Royal North Shore Hospital in Sydney, where I interviewed two British nurses who had worked for the NHS at home but had emigrated to Australia and were very happy that they had made the move.

Some very tough-looking traffic cops whom I interviewed at the roadside told us that they were authorised to stop any vehicle at any time. While we were there they actually stopped several drivers for random breath tests, and so, seizing the opportunity, I interviewed some of them too. The majority of them not only accepted random testing but thought it was a good thing, since it really did help to reduce the number of accidents.

Possibly the best-known Australian to British audiences is Dame Edna Everage. The Great Dame didn't have anything particularly sensational to say to me, but interviewing her was certainly a bizarre experience. Since the interview was on radio Dame Edna's creator, Barry Humphries, quite rightly saw no reason to turn up in full drag. It was slightly off-putting that sitting opposite me was a rather beefy and obviously masculine Barry, yet in answer to my questions out of his mouth came the voice of Dame Edna. The Dame herself would probably describe it as 'spooky'.

Perhaps the most fascinating interview concerned Australian wildlife, and if you are arachnophobic I should skip the next bit. Australian spiders vary in size. The bird-eating

245

ones can grow as large as four to five inches across. There is the white-tailed spider, whose venom contains a bacterium that causes necrosis, an ulcer that eats away at your skin and is extremely difficult to cure. Then there's the redback spider, which is similar to the black widow and extremely poisonous. The redback particularly likes to hide under toilet seats. Think of it as an opportunity not only to get a bite where you really don't want one but also to find out who your true friends are.

My serious political interview was with the Prime Minister, Bob Hawke. Mr Hawke is a short, stocky man and he's tough, both mentally and physically. He may not be big, but you feel he would be a good guy to have on your side in a punch-up in a dark alley. He was having a very busy day and so, at his request, we did the interview at Sydney airport. He made it clear that he was keen to get it over in the shortest possible time.

As the recording engineer, my producer, my chief researcher, Mr Hawke and I bustled along corridors on our way to a quiet place to record I found myself engaged in a very animated conversation with the Prime Minister over the length of the interview. I was after twenty minutes and he was offering, at the most, five. As we bustled I pleaded, but Mr Hawke was adamant. In fact his replies got shorter and shorter until they consisted of just the one word, 'Bullshit'. He 'Bullshitted' me all the way to the room where we were to record. The recording engineer quickly set up and I thought I would have one last go.

'Twenty minutes, please?' I said.

'Bullshit,' replied Bob—on tape.

Since I had nothing to lose I thought I'd pick

him up on his rudeness and his use of the word 'bullshit'. He roared with laughter, as did his wife who was also present. Mr Hawke then apologised and, even better, gave me the longer, wide-ranging interview I was seeking.

We talked about the Australian economy, and about the upcoming bicentennial celebrations due in 1988. Mr Hawke also said that he was considering the possibility of Australia breaking away from the Commonwealth. Since that date a referendum has been held in which Australians were asked to vote on whether they wished their country to become a republic. The result in 2000 was 'No', but it was a fairly close-run thing.

*   *   *

Another part of the Commonwealth that was much in the news in the late twentieth century was tiny but economically significant Hong Kong, sometimes described as 'the buzzing last outpost of Empire'. Early in 1989 I interviewed Dame Lydia Dunn, the senior member of Hong Kong's Executive Council, who was visiting Britain to discuss Hong Kong's future with the Prime Minister, Margaret Thatcher. The British colony was due to be handed back to Chinese rule in 1997, when the ninety-nine-year lease from China ran out. During the course of the interview Dame Lydia said, 'If you really want to know what life is like there, you should come out and do your programme from Hong Kong.' So, always keen to be at the centre of the action, in November that year we flew to Hong Kong to find out how its citizens felt about their future.

Kai Tak airport was surrounded by steep hills, a busy harbour and thickly populated urban areas, and I had seen the approach to it described as 'one of commercial aviation's most gut-wrenching finales. Kai Tak is the eye of a needle and you are a flying piece of thread.' I decided that, if possible, I should try to be up front with the pilot to observe it.

I've never been one to push myself forward and so I was reluctant to ask, but at the last minute, just as we were about to begin our approach, I was asked if I would like to go up to the sharp end. The pilot confirmed that what I'd been told was correct. Away in the distance I could just make out a very small Coca Cola sign, and the pilot explained that the approach to Kai Tak was, in fact, fairly basic. He said that you just aimed at the Coca Cola sign, and when you got up to it it was simply a case of right hand hard down. Sure enough the Coca Cola sign got bigger and bigger and then, just when I was wondering whether he meant through it rather than up to it, right hand down it was.

The next bit was even more spectacular. From then on we literally flew between the houses of suburban Hong Kong. Looking out of the side windows, we could see families eating their meals or watching the television. I'd never seen anything like it and don't suppose I shall again either.

Incidentally, if you're a nervous flyer and are about to fly to Hong Kong, don't worry. They've moved the airport.

Despite much apprehension in the West about Hong Kong being handed back to China, there were no such fears among many of its residents. In fact quite a few of them seemed to be looking forward to the change of rulers. Which is not surprising, really, when you think how many of them originally came from China, and still have family and friends living there.

We flew up to the border with China by helicopter and were then taken to an observation post on a high hill overlooking the Chinese town of Shenzen. 'Our boys' stationed there had the job of guarding the border against illegal immigrants. A very important member of our party was our ace engineer George Legg; the BBC always prided itself on its prestigious engineering department, and George was one of its most senior members. Unfortunately, for our close encounter with the Chinese border George was carrying all the bulky, heavy recording equipment on his back. It was a very hot day, and carrying that lot on flat ground was bad enough—but as we scrambled up the hill I watched anxiously as George's face got redder and redder and the sweat poured off him. Fortunately he survived, none the worse for what must have been a gruelling day's work.

Among Hong Kong's political figures whom I interviewed were Emily Lau, a member of the national legislature and a long-time pro-democracy activist, and Martin Lee, then leader of the Hong Kong Democratic Party and perhaps the most outspoken advocate of democratic freedoms in Hong Kong. And once again I talked to Dame Lydia Dunn, whose career accomplishments included being a director of the Hong Kong and Shanghai Banking Corporation Ltd and of the powerful John Swire and Sons which, among its other business interests, controlled the Cathay Pacific Airline. These interviews were all taking place just four months after the savage assault on student demonstrators in Tiananmen Square in Beijing, which represented an enormous setback to Hong Kong's hopes of a harmonious future with China. Dame Lydia summed up the situation: 'In one week China has wiped out what it had accomplished in ten years. Fears now have to be recognised.'

However, one reviewer wrote that 'the most compelling encounter of the week' had taken place between myself and a Vietnamese boat person in a Hong Kong refugee camp. If he meant that the emotions I felt communicated themselves into the interview, I'm not surprised.

The camp itself was overcrowded, filthy and surrounded by barbed wire. Some families had been there for so many years that they had children who had been born there and had known no other life. 'Bob', as he was known for the purpose of the interview, told me he had made the journey to Hong Kong in a 'very overcrowded boat'. When I asked him whether the dangerous journey had been worthwhile he simply said, 'It was the most important moment in my life.' Bob was an 'official' political refugee who had already been in the camp for seven years and I asked him what were his prospects for the future. He replied simply: 'I have to sit here and wait for a country to accept me.'

That was in 1989 and he'd already been 'sitting there' since 1982. I wonder if he's still sitting there as I write this in 2003. Or did he simply die waiting?

I know that interviewers are not supposed to get involved in personal tragedies. Just do the interview and get the hell out of there is the basic rule, but sometimes you can't help wondering. It happened to me in a Moscow railway station when I was surrounded by homeless little children. And it happened again—to a lesser extent since he was a grown man—with Bob. What happens next? What is their future?

It's easy for us. We fly in, do the interviews, then hop back into the great silver bird and fly off again, sipping our large gins and tonics and hoping for commendations from our bosses. But what of the poor sods we leave behind and in whom we may, for the purpose of a good interview, have raised false hopes?

Or am I being too soft-hearted?

CHAPTER TWENTY-NINE

EUROPEAN VIEWS

Our foreign trips were usually planned with military precision from Broadcasting House, and the JY team had travelled across most of the world without a hitch. But in September 1995, when we went to Rome, something went wrong. We arrived at our hotel only to find that no room had been booked for Alicia and myself. Since this was the first time that Alicia had accompanied me on an overseas trip we weren't getting off to the best possible start.

My producer John Gurnett and his wife Margaret very kindly said we could have their room and they would find accommodation in another hotel. A kind gesture that had unfortunate results.

John and Margaret checked in elsewhere, but their first hotel meal gave them severe food poisoning and they were very ill for the next two days.

For the rest of us it was work as usual—but not without its compensations for some. When I interviewed the Mayor of Rome, Francesco Rutelli, he completely bowled over the female members of our research team and made the men extremely envious. The ladies thought he was one of the most attractive politicians they had ever met. Not only was he so damned good-looking—just like Paul Newman—but he wowed everybody with his charm.

His English, which was perfect, he told me he had learnt by listening to Beatles records. He was also very good at presentation. He arrived with his bodyguards—who didn't look in the least like bodyguards. They were two very sexy-looking policewomen who looked more like models than cops but still gave one the feeling that they would be very capable if required to be.

We were told that one of the Mayor's most remarkable, and unlikely, successes had been in sorting out Rome's notorious traffic problems. He had even persuaded the citizens of Rome to start parking their cars in an orderly fashion. In terms of charisma and brains he appeared to have everything going for him, which was perhaps confirmed by the fact that when he came up for re-election in 1997 he won a massive 60 per cent of the vote in the first round.

Then we went to a very fashionable suburb of Rome where I interviewed an Italian journalist in his home. Although he was an extremely successful journalist the house was very small by English standards, and he explained that the pressure on building space in Rome meant that most of the modern houses there were like that. A British estate agent would probably flatter them as 'snug' or 'compact'. His small son spent most of the time racing round the room on his scooter which didn't help the interview too much, but we were made extremely welcome and were treated to a beautiful Italian family lunch cooked by his wife.

We also visited the Venerable English College in Rome, where the crème de la crème of Catholic priests from England are trained. Two rectors of the Venerable English College, Arthur Hinsley (rector 1917–29) and William Godfrey (rector 1929–39), went on to become Cardinal Archbishops of Westminister. Sitting in the beautiful College gardens, I was able to interview two young Englishmen who were just completing their training prior to returning home—no doubt hoping that in time they too might become Cardinal Archbishops.

Apart from that little hitch with the hotel and the resultant misery for John and Margaret, our visit to Rome had been thoroughly enjoyable and light-hearted. But elsewhere in Europe there were more serious matters on the agenda.

*   *   *

A few years earlier I broadcast live from Berlin, just after the Wall had been pulled down. But before I talk about that I would like to go back for a moment to 1938. The night of 9–10 November that year became known as *Kristallnacht*—the Night of Broken Glass. Gangs of Nazi youths

253

roamed through Jewish neighbourhoods breaking the windows of businesses and homes, burning synagogues and looting. During this night of terror 101 synagogues and almost 7500 Jewish businesses were destroyed. Some twenty-six thousand Jews were arrested and sent to concentration camps. Others were physically attacked and beaten, and 91 of them died as a result. It was the beginning of what is now referred to as the Holocaust, and it was on its fiftieth anniversary in 1988 that I spoke to one of Britain's most famous actors in an interview that had strong links with Germany.

The actor in question was born on 28 March 1921, making him just six months older than me. However, he made a much more spectacular entrance into this world than I did. Dirk Bogarde was born in a taxi in Hampstead, North London. The eldest of three children, he was actually named Derek Jules Gaspard Ulric Niven van den Bogaerde. In fact he made his West End theatre debut as Derek Bogaerde, and it was some years later that his agent decided he should change his name to Dirk Bogarde. Naturally we talked about his acting career during our interview but, although we touched on it only briefly, it was one aspect of his service as a wartime Army officer that most affected me.

While serving with the Signal Corps Bogarde took part in the liberation of the Belsen concentration camp in Germany. Belsen was a place of unbelievable horror and brutality, and Bogarde was one of the first liberators to enter the camp. He was never able to bring himself to describe in detail what he saw there, but he told me that it was like 'looking into Dante's *Inferno*'.

In 1990 we were flying into a vastly different Germany, a several-generations different Germany. Nevertheless, to someone of my generation, flying into Berlin was a strange experience. I couldn't help imagining how our wartime bomber crews must have felt as they flew over Germany, wondering if they would live to tell the tale.

Until just before our visit Berlin had been, literally, a divided city. After World War II the victorious Allies—Britain, the USA, France and Russia—divided Germany, and Berlin itself, into four sectors, each under the control of one of the Allied powers. The US, British and French sectors combined to form a democratic state, the Federal Republic of Germany or West Germany. The Soviet sector became a Communist state, the German Democratic Republic or East Germany, within which lay the tiny, divided 'island' of Berlin.

Most of the residents of East Berlin and East Germany didn't like the Communist regime. In fact most of them weren't Communists at all. Many tried to escape to the West, to friends or relatives, and some succeeded. East and West Germany were already separated by hundreds of miles of minefields, barbed wire and watchtowers— Churchill's 'Iron Curtain'. In 1961 the Communists decided they needed to build a wall across Berlin to keep the population of the Eastern sector from escaping to the West, and on 13 August they began building one. The Wall was made of steel, cement, and barbed wire fences with traps and explosives. It also had guard towers manned with machine guns and other weapons. During the twenty-eight years that the Wall was standing over five thousand people tried to escape to the West. Over a hundred died in the attempt, most of them shot by East German guards.

East Germany, however, began to reform in 1989, and by the time we got there in 1990 the Wall was but a shadow of its former self. Souvenir hunters, dubbed 'Wall woodpeckers', had started attacking it with hammers and chisels and we, being children at heart, were able to straddle it with one foot in the West and the other in the East.

We were taken around Berlin and saw the Reichstag (Parliament) building, still showing the pockmarks caused by Soviet shells and bullets as the Russians forced their way to Hitler's Bunker in 1945. We walked around the Brandenburg Gate, the symbol of Berlin, which had until recently stood in East Germany.

And as we toured we found it impossible to miss the stark contrast that still existed between East and West. There was the Kurfürstendamm, the main thoroughfare, in the West filled with department stores and brightly lit shops, cafés and restaurants. In the East there were dark streets with few people and very few cars on them, and hardly any shops at all. The studio from which we were to broadcast was in East Berlin, and scenes from wartime films used to pass through my mind as we made our daily journey to it via Checkpoint Charlie where the Russians and the Americans used to exchange their spies.

Now, of course, all that has changed. On the surface at least, the old East seems as prosperous as the West. Reunited Germany is a large country, a strong leading member of the European Union.

*   *   *

I've interviewed a few Prime Ministers in my time, but only one confessed that a lot of people hated him. Before you read on I wonder if you can guess which one.

The answer is John Major. And what was the reason for the hate? Europe. Mr Major was attempting to promote his pro-European views after a Danish referendum had come up with a 'Yes' vote in the Maastricht referendum. Perhaps I should put that in context.

You may remember that the Danes originally voted 'No' in the Maastricht referendum on whether they wished to join the EU. However, our European masters weren't best pleased with that result and so, working on the basis that if at first you don't succeed keep trying until you do, they decided they'd keep having referendums until they got the answer they wanted. The Danes, being extremely intelligent people, realised they were playing with the dice loaded against them. So, to save themselves the aggravation of referendums stretching far into the future, they took the easy way out and voted 'Yes'.

It was following that vote that Prime Minister Major came on to the programme on 19 May 1993. He spoke of the venom and vilification heaped on him since he became Prime Minister, and when I asked him the reason he replied, 'Europe.' He blamed what he described as the 'great passions' aroused by the issue of Europe and said, 'Even the Archangel Gabriel would have been the victim of criticism if he had been Prime Minister at this time.' He then hailed the Danish 'Yes' vote as ending a 'debilitating period for Denmark, the

Community and Britain' and, predictably, said that Britain should be 'at the heart of Europe, not standing on the sidelines throwing stones at all our partners'.

Writing this ten years later, I find it interesting that, despite years of peddling the concept of pro-European integration by so many leading politicians, the great British public is convinced that it is they, rather than the politicians, who have got the issue in a proper perspective and balance. Trade with mainland Europe—certainly. But 'ever closer union'? Forget it.

The British people have always been suspicious of the motives of France and Germany, the driving force behind the European Union. When Mrs Thatcher wrote her memoirs she chose two attitudes to describe the German national character: angst and aggressiveness. If you add apprehension, those three words probably best describe British feelings towards 'ever closer integration'. In 2003 France's President Jacques Chirac and the German Chancellor Gerhard Schröder spoke of their joint future at the heart of the European Union. In Chancellor Schröder's words, 'Europe cannot develop without the French–German friendship.' Those two countries dominate the new blueprint for the European Union, and their openly political vision of the future is vastly different from the Common Market and free trade agenda to which the British people thought they were being signed up.

Could it be that, as is so often the case, the ordinary man and woman in the street show greater wisdom than our leaders?

The controversial subject of the single European currency, the Euro, was in the news again in 1998. It was prompted by a poll, paid for by Brussels, which claimed that only 49 per cent of the British people were against it. This figure was so madly out of kilter with the messages we were getting from our listeners that we immediately announced a phone-in poll of our own. Within one hour we received a massive 31,000 phoned-in votes, an amazing 91 per cent saying 'No' to scrapping the pound in favour of the Euro.

At the time of writing there is a referendum due on abolishing the pound and adopting the Euro, and had I still been on Radio 2 I would have mounted completely unbiased, explanatory programmes about that issue. With the help of experts both for and against I should have explained to my 5.75 million listeners the advantages and disadvantages of keeping the pound or dropping it in favour of the Euro. Then, as I have always done, I should have left it to the listeners to decide what they wanted to do.

That is not what the government wants. The government is pro-Euro. So when the referendum comes, watch the media line. The BBC, for example, should be dispassionate. It should present you with both sides of the argument and leave you to decide. Which of course it will probably do . . .

As I write this, Britain is doing better than most countries in the Euro-zone. If we decide to keep the pound, we can certainly co-exist with the Euro by treating it as just another foreign currency.

I'm not taking sides one way or the other. All

I'm saying is beware of the propaganda. Beware of the politics. Beware of the bullshit. You have been warned.

CHAPTER THIRTY

RUSSIA REVISITED

In 1994 the BBC decided that we should return to Moscow to update our listeners on the monumental changes that had taken place since our first visit in 1977.

President Gorbachev's introduction of *glasnost* and *perestroika* had resulted in a gradual liberalisation of hard-line policies, both internal and external. In 1991 the old Soviet Union had finally disintegrated and many of its former members became independent states or joined with other regions to form independent alliances.

In 1977 we had been booked into the vast and unmanageable Rossia Hotel, an experience we would all prefer to forget. In 1994 things were very different. This time we stayed at the Radisson Slavyanskaya Hotel, described as one of the very first Western-style hotels in Moscow. And it was true that you had to go outside to remind yourself where you were. Had you been parachuted directly into the hotel, you might have thought you had landed in America. All the hotel amenities were geared to US standards of comfort. The receptionists even spoke with American accents.

Our trip took place at the same time as the Queen's first state visit to Russia, and we went to a specialised English school that had been visited by Her Majesty. It was the school at which our wonderfully helpful guide and mentor Elena Romanova had been educated, and she was able to arrange for me to interview some of the school's staff and pupils. We also spent a charming morning recording an interview, drinking coffee and talking with a young couple in their dacha just outside Moscow.

Perhaps a few words about what a dacha is would be in order. We might loosely translate the word as a country cottage, but it can mean anything, in fact, from a little cabin to a substantial house. In Soviet times trades unions obtained land for dachas and distributed it among their members. Not equally, of course. The 'workers' paradise' was never as equal as that. Ordinary party members got ordinary dachas in ordinary locations. Senior party members got very special dachas, more like luxury palaces, in beautiful locations. A dacha was often a favourite hobby—one of the most desirable parts of the lifestyle desired by most of Russia's city-dwellers. It was a place with a different pace and priorities. It was a place to rest or to work as you chose. In short, it was a dacha. If you thought that having 'a place in the country' was a peculiarly British ambition, forget it. The Russians were after it a long time ago.

We also saw signs of the dark side of Russia when I talked to members of the Salvation Army outside one of Moscow's railway stations. As I was interviewing them I was surrounded by small children, some of them as young as five. They were part of Russia's millions of homeless boys and girls. Some had fled from unhappy homes, some had

261

escaped from the harsh discipline of state-run orphanages. As the children tugged at my clothes and held out their hands to beg they almost reduced me to tears. By day many of them roamed the city, begging in subways or stealing from shops. Some of the boys and girls worked as prostitutes, risking hepatitis or HIV. At night they returned to their filthy and often violent home in the railway station. Knowing that there were too few shelters to cope with the numbers, the police made almost no effort to evict them.

Inside the station none of the children seemed to think very much about their future. One said, 'They are not killing us outright, they are killing us gradually.'

On Moscow's streets things had changed for the better since our last visit. There were no problems now with getting about. Taxis were abundant. Gone were all the clapped-out old bangers. Well, with the exception of one—and trust my intrepid team to find it.

We had finished our final broadcast and were standing on the pavement outside the studio waiting, so I thought, to hail a taxi to take us all back to our hotel. However, the team had other ideas. They wanted to go shopping. Accordingly they hatched a plan. Elena, our guide and interpreter, informed us that, under Moscow rules, you were allowed to flag down a passing car and, in effect, use it as a taxi if you could persuade the driver to take you to your destination and agree on a price.

You won't need me to spell out the plan for you. Jim was about to be given some money for the fare and dumped in some passing Russian citizen's car.

To complete the scenario a vehicle appeared in the distance. It made its uncertain and noisy way towards us surrounded by a haze of blue smoke. It was an old Lada, and the appearance of its driver was that of a low-order Russian spy in a James Bond film. He was wearing a black leather cap and a black leather trench-coat. And to me, given my increasingly apprehensive frame of mind, he looked rather sinister.

Elena flagged him down. He stopped and wound down his window. Rapid exchanges in Russian ensued. Then Elena turned to me and said, 'I've agreed a price for this gentleman to take you to your hotel, so if you'll just hop in we'll see you there later.'

I still thought this wasn't a very good idea. But what could I do? I hopped into the back seat. Elena slammed the tinny door and orft we jolly well went.

Well, not very jolly as far as I was concerned—although, as I gazed through the back window, I could see the team standing on the pavement literally falling about with hysterical laughter.

The team vanished from sight, and as the car rattled along I reviewed the situation. The first thing I discovered, and this really was a bit scary, was that I could not for the life of me remember the name of our hotel. So, here was I, a non-Russian-speaking Englishman, somewhere in Russia—because we were not yet even in the centre of Moscow—in the back of a car being driven by a non-English-speaking Russian, and I didn't even know where I was going.

Fortunately, the driver remembered Elena's instructions and we duly arrived at the Radisson

Hotel. However, my troubles were not over. I handed the driver the money which Elena had given me to cover the fare, only to have it thrown back at me. Accompanied by ugly stares and a lot of what I assumed to be not very complimentary Russian language. When I attempted to get out of the taxi to ask the hotel porter to sort things out, the driver refused to unlock the door. Seeing my predicament, the porter put his head through the taxi window and spoke to the driver.

'The driver wants three times as much as you gave him,' was the message.

I explained that Elena had negotiated a fee, but that cut no ice at all. I was being held hostage in a Russian taxi and, unless I paid the exorbitant ransom money, I wasn't going to get out. The trouble was that on foreign trips I, rather like the Queen, wasn't normally allowed to handle money. Our money supply was controlled by my producer, John Gurnett, who had a long-established reputation as a frugal man. On his instructions Elena had given me the number of roubles she considered sufficient to pay for the taxi, and that was it. I hadn't got any more with which to pay him even if I had wanted to.

We were in what I believe is known as a Mexican stand-off. The driver wouldn't let me out of his cab without the extra money, and I hadn't got enough on me to persuade him to let me out. In the event, and somewhat embarrassingly, the hotel porter rescued me.

'Leave it to me, sir,' he said in perfect English.

He went into the hotel foyer where he conferred with a colleague, then returned holding an enormous wad of rouble notes. He spoke with some force to the taxi driver, no doubt knocking him down from his robber baron 'foreigner' tariff to a more reasonable Russian tariff. Finally he peeled off sufficient notes to settle the bill before stuffing the rest of the huge wad back into his pocket.

'Pay me back when you're able to, sir,' he said nonchalantly.

Talk about the rise of Russian capitalism.

CHAPTER THIRTY-ONE

POLITICAL LIFE AFTER THATCHER

Although I interviewed a powerful Tory woman, Margaret Thatcher, on several occasions both before and after she came to power, I seldom had the privilege of interviewing another front-bench politician, Margaret Beckett. However, that pleasure was to come my way in 1993. What was at issue was her position as deputy leader of the Labour Party, for which post John Prescott was being touted as a serious contender.

Brushing aside allegations that she was 'sullen and petulant', she added, 'I think that John Prescott would make a superb deputy leader but— and I realise it is a difficult thing for anyone to say—I am afraid I do think that I would be the better one.' For his part John Prescott said, 'I see Mrs Beckett working and she gets on with the job. Frankly I am fully supporting her.'

As we all know, it was John Prescott who ended up as deputy leader of the Labour Party. Talk about the greasy pole.

*   *   *

On 22 July 1994, his first day as leader of the Labour Party after the death of John Smith, Tony Blair came on to my programme to lay down a few guidelines. I asked him if, under his leadership, Labour's traditional relationship with the trades unions would change. He made it clear that it would. And if he became Prime Minister, would the unions have easy access to Labour ministers and a strong influence on policy? Any union leader hoping for a return to the 1970s' days of beer and sandwiches at No. 10 would have been disappointed by Mr Blair's reply: 'Trades unions are an important part of our democracy and they will be listened to, but I shall never bend the knee to unions on policy. They will have no special or privileged place within the Labour Party. Fairness, not favours, is the way we are going to run things in future.'

On the matter of whether he would raise income tax, even when I pressed him hard he was quite definitely not going to give anything away to me. 'I am not prepared,' he said, 'to write the tax policies of the next Labour government on your programme.' However, he did deny that a future Labour administration under his leadership would return to the 83 pence in the pound—and with the surcharge 98 pence in the pound—penal income tax policies of previous Labour governments. But under further strong pressure from me he admitted that anyone earning more than £64,000 a year might well face tax rises. There were rumours that

Labour was secretly considering plans for a 60 per cent 'supertax' on annual incomes over £100,000. But Tony Blair, keen to get his party back into power for the first time in nearly two decades, was already setting out his stall as a reasonable man for whom the Tories of middle England could safely vote. So they remained just rumours.

*   *   *

In 1996, with a General Election in the offing and Labour all geared up to win, the Conservative Party was going through another of its now frequent episodes of turmoil, squabbling and virtual civil war. A newspaper article under the by-line 'Cassandra', written by someone who claimed to be a 'senior Conservative', was viciously critical of John Major, Mrs Thatcher's successor in Downing Street. Specifically it said, 'More and more Tory MPs are waking up to the fact that John Major is terminally inadequate at defending Britain's interests and leading our party.'

In replying on my programme, the Chancellor of the Exchequer, Kenneth Clarke, really laid about 'Cassandra'. His initial reaction was, 'I have never heard a more preposterous remark in my time', before launching into a savage attack on Conservative back-benchers. He dismissed 'Cassandra' as 'probably one of those MPs who have made it so difficult for John Major to lead our party'.

Then, going a shade too far—as people have been known to do in the relaxed atmosphere of my studio—he came close to painting some sections of the Tory Party as being ungovernable. He said,

'You can lead a party. John Major can lead a party. But there are sometimes parties that are simply not capable of being led.' It sounded to me like a propaganda gift to Labour.

John Prescott certainly thought so. His immediate reply was, 'Once again Kenneth Clarke has let the truth slip. People know a party that is incapable of being led is a party that is incapable of governing.' In 1997 the opportunity to do so was removed by the electorate and handed to Labour.

*   *   *

Often described as a 'maverick', although not by my listeners, Frank Field is Labour MP for Birkenhead. Quietly spoken and always polite, Frank nevertheless has a devastating turn of phrase when required. A former director of the Child Poverty Action Group, and of the Low Pay Unit, he has been at various times Labour's spokesman on Health, Education and Social Security. In fact on the subject of social security, and perhaps in particular pensions, Frank had very definite, firmly held and constructive views. What's more, he was always outspoken about them on my programme in ways which were welcomed by many of my listeners but which did not endear him to the Labour leadership.

I don't think this worried Frank at all. As he demonstrated when, appearing on my programme in August 1998, he attacked the government's spin doctors and called them a 'cancer within the Labour Party'. Even before the broadcast ended 'anonymous Government sources', in other words the very same spin doctors, were quickly at work on two fronts. On the one hand saying that the government was 'not engaged in a war of words with Frank', while on the other describing Frank as 'childish', 'pathetic', 'a complete disgrace' and a 'failed joke'. My listeners, even when they disagreed with him, described him as that rare breed, a 100 per cent honest MP and a man of the very highest integrity.

Someone else who always sparked enormous interest from listeners is the Rt Hon. David Blunkett, the Labour MP for Sheffield Brightside. David has certainly not allowed his blindness to hold back his career, having been Labour's front-bench spokesman on the Environment, Health, Education and Employment. As I write this, he is Labour's Home Secretary. A man of great courage and determination, he robustly defends his plans whether the opposition to them comes from outside or inside the Labour Party.

And while we're talking about honest, fair-minded politicians who tend to plough their own furrow rather than slavishly toe a party line, one of the most astonishing changes in 'personality perception' on my radio programme concerned the Rt Hon. Anthony Neil Wedgwood Benn MP. In his days as a Labour minister Tony Benn was usually depicted in Conservative-supporting newspapers as a foam-flecked, wild-eyed leader of the Loony Left. My Radio 2 programme listeners, on the other hand, were generally thought to be sane, sensible and, in most things, pretty middle-of-the-road. It seemed unlikely that the people who supported me would also support Mr Benn.

On the contrary. Every time Tony appeared on my programme we were inundated with telephone calls praising his clear-sighted and well-expressed views. He also has an excellent sense of humour and fun, which he used to great effect when confronting his fiercest critics. In short, on my programme he became something of a broadcasting icon, even among those who bitterly opposed his politics.

He then branched out into presenting *An Audience with Tony Benn* in theatres and I read that he did sell-out business everywhere. Hearing that he would be appearing at a local venue, the Richmond Theatre, I booked some seats.

When Alicia and I entered the auditorium, we saw Tony sitting on the steps leading up from the stalls to the stage chatting informally with a few members of the audience. The stage was bare except for a chair with a jacket draped over the back of it, together with a table on which stood a mug and a flask containing Tony's favourite beverage, tea. When the theatre was full and kick-off time arrived, Tony simply walked up the steps, sat down on the chair and the *Audience with* began. For forty-five minutes he talked to a quiet, rapt auditorium, then announced that we would have an interval after which he would answer questions.

His agent had said that he wanted to book me to present *An Audience with Jimmy Young*, so I was very pleased when Tony came over during the interval for a little chat. The general thrust was that he thoroughly enjoyed his theatre appearances, and thought that the sooner I started to do some myself the better. Tony, of course, started with the great advantage of many years of public speaking behind him. I suspect that although the *Audience with*

270

format seems simple it is probably much more difficult to pull off successfully than it looks. But I'm going to give it a go anyway.

*   *   *

Until he gave up his inherited title in order to remain an MP Tony Benn was Viscount Stansgate, and the only seat he would have been allowed to take was in the House of Lords. In August 1999 a Labour man from the other end of the social spectrum, John Prescott, came on my programme to throw a few left hooks into the class war.

Asked if he thought there were too many upper-middle-class toffs in the government he replied, 'There are too many upper toffs around generally, particularly in the Tory Party.' He added, 'And don't make no mistake about it, I'm proud of being working-class. I'm not changing my attitude or culturing my voice or even getting my grammar correct.'

We get the message, John, even if sometimes we don't understand it.

*   *   *

That year the Tory leadership was once again under fire. William Hague, who had stepped into John Major's shoes, appeared on my programme just as a MORI poll revealed him to be the 'least attractive of any Opposition leader since Neil Kinnock in 1988, with a dissatisfaction rating of 54%'.

I asked him how he reacted to that verdict, and when he thought people would start loving him. He didn't answer the second part of the question, and gave a very short answer to the first part. 'We don't take too much notice of MORI polls.'

Oh, so that's all right then.

Commenting on the interview, the Liberal Democrat MP Andrew Stunell said, 'The Prime Minister is more likely to be held to account by Jimmy Young than he is by the Leader of the Opposition.' Poor old William Hague. Witty and erudite, he was brilliant in parliamentary debate, where he often kicked great lumps out of Tony Blair. But he still failed to convince either the Tory Party or the country that he was the leader they wanted. As a Yorkshireman he might well muse on the old Yorkshire saying, 'There's nowt as queer as folk.'

In fact the leadership of the Tory Party was being contested yet again in August 2001, and I had the two leading contenders in my studio to put their case. You could say that Ken Clarke had an advantage because he went second. While I was interviewing Iain Duncan Smith Ken was watching through the glass, listening to what Iain was saying and preparing his counter-blasts.

Duncan Smith's approach was conciliatory. He said, 'I offer a lifeline to people like Ken who may disagree with me on the European issue.' He went on to speak of tolerance and honour.

No doubt working on the motto that 'Nice guys finish last', there was not much tolerance on offer from Ken Clarke. Often portrayed as laid back, with a pint in his hand, Ken proved that he's quite handy on the cobblestones as well when necessary. A lengthy interview boiled down to one key and, Ken must have thought, killer sentence which summed up his view of Duncan Smith: 'He's a hanger, he's a flogger, regarded in the old days as the epitome of a right-wing Tory.'

As it happens, in this case the 'nice guy' finished first. And as I write this in 2003 Iain Duncan Smith is still clinging on as leader of the Conservative Party. He has not, so far, revived hanging or flogging. But then, he hasn't exactly revived the Tory Party either.

Regularly, falsely and annoyingly accused of doing soft interviews, I had in fact been politely firing tough questions at politicians ever since 1973. However, it took an interview with Prime Minister John Major twenty-one years later, in March 1994 in his fourth year of government, to convince some sections of the press that perhaps there was more to my interviewing than met the eye. The following day the *Today* newspaper's headline read, 'PM is KO'D by JY'. *The Independent* wrote, 'After his polite savaging of John Major Young is called the "Radio 2 Rottweiler".' The *Daily Telegraph* asserted: 'During the 40-minute interview Mr Young subjected Mr Major to some of the toughest questioning he has ever faced.' While the following weekend's *Sunday Telegraph* referred to 'Young asking one deadly question after another in a friendly tone completely at odds with what he was actually saying'.

I had put it to Mr Major that he was widely perceived as being 'a poor little grey thing who lacks oomph and is grey and boring, weak and indecisive'. As you might expect, that brought a robust denial: 'If that were true,' retorted Mr Major, 'I doubt that I would have survived the last three and a half years.'

However, the question which provoked one of Mr Major's aides to mutter, as the party left the studio, 'He won't be coming back here again', came later. I had suggested to the Prime Minister that, while strong leaders like Mrs Thatcher could survive hatred and vitriol, 'once people begin to make fun of you and draw silly cartoons of you with your shirt tucked into your underpants it is almost impossible to regain your credibility'. Responded Mr Major, 'You don't need to shout, scream and bang the table to get across the message that you are a strong leader.' Which may be true. But cartoons often convey strong messages and ridicule is a powerful weapon.

The following day's *Times* carried an interesting review of the interview:

In 45 minutes yesterday Jimmy Young managed to tease more out of John Major than the country's leading political editors did in three days during the Prime Minister's recent trip to America . . . . The secret of Young's success is his painstaking research which involves digging out every press cutting on his chosen subject and committing them to memory. He also has the advantage that he has neither the need nor the inclination to court politicians.

I got a similar write-up after my programme on 10 April 1997, when I was pressing Tony Blair very hard over Labour's muddle and confusion about the future, and possible privatisation, of the air traffic control system. Specifically, I repeatedly asked him which member of Labour's Transport team had ruled out privatisation. Eventually he gave me a clear answer: 'I'm not sure. I simply don't know.'

You don't often get a senior politician to admit that, I can tell you.

It was once again the *Times* which carried an interesting review. Peter Barnard wrote, 'In his recent interview with Tony Blair Young shunned the obtuse cleverness that most political journalists tend to go for. Instead his first question had the blunt common touch that characterises his technique, "If the Tories have been such a disaster, why are you adopting so many of their policies?"' Peter went on, 'He pursued the line with a relentlessness that clearly discomfited Mr Blair, and I know of three political writers who regarded the Young interview as one of the best of the campaign.' And as a final thought he added, 'Young is undoubtedly the best argument against ageism in radio, and it is fervently to be hoped that in attempting to lower the age profile of the Radio Two audience the Controller, James Moir, leaves him alone.'

Peter's argument appeared irrefutable to my listeners, but was ignored by my Radio 2 bosses.

Rarely have I been as furious as I was over a BBC statement in 2002 that revealed an extraordinary lack of knowledge of the history of the *JY Programme*. A senior BBC spokesperson said that it was necessary to replace it with a 'harder edged' programme in order to generate more headline newspaper coverage. Had he, or she, bothered to look through the press cutting files they would have discovered that, over the years, the *JY Prog* has consistently generated more 'headline press coverage' than just about any other current affairs programme on either radio or television.

CHAPTER THIRTY-TWO

FORKED TONGUES

It was quite by accident that I discovered that for two years, behind my back and despite my continuing success, my job had, allegedly, been offered to other presenters. Nicky Campbell, one of those who had allegedly been approached, admitted it later in a newspaper interview. On 1 November 2001 the *Daily Telegraph* carried an article in which Campbell, describing the BBC as a ruthless organisation, claimed he had been courted by senior Radio 2 bosses who offered him my job. He said that Jim Moir and his deputy, Lesley Douglas, had, over a period of eighteen months, had talks with him at his home and 'over champagne in out of the way hotels and restaurants'. All of which may sound a bit sneaky. But then you can't be too careful if you're doing sneaky things, can you?

Mr Campbell quoted Mr Moir as saying, 'You are the anointed one. You are the one who can interview Gordon Brown and play "Golden Brown".' That's odd. That's exactly what I'd been doing with such enormous success that I'd raised the programme's listening figure to 5.75 million.

Sounding like a practical guy, Campbell expressed sympathy that I had not been told what was going on and then added, 'But the BBC is like that. They're dumping on Jimmy Young now but I shall be the one being dumped on in five years' time.' Of Campbell's allegations the *Guardian* said, 'It puts Mr Moir, a respected figure, in an awkward position.'

You can say that again.

Dubious practices in general are par for the course in broadcasting. But you have to be particularly tough and resilient to sit at your table at the Controller's Christmas knees-up, listening to your leader eulogising you, when in the same week you are reading that he, or she, is running around behind your back selling you right down the Swanee.

I continued to get support from the most unexpected sources. In 1998, when the Beeb was apparently having one of its 'never mind what the listeners want we've got to get rid of Jimmy Young' frenzies, I was working at home one morning when my telephone rang. The caller introduced himself as the producer of *The Big Breakfast*, and asked me if I was watching television. When I replied that I wasn't, he asked me to switch on Channel 4.

Johnny Vaughan was interviewing a sixteen-year-old young lady named Louise Thomson from Kingston, who had originally written a letter to the *Daily Mail* protesting about the BBC's campaign to get rid of me. She was repeating the message to Johnny Vaughan and telling the BBC in no uncertain terms what she thought of them. Quite explicitly, and speaking on behalf of all her teenage mates, she said that she, and they, were publicly warning the BBC to get their hands off me. She added that her friends thought her protest was really groovy.

During the interview with Johnny, Louise had to answer a question about my number one hit records in the 1950s in order to win a prize. That presented no problem at all. She then had to choose between pop concert tickets to see the band E17 and visit them backstage, or having tea with me. She chose tea with me.

Extremely flattered, in due course I met Louise and her mother on the top floor of a hotel with a panoramic view of Broadcasting House and London beyond. Our meeting was very enjoyable. It was also very interesting, because Louise substantiated personally what she had said on television. Not only were she and her school friends great fans who listened to my programme whenever they could, but she confirmed that I appeared to have a very large audience among younger listeners. This was something that the BBC was apparently never able to accept.

I was, and still am, very grateful to Louise and her young friends who fought so hard for me, but of course they were never likely to succeed.

*   *   *

The BBC's paranoia over so-called 'more rigorous', as opposed to what it perceives as less rigorous, programmes surfaced again that year, 1998. Someone named Richard Clemmo, the BBC's head of News Programmes, accused the government of dodging serious programmes like *Newsnight* and *World at One* and instead putting ministers on mass audience shows where they would face softer questions. Fortunately the Prime Minister's press secretary, Alastair Campbell, was on hand to give Mr Clemmo the kicking he so richly deserved.

Said Alastair, '*Newsnight* is on late with a dwindling audience. And very few people in politics or the media take the *World at One* seriously, so regular appearances by ministers are unlikely . . . Also,' he added, 'anyone who suggests that Jimmy Young is a soft interviewer knows nothing about interviewing, and even less about Jimmy Young.'

Well said, Alastair. But don't expect the BBC's elite trying to defend their 'serious' programmes with tiny audiences to admit it.

Fortunately I have, to a large extent, been my own master since 1973 and one of my basic broadcasting principles is, 'What on earth is the point of broadcasting if nobody's listening to you?' Putting bums on seats to listen to, and take part in, important and interesting discussions is the name of my game.

US television is much derided by elitists in this country, yet an interesting comparison can be made between *Panorama* and the American *60 Minutes* programme. The *60 Minutes* format is usually to deal with three issues per programme, and its editors travel extensively to cover their stories. *60 Minutes* is transmitted from 7pm to 8pm on Sundays—hardly prime time. Yet it has remained in the top ratings since it first appeared in September 1968. I've even seen it at number one. When did you last see *Panorama* in the Top Ten ratings?

And what does that say about British and American audiences? Are Americans more intelligent than us, or is it that broadcasters there are better at doing what I used to do on Radio 2—

make current affairs so interesting that lots of people want to listen to and watch it?

Incidentally, for a country usually thought of as youth-oriented, America's *60 Minutes* makes an interesting point for the seemingly age-obsessed BBC which allegedly replaced me because I was considered unlikely to attract the younger listener. There are four prime movers on *60 Minutes*. Morley Safer, who has been Co-Editor since 1970, is seventy-three at the time of writing. Don Hewitt, Executive Producer and creator of the programme, is now eighty-one. Andy Rooney, a correspondent with the programme for twenty-five years, is eighty-four. And Mike Wallace, Executive Editor since the programme's inception, is eighty-five. As I write this in January 2003 none of the four shows any sign of voluntarily retiring. Indeed Don Hewitt has just accepted a ten-year contract as a 'troubleshooter', on the expiry of which he will be ninety-one.

* * *

I interviewed the Prime Minister again on 24 January 2002, after my forthcoming departure had become public knowledge. As always the interview was wide-ranging, and as always Mr Blair was evasive. But he must have been even more so than usual because I finished the interview by saying, 'What you've done, in your incomparably charming way, is to say, "I'll answer your questions but then decline to answer them." But then, you didn't get to where you are today by answering questions, did you?' Predictably, it became the top Quote of the Week.

Actually, honesty is often the best policy, and ducking, diving and being evasive and clever in interviews can sometimes be counter-productive. As Michael Vestey wrote in the *Spectator*, 'More of the true nature of Blair emerged in the Young interview than I've heard elsewhere. The almost manic spinning, the casual untruths, the false modesty, the actorish style of the man.'

Following the interview I received an immediate and warmly congratulatory telephone call from my Controller, Jim Moir, followed by an equally congratulatory email from him saying that I had been at my most rumbustious. At the same time Jim informed me that my latest listening figures were remarkable. Absolutely wonderful.

Jim, you will remember, had already been accused of chatting up my potential replacement. The words 'forked tongue' come to mind.

Michael Vestey concluded his *Spectator* article by writing, 'I can only think that, for the Radio 2 Controller, Young's departure became a matter of managerial pride. Decisions are rarely reversed even when they are demonstrably wrong and silly. It happens quite often at the BBC.' After such newspaper headlines as 'Jimmy Young's searching interview with the Prime Minister' and 'Sir Jimmy pulled no punches with Teflon Tony' one commentator wrote, 'Maybe the BBC is right to move Sir Jimmy Young from the *Jimmy Young Programme*. Clearly, after his performance, he would make a better job of presenting *Newsnight* than Jeremy Paxman, who is a teddy bear by comparison.'

CHAPTER THIRTY-THREE

SHAFTED

On 1 September 2001 I was getting ready to leave home for Heathrow airport en route to a short break in Jersey when my PR consultant, Shimon Cohen, telephoned me. He said he had received a call from a Sunday newspaper saying that they were going to run a story to the effect that I was about to retire. Shimon said, 'I think it's about time you killed these rumours.'

We agreed the wording of a statement that I had no intention of retiring, although it could be that someone, in pursuit of an ageist policy, might decide to fire me. Alicia and I then left for Jersey.

The following day the *Sunday Express* ran a large feature story, which was picked up by most other newspapers. Then everything hit the fan. No doubt to the dismay of the BBC, young people mounted a 'Save JY Campaign' on the BBC's own website. Its message was reinforced by mail, faxes, emails and phone calls from listeners demanding that the BBC keep me on, and Liberal Democrat MP Nick Harvey tabled a motion in the House of Commons, signed by more than eighty MPs, calling on the BBC not to fire me.

A deeply embarrassed BBC put up a spokeswoman who denied that the BBC intended to sack me. 'There is a big difference between sacking someone and not renewing their contract,' she said. Have you ever heard such weasel words? The end result is exactly the same, dear.

I have already mentioned Nicky Campbell's interview in the *Daily Telegraph* in November 2001. It was against this background that Alicia and I set off for a prearranged holiday in Florida. A holiday from which we were to return absolutely knackered because of the phone calls, faxes and emails which flew in both directions across the Atlantic several times a day.

Suffice to say that, when we went to Florida, the BBC was resolved to replace me at the end of April 2002. Thanks to tireless work by my lawyer and PR consultant, plus sleepless nights and shredded nerves for Alicia and myself, by the end of the holiday my execution was postponed first from April to October and then, after a lot of arguments, from April to December.

However, the price for that concession was that I should agree to present a weekend programme instead. I was also instructed by the BBC that I must announce in a 'positive manner' my move from my five-days-a-week flagship programme with a superb back-up team to a once-a-week weekend programme without them. I must not refer to being 'gutted' or 'disappointed', or use any similar terms. I must not say anything about the change being forced upon me that could be construed as being negative for the BBC image. In other words, I was being ruthlessly shafted by the BBC but I had to pretend I was enjoying it.

On 17 January 2002 the first stories began to appear to the effect that I was leaving the *Jimmy Young Programme*. Most referred to me 'stepping down'. The *Daily Mirror* went further: 'Yesterday, Jimmy Young announced his retirement from Radio Two.' Since all this suited the BBC rather

283

well, it didn't exactly go out of its way to correct the impression that I was leaving voluntarily.

Fortunately, the *Sun* newspaper was rather more accurate. I quote: 'The BBC had a black day yesterday. Sir Jimmy Young, that great Radio Two veteran who the nation adores, has finally been forced out. Young was loved by the people and hated by the BBC's biased bosses. That says it all. Young is a very special man, and a national treasure because he dared to bring the views of middle England on to the BBC.'

I decided against doing the sop weekend programme for two very good reasons. First, because I would not have my wonderful team with me—they would be working five days a week with my replacement. And, second, since it had previously taken me five days a week to cover current events fully I certainly wouldn't be able to do myself or my listeners justice by allowing the BBC to truncate five days to one. Rather than allow the BBC to shunt me up a siding and probably get rid of me after a year I decided that letting them do that while I was still clearly at the top was the better idea.

CHAPTER THIRTY-FOUR

SIR JIMMY

Fortunately, January 2002 also brought a piece of better news. I had been awarded a knighthood. I received the most wonderfully warm, sincere congratulations from my friends and colleagues, from the Great and the Good and, it seemed, from most of my millions of listeners.

I also received congratulations from Jim Moir and his boss Jenny Abramsky. Mr Moir told me that they knew this was a big news story but had no idea it would be as enormous as this. He added that there had been an enormous outpouring of warmth such as had seldom been seen. I replied that if he and others at the top of the BBC had only acknowledged the strength of my programme and the affection in which it was held we wouldn't be in the embarrassing position in which we now found ourselves. However, I knew that once a corporate decision had been taken, it would not be reversed.

*   *   *

When I was invested with the OBE, and again with the CBE, I was allowed to take only two guests, but for the knighthood investiture that number was increased to three. Thus I was able to take not only Alicia and my daughter from my first marriage, Lesley, but also my cousin Ann. Ann came up from Gloucestershire with her husband John, but John had to be content with going to the Zoo to study the gorillas while we went to the Palace.

The next question was—how to get there. On the two previous occasions I had driven myself and I was keen to do so this time. However, this raised the delicate question of the condition of my car. It was getting on a bit in years at the time of the two previous visits, but by now it was a venerable eighteen years old. And looking it. So—what to do?

I've enjoyed a long association with BMW, so I

decided I would ask for their help. They said they would be delighted and, bearing in mind that the three ladies would be wearing hats, thought a BMW X5 would be needed for the occasion. Thus, on 27 June, we set off for the Palace in some style. I was driving £40,000 worth of motor car and feeling rather like Lord Muck.

We duly rolled up at the gates of Buckingham Palace, and that's where embarrassment set in. At the gates I was stopped by the policeman on duty, and rolled down the window so we could speak.

'Good morning, Jim,' he said. 'That's a lovely motor you've got there. Could you just open the bonnet and boot for me, please, so we can do a security check?'

A simple enough request, you might think. Certainly simple if you know where the levers are to open them. Not so simple if you don't. After some lengthy, and unsuccessful, fumbling on my part the policeman solved the problem by opening the car door and doing it himself. Meanwhile his colleague had passed a mirror under the car and, once they were satisfied that we constituted no danger, we were allowed through the gates.

I then drove across the courtyard, through the archway and out into the large open area behind the Palace. This serves as a car park when you arrive, and is where the interviews, press photographs and personal photographs are taken after the ceremony is over. Having parked, you approach the rear entrance of the Palace, and that is where the separations begin.

First you are separated into two groups, 'recipients' and guests. Once the recipients have entered the Palace they are separated again into

MBEs, OBEs, CBEs and so on, and kept in little groups where they chat away while waiting to be called. But for me, today was slightly different from my two previous visits to the Palace. Those about to be honoured with a knighthood were shown into a special room where we were briefed.

The Comptroller of the Lord Chamberlain's office, an extremely tall gentleman in full ceremonial dress, lined us up in military fashion. He then addressed us rather in the manner of a sergeant major trying to drill some sense into a bunch of particularly thick recruits. A stool was placed in position, and he explained and demonstrated what we were required to do: 'Due to the absence of HM The Queen your Investiture is being carried out by HRH The Prince of Wales. When your name is called walk forward until you are level with the Prince. Turn to face him. Bow. From the neck only—*not* the whole body. Move to the stool and kneel. The Prince will tap you lightly on both shoulders with his sword. He will not say anything.' So much for the tradition of 'Arise, Sir Jimmy.' 'The Prince will place a ribbon over your head. As he does this you should bow your head slightly so he can place the ribbon over your head more easily. Except for Sir Jimmy—he won't need to bow.' Laughter all round because I am short. 'Get up from the stool and the Prince will speak to you. When he has finished he will shake your hand. Take four paces back, bow, right turn and walk off.' The Comptroller then took me on one side and explained that I would have to be announced as 'Leslie Ronald Young' because that was my legal name, even though I was being honoured for my services to broadcasting as Jimmy Young.

287

My moment arrived. Leslie Ronald Young was announced and I commenced my walk towards Prince Charles. HRH was exchanging notes with his aide and taking up the sword with which to dub me. Thus I was almost level with him before he looked up and did a rather startled double-take as he realised that Leslie Ronald Young was actually the Jimmy Young who had interviewed him at Sandringham.

After I had knelt, been dubbed and arisen the Prince exchanged a few words with me. He asked me whether I intended to continue with my programme and for how long. Since I already knew of the BBC's intention to replace me at the end of the year I was able to answer him with absolute accuracy. Actually, my overwhelming feeling was of great relief that so far I had managed to execute the required stepping and kneeling without falling over.

As I exited, waiting in the wings was a royal aide. He removed the insignia from me, smoothly and skilfully folded the ribbon, slipped the ribbon and the insignia into a ceremonial box and handed it back to me.

When you are honoured with a knighthood you are entitled to use the prefix 'Sir' from the time of the official announcement. However, for me, it took the actual ritual of the visit to the Palace and the dubbing to feel that the process was complete. The next worry, of course, is how your friends are going to react to this. The next time they phone is it going to be, 'Hello, Sir Jimmy,' or 'Hello, Lady Young'? Because that would be terrible. I remember that, when a friend of ours was honoured with a peerage, I called him at home to congratulate him. He answered the phone, I said, 'Hello, Lord ——', and he went absolutely potty. But I know now how he felt.

While you're delighted with the honour, you really do wonder whether it will in some way affect the way your friends approach you. Although, I suppose, that may be more the case with an elevation to the peerage than with a knighthood. I'm happy to say that nothing has changed in that respect—and I think it's unlikely we shall have to worry about me being elevated to the peerage.

Incidentally—and I don't know whether this was BMW's intention—there was a consequence to the visit to Buckingham Palace. Having driven a brand-new BMW there I came to the conclusion that my eighteen-year-old vehicle really would have to go. So I suppose you could say that the knighthood actually dented my bank balance to the extent of a new 2.5 litre BMW.

Even if it did, it was well worth it.

CHAPTER THIRTY-FIVE

MRS YOUNG AND THE HIP SAGA

The last week of June turned out to be a rather special time for the Young family. Having celebrated our visit to the Palace on the 27th we were about to celebrate Alicia's fiftieth birthday on the 29th. Her birthday had actually been in March, but we were in Florida at that time, so this year she managed to have two birthdays.

I have to confess to a blind spot here. I'm not

really a party animal, as I've said earlier, and I have never been one for celebrating birthdays. And before you cry, 'At your age, I'm not surprised', I mean I have *never* been one for celebrating birthdays. I can understand celebrating winning the lottery (filthy lucre), or getting promoted to office manager (one in the eye for your rivals), or winning the 100-metre dash at the Olympics (ditto). But why celebrate your birthday? After all, you had nothing to do with it. It's no great achievement on your part. You weren't present at the conception. You are simply the result of a gleam in someone else's eye. You are the end product of a lustful itch in someone's loins. What's to celebrate about that?

Anyway, different strokes for different folks. So, on Saturday, 29 June 2002 we assembled to celebrate Alicia's fiftieth for a second time. She had booked a room in the Petersham Hotel at Richmond for the purpose and, as she usually does, made a superb choice. Tony Blair based his election campaign on education, education, education. Estate agents base their business on location, location, location. Believe me, the Petersham Hotel succeeds magnificently in terms of location.

Situated high on a hill, it overlooks a river scene of outstanding beauty. The Thames, shimmering in the sunlight far below as it curves its way through lush green meadows, was captured wonderfully on canvas by many famous painters. By Sir Joshua Reynolds in 1772, by J. M. W. Turner in 1819 and by an American, Jasper Francis Cropsey, who called his painting *Richmond Hill in the Summer of 1862*. That was the scene on which we looked down as we drank Alicia's health. As birthday bashes go, it was certainly a good one.

* * *

March 1996 had seen another momentous occasion in our personal lives, although celebrated in a much more low-key fashion. Having been married twice and divorced twice, I had come to the conclusion that marriage and I were simply incompatible and I should never attempt it again. What is more, Alicia and I had lived together perfectly happily for the past quarter of a century. As the old and much-quoted saying goes, 'If it ain't broke, don't fix it.' However, it was as though someone somewhere had decided that living together simply wasn't good enough. And so it was that, despite my knowledge that a second—never mind a third—marriage is a triumph of hope over experience, I proposed.

The circumstances were bizarre rather than romantic. For many years I had been suffering a great deal of pain in my right hip. However, because of the insecurity associated with my job I had done nothing about it. My desperate attempts to put off having an operation led me to take anti-inflammatory drugs, but I had to stop when they caused serious internal bleeding. When eventually things reached such a state that I could, literally, hardly put one foot in front of the other I agreed to be admitted to hospital. There they discovered that, because of my years of delay, my right leg was now two inches shorter than my left leg. Which didn't exactly delight the surgeon who was about to perform the operation. All that my years of procrastination had achieved was to make his job much more difficult and my chances of having a future free of hip problems less likely.

So it was in the context of an imminent hip replacement operation that I said to Alicia, 'There's always a risk when you have a general anaesthetic. If anything should happen, do you want to be left as Miss Plastow or Mrs Young?'

She replied, 'Mrs Young, thank you very much.'

We were married in our beautiful Florida apartment overlooking the Atlantic Ocean on 11 March 1996. To say it was a quiet wedding would be an understatement. Apart from Alicia and myself, the only other people present were the notary who conducted the ceremony and the photographer we'd hired to take the pictures. He also performed the vital role of witness.

After the ceremony we went downstairs and posed on the beach for photographs. March in Florida can mean beautiful, balmy weather, and 10 and 12 March were exactly like that. But Murphy's law was at work on the 11th. The skies were overcast, rain threatened and—by Florida standards—it was really cold. Not too bad for me, since I was wearing a formal suit and collar and tie. But Alicia, wearing just a thin outfit which would be ideal for a normal Florida spring day, was freezing. Rather ungallantly I noted that, in the colour photos, the tip of her nose glowed a delicate shade of pink.

We are all familiar with the stories of couples who have lived together very happily for many years. They then decide to get married, and in practically no time at all end up getting divorced. I was desperately worried lest the same thing should happen to us. And as the big day approached I wondered what my feelings would be as I stood there during the ceremony, and after it when the full significance of what I'd just done would hit me. In the event my fears simply didn't materialise. I was very glad that Miss Plastow was now Mrs Young and, I knew, so was she.

Two months later I was in hospital for surgery, as arranged. However, even operations can have their funny side. The following day Alicia, worried and anxious, came to visit. She took one look at me, fainted and collapsed in a heap on the floor. She ended up in the bed next to me in the high dependency unit.

*　　　*　　　*

If the first half of 2002, culminating in the visit to the Palace to be dubbed Sir Jimmy, had gone quite well, 3 July was the beginning of my (semi) *Annus Horribilis*. Six years earlier the surgery on my right hip had been a great success and I had had no problems since that time. However, on that day I woke with a pain in it. But I thought it might be due to no more than having slept in an awkward position, so I assumed the problem would go away once I was up and walking.

Not only did it not go away, it gradually began to get worse. In fact by the time I left home it was really painful. With some difficulty I drove to work. I then had to get to the BBC Concert Hall to have my photograph taken for *Radio Times*. I just about managed that. The next hurdle was getting myself to the studio to do my normal midday broadcast. I never made it to the studio.

I had got almost as far as the studio door when I

293

had to accept that I just wasn't going to make it, and collapsed on to a sofa in an annexe. By this time I was also running a very high temperature. I called Alicia to get her to collect me and take me home.

Radio 2's Controller, Jim Moir, happened to pass on his way to see someone else and I called him over. We rang for a BBC nurse to come over and inspect the damage. She brought with her an oxygen tank, and when she had taken a look at me she suggested an X-ray and arranged for me to go immediately to Medical Express in Harley Street. By this time the situation was deteriorating rapidly and walking had become impossible. However, having been lifted into a wheelchair and then into a car I managed to get to Harley Street for the X-ray, followed by a consultation with an orthopaedic surgeon.

After looking at the X-ray, the surgeon announced that I needed further surgery. 'Get yourself back to the man who did the hip replacement operation as soon as you possibly can,' he advised.

I telephoned the hospital where I'd had the original operation and, unaware of the seriousness of my condition at that stage, was told that the earliest they could admit me was in five days' time—the following Monday. However, as the day progressed so did the pain. I could alleviate it slightly by lying flat on my back, but even those periods of relief rapidly began to get shorter. Alicia and I knew there was no way I was going to get through to Monday, so she called the hospital and explained the situation. They arranged for me to be admitted as an emergency the following day.

After a sleepless night we arrived at the hospital at 9.30 on the morning of 4 July. With a very high temperature and in a great deal of pain, I was described as 'very poorly'. The surgeon wanted to get me into the operating theatre as soon as possible, but that could not be before 6pm. In the event I was taken to theatre at 5.40pm and the operation took until 9pm.

It was only afterwards that the surgeon told me, 'We hadn't realised how desperately ill you were until we got you into the theatre. When we opened up your hip the cavity was full of the most terrible infection, including acute septicaemia. To be honest, had the hospital not admitted you until Monday it would have been touch and go as to whether you would have survived.'

It seems that the normal procedure would have been to remove the old hip replacement, thoroughly clean out the cavity to get rid of any bugs, then wait for three to six months before fitting another replacement. In my case it was all done in one go, and I was very grateful for that. However having undergone, in effect, two operations in one resulted in quite a lot of pain, and I was given very strong painkillers to cope with it.

Unfortunately the downside of the ultra-strong painkillers was that they made me hallucinate. Alicia, who was with me the whole time, reported me as being 'very confused and not speaking any sense at all'. Apparently I was convinced I was in South Africa. At one stage I thought I was at a cricket match where I reported the score as being 82 for 1. I then switched to tennis, where I was very critical of the way the ball boys were performing.

After that I found myself present at a court case, of which even Alicia could make neither head nor tail. I then demanded a hot cup of tea in thirty minutes. And I rounded off by saying to Alicia, 'She wouldn't be a hooker, would she, you silly tart.'

By this time I had also lost 16 pounds in weight which, from a starting weight of only 143 pounds, was not exactly good news. What was even worse was that I had completely lost my will to eat. Just the mention of food made me feel sick and the worry was that I would simply continue to fade away. The instruction from the medical staff was, 'You must force yourself to eat.' I don't know if any of you have ever been in that position, and if you haven't I hope you never will be. The fact is that it's almost impossible to do. However much you realise that it's what you should be doing, in an extreme situation such as mine even the mere sight of a piece of bread and butter makes you want to be sick.

The fact is that I was on such a high dosage of antibiotics, both by mouth and intravenously—at one stage I was on four times the normal dosage of one particularly strong one—that they were making me feel nauseous. Thank God for my very wise doctors who were able to balance my medication. They gave me sufficient drugs to keep the bugs at bay while taking me off some of the more extreme ones, which enabled me to regain at least a little of my appetite. Initially I was only able to cope with a few Rice Krispies and we had to make gradual, although very slow, progress from there.

Having been admitted to hospital on 4 July I was still there on the 22nd, but at least everyone now seemed to be looking at me getting out very soon. I had been tested for just about everything under the sun—blood, kidney, liver, heart and so on—and all the results had come back negative. In fact we were all feeling positively upbeat, and speculating that I might be released from hospital the following week and back at work by mid-September. That, however, was before the arrival of the spots.

They started on my legs and spread to my arms, and were a sort of warm-up act for the rigors and high temperatures that speedily followed. A rigor is an interesting experience. If you associate the word with the stillness of rigor mortis, forget it. In a rigor your body shakes from head to toe. It's not very pleasant, and in my case it was accompanied by wildly fluctuating temperatures, sometimes subnormal, sometimes as high as 103°F.

The variations in temperature worried the doctors and they were concerned to find out what was causing them. I went through a variety of tests: X-rays on my hip and chest, ultrasound on my stomach and so on. According to the tests, everything was OK. Yet the problems with my temperature persisted. I had been fitted with something called a Hickman line to enable me to receive treatment intravenously and my surgeon wondered whether that could have become infected. It was removed and sent to the laboratory to be tested. The report came back that it was not infected.

By this time the medical experts were getting increasingly frustrated. Every sample that was sent for testing came back with an all-clear verdict, yet the infection was still raging throughout my body. They decided they would change my antibiotics, and that reduced my temperature to normal.

However, the infection was still there and we were no closer to finding its source.

By 1 August my doctors had decided that, in a further effort to establish the location of my infection, I should undergo a white cell scan. Not all hospitals are equipped to carry out that particular test, but the Cromwell Hospital in London is, and that was where I was sent. The test results contained—as they so often do—good news and bad news. The good news was that the tests had revealed that the infection was located around the femur. The bad news was that it seemed to be located in the bone, where infections are particularly difficult to treat.

However, by 19 August I had improved so much that I was discharged from hospital. Free at last!

But not for long. My freedom lasted just two days. At 9.45pm on the 21st, having been sitting upright on a high chair, as instructed, I got up to get ready for bed. The immediate result was excruciating pain—my right leg was two inches shorter than my left and it was turning blue. Any attempt at movement produced agony. I had dislocated.

By this time we were on such close terms with the hospital that when Alicia telephoned them they agreed to admit me as an emergency immediately. We arrived there at 1.30am on the 22nd. Some weary nurses were already waiting in the operating theatre and we were joined there thirty minutes later by my long-suffering surgeon. By 2.30am it was all over, and I was discharged from hospital a week later, on the 29th.

My joy at being dislocation-free was to last just one day short of a month. On 28 September at

11.30am out it popped again. Back into hospital I went, where the surgeon had to open up the hip again in order to put things right. It took me until 4 October to get out of bed and on to a walking frame, and another three days before I was finally discharged.

I would like to record my thanks to the surgeons, doctors and nursing staff, not only for their high levels of skill and efficiency but also for their unflagging good humour. Even though they must have been frustrated beyond belief by the setbacks which transformed a simple surgical procedure into a seemingly endless saga, they never showed it. They jollied me along through all the reverses and, difficult though it must have been, somehow managed to keep up a cheerful appearance.

By now I had been absent from my programme for three months and had not yet even progressed to walking with two sticks. I had also had four operations requiring general anaesthetics in that time, and it seemed unlikely that I would be able to get back to the *JY Prog* before the end of November. At one stage I despaired of getting back before the end of my BBC contract on 20 December, but my close friends and advisers urged me to do so for at least a couple of weeks if possible because rumours were being fed to the press that I was no longer capable of doing the programme. My friends knew I had to demolish these allegations in public.

My surgeon had already told me that it would take twelve to eighteen months to recover from all the anaesthetics, but I was determined to return to work. Indeed, having been told of the rumours I knew there would be no future career for me if I didn't.

By the beginning of December I had put back on 8 of the 16 pounds I had lost, and I decided the time was right to get back in harness. Having been off for five months I found the studio controls felt decidedly strange, but I haven't been called 'shit hot on the buttons' for nothing. And I most certainly wasn't going to fall over the furniture on this occasion.

CHAPTER THIRTY-SIX

LOOKING BACK, LOOKING FORWARD

On 9 December 'orft we jolly well went'—at full throttle plus an adrenaline-boosted supercharger. In flooded the emails and telephone calls welcoming me back and saying that I sounded as though I'd never been away. 'You're on top form, Jim' was the verdict, and I was delighted to see it confirmed in the press. I knew that none of it would stop the BBC axing my programme, but at least I had demonstrated publicly and emphatically that I was up to the job.

The day after I returned to work Jim Moir came to my studio to tell me how wonderful I was sounding, begging the obvious question: 'So why are you getting rid of me?' On my last day, the 20th, Jim visited briefly, and his boss Jenny Abramsky brought champagne and flowers. It was a sad day but I reminded myself that, as Michael Vestey had written in the *Spectator*, once they are taken, corporate decisions, however stupid, are never reversed.

The following day the results of an interesting poll appeared in the influential *Manchester Evening News*. The question the paper had asked was whether the BBC had been right to let me go. The answer its readers provided could not have been clearer. 'Yes,' said 7 per cent; 'No,' said the remaining 93 per cent. It was too late for Manchester readers to change the BBC's mind, but would they have listened anyway? You already know the answer to that. Of course they wouldn't.

I was never in any doubt that I would suffer the most enormous withdrawal symptoms from my five-days-a-week programme. I am proud of the fact that I successfully managed to introduce politics and current affairs on to a popular music network in 1973. And I treasure the comment of Professor Ted Wragg of Exeter University who, in a letter to the *Guardian*, praised me for my part in 'educating the nation'. I am proud of the fact that I always conducted my programme in an even-handed and apolitical way. I am particularly proud of the fact that listeners frequently commented that they had no idea what my politics were. In my opinion that is exactly the way one should approach political interviewing, but I am well aware that it is not the view of everyone employed by the BBC.

And just how independent an organisation is the BBC itself? Despite its claim that it operates fearlessly as an independent organisation, it is inevitably closely linked to the government. How could it be otherwise, when it is the government that ultimately decides the level of the licence fee?

Consider the situation in 2003. The top two men in the BBC, Gavyn Davies and Greg Dyke, are well-known supporters of, and past contributors to, the Labour Party. Both are thoroughly honourable men, but would it be surprising if an increasingly cynical public thought they detected the BBC leaning a little to the left?

Then there is the question of the licence fee itself. A case can be made for the BBC, as a public service organisation, to be funded by a licence fee—although even then many would argue for alternative methods of funding. But as the BBC aggressively expands into commercial activities, the licence fee becomes increasingly difficult to defend. In other words, at what point does a public service organisation cease to be purely a public service organisation?

The BBC licence fee is regarded by many people as a poll tax levied on ordinary members of the public who think it should go. In my *Sunday Express* newspaper column I asked readers for their opinion about the licence fee. Did they think it was the best way for the BBC to be funded? Did they think the BBC provided good value for the licence fee? Were they happy for it to continue?

Overwhelmingly, their verdict was that it should go.

*　　　*　　　*

Was I angry when the news broke that the BBC was going to replace me? Of course I was, and so were my listeners, as they showed in the thousands of letters I received and their reaction on the Radio 2 website. However, my initial angry reaction was quickly replaced by hurt. I was very hurt indeed that the BBC never explained to me why they were getting rid of me. I knew it couldn't be because my performance had slipped. It hadn't, and my Radio 2 Controller had not only confirmed that but also had been generous in his praise. I knew it couldn't be because my ratings were slipping. On the contrary, they kept going up. And I knew it couldn't be because we were suddenly failing to get top-quality guests on the programme, because we were as successful as ever in doing that. So what could the reason be?

My listeners, perspicacious as ever, suggested that the answer, as far as the BBC was concerned, might lie in the opening line of the song that launched my career. All you have to do, they suggested, was change one word. It was in 1951 that I sang, 'They Tried to Tell Us We're Too Young'. The only conclusion was that I was considered to be too old. It didn't matter that I was achieving excellent results—what mattered was that I was seen as too old.

Well, that's a reasonable conclusion for management to reach. What was not reasonable, and was extremely hurtful, was that they lacked the courage to tell me that face to face. I've been a freelance all my working life, and freelancers expect to be hired and fired. But no one in Radio 2's senior management had the courtesy to invite me along for a drink and a chat to explain why I was being replaced. No one had the courage to say, 'Look, Jim, you've done and are still doing excellent work and are getting excellent results for us. But the fact is that Radio 2 is trying to project a younger image and at eighty-one, quite frankly, you don't fit into that image.'

All I needed was an explanation. I never got one,

303

and that was what turned initial anger and disappointment into hurt.

*   *   *

Of course there is life after the BBC, and its decision to part company with me has opened up other interesting possibilities. I am currently writing a column for the *Sunday Express*. We began on a three months' contract, and after just two weeks the response from readers was so great that my editor asked if I would agree to extend the contract to twelve months. And I am going to present *An Audience with Jimmy Young* in theatres. So it seems there is some truth in the saying that as one door closes others open.

As I write this book in April 2003 I am in the happy position of being able to say things I wasn't able to say before, and I look forward to meeting many of my former listeners as I travel around the country when it's published. I'm certainly attracted to the idea of *An Audience with Jimmy Young* because it will give me the opportunity to meet in the flesh, so to speak, many of you whom, up to now, I've only known through the microphone. I'm quite looking forward to 'treading the boards' again, which I did for the first time back in 1951 at the old Croydon Empire. And I hope you will come to see me and say hello.

It's often said, and in my case it looks like coming true: what goes around comes around.

PHOTOGRAPHIC ACKNOWLEDGEMENTS

All photographs are from the Author's Collection.